Geographies of the Heart

EDITED BY

Raymonde Tickner, Amea Wilbur, Zahida Rahemtulla,
and Kerry Johnson

Geographies
of the
Heart

Stories from Newcomers to Canada

PURICH
BOOKS

Printed in Canada on FSC-certified ancient-forest-free paper (100% post-consumer recycled) that is processed chlorine- and acid-free.

UBC Press is a Benetech Global Certified Accessible™ publisher. The epub version of this book meets stringent accessibility standards, ensuring it is available to people with diverse needs.

Library and Archives Canada Cataloguing in Publication

Title: Geographies of the heart : stories from newcomers to Canada / edited by Raymonde Tickner, Amea Wilbur, Zahida Rahemtulla, and Kerry Johnson.

Names: Tickner, Raymonde, editor. | Wilbur, Amea, editor. | Rahemtulla, Zahida, editor. | Johnson, Kerry (Educator), editor.

Description: Includes bibliographical references.

Identifiers: Canadiana (print) 20240300920 | Canadiana (ebook) 20240301013 | ISBN 9780774881012 (softcover) | ISBN 9780774881029 (PDF) | ISBN 9780774881036 (EPUB)

Subjects: LCSH: Immigrants—Canada—Biography. | LCSH: Canada—Emigration and immigration. | LCSH: Immigrants—Canada—Social conditions. | LCGFT: Biographies.

Classification: LCC FC104 .G36 2024 | DDC 305.9/06912092271—dc23

  Canada Council Conseil des arts
for the Arts du Canada

 Canadä

BRITISH COLUMBIA
ARTS COUNCIL

BRITISH
COLUMBIA

UBC Press gratefully acknowledges the financial support for our publishing program of the Government of Canada, the Canada Council for the Arts, and the British Columbia Arts Council.

UBC Press is situated on the traditional, ancestral, and unceded territory of the xʷməθkʷəy̓əm (Musqueam) people. This land has always been a place of learning for the xʷməθkʷəy̓əm, who have passed on their culture, history, and traditions for millennia, from one generation to the next.

Purich Books, an imprint of UBC Press
University of British Columbia
www.purichbooks.ca

CONTENTS

Bearing Witness

IN *GEOGRAPHIES OF THE HEART,* readers are invited to push the boundaries of their identities and explore uncharted territories within their hearts. The stories within this book bridge the gap between the familiar and the unknown, and are illuminating narratives that have shaped and will shape Canada. They compel us to confront both our beauty and complacency, and force us to acknowledge truths we like to avert our gaze from. How can we mourn the loss of historic sites but not give aid to people who carry endangered traditions? Newcomers are treasures of experiences, bearers of human heritage – stories, recipes, languages, perspectives, and philosophies – and this book is an antidote to the prevailing misconception that refugees are burdens to shoulder or threats to fear.

Even when we are willing to open up to untold stories, the injustices endured by others can evoke visceral reactions. We sympathize with their burdened souls, yet often feel powerless to alleviate their suffering. Some may

> *Newcomers are treasures of experiences, bearers of human heritage.*

turn away, attempting to shield their hearts from further shattering. But in this vulnerability lies a crucial mistake – looking away does not protect us, nor does it diminish the lingering pain in our world.

How, then, do we bear witness to heart-wrenching tales without succumbing to despair? In the profound words of the Dalai Lama and

Desmond Tutu in *The Book of Joy,* how do we cultivate "a shift in perspective, from oneself and toward others, from anguish to compassion"?

I grappled with this wisdom for years, striving to witness suffering within and around me without losing my anchor. Oppression, a relentless historical force in my birthplace, Kurdistan, often left me adrift like suspended particles.

A transformation occurred within me when I began to look beyond my ancestral struggles, to read literature on the horrors of gas chambers, internment camps, and plantations. It was an arduous journey, one that demanded frequent breaks and long walks, but gradually, the meaning of suffering shifted for me. No longer a marker of my (generational) unworthiness, it became a universal aspect of humanity – like living in bodies that inevitably decay and die. I wondered what would happen if I shared my challenges with others, and merged my pain with theirs. Our suffering intertwined! What would that make us?

In my fervent years of writing and activism, I immersed myself in the narratives of victims of torture, those on death row in Iran, and families shattered by executions. My error was not in listening to others' stories, but in naively assuming I had to carry their pain.

Exploring injustice in my novel *Daughters of Smoke and Fire* left me incapacitated and drowning in pain for hours, sometimes days. It caused me unnecessary suffering, yet it revealed to me the immense endurance of the human spirit. We are remarkably fragile and yet unbelievably resilient. I witnessed how grief wounds us but presents an opportunity to deepen our empathy, sometimes to the point of blurring the distinction between self and other.

"Pleasure is an attempt to fill yourself. Joy is what you are," writes Byron Katie in *A Thousand Names for Joy*. If our essence is joy – unlike happiness that depends on external conditions – it must be possible to remain rooted in joy, in our true nature, while bearing witness. We all enter this world crying and leave alone, and yet we experience immense joy in the wild ride, often unexpectedly. I've interviewed people who fall in love while imprisoned, who pause to taste chocolate while bullets rain around them in a war zone, and who have profound epiphanies in refugee camps.

Bearing witness – being present without absorbing pain – is a skill I'm still practicing. It's not easy, but it is possible. I practice because I healed when someone acknowledged my pain, a pain that I had gaslighted for years. It was the most precious gift I've ever received, and it's one I wish to offer whenever I can. Readers who pick up *Geographies of the Heart* might share that desire.

To build a capacity for bearing witness in a healthy manner, I deliberately distanced myself from the media and immersed myself in literature. The modern cacophony of media, where disaster overshadows hope, can ensnare us in despair. Literature, on the other hand, portrays both sorrow and resilience, both destruction and reconstruction. The narratives in *Geographies of the Heart,* which amplify the voices of writers from across the planet, deepened my understanding of individual and collective realities, grounding me rather than uprooting me.

When I am triggered by certain stories I read, write, or hear, I take refuge in nature – listening to bird songs, kissing the earth beneath my feet with each step, inhaling the scents of plants and trees. When nature isn't accessible, I turn to videos of waterfalls, sea worlds, anything that reminds me that on Earth horror and beauty coexist. When even that seems out of reach, I focus on one breath at a time. This breath. And now, this breath.

Grief wounds us but presents an opportunity to deepen our empathy.

There's a Tibetan saying: "Wherever you have friends, that's your country; and wherever you receive love, that's your home." I hope that we can make Canada a home for more people by extending the geographies of our hearts.

AVA HOMA, Author of *Daughters of Smoke and Fire*

ACKNOWLEDGMENTS

ON NOVEMBER 9, 2019, Muhialdin Bakini and I had a chat over coffee at Café Amarti, a lovely coffee shop in Abbotsford, British Columbia. Our conversation that day became the inspiration for this book. I owe a debt of gratitude to Muhi for sharing his migration story, for his willingness to contribute to the book, for trusting me with his narrative, and for referring two of his friends – Albino Nyuol and Jummeiz Kambidi. From this beginning, the list of acknowledgments continued to grow.

Mary Gene Saudelli from the University of the Fraser Valley (UFV) invited me to her office for tea after I approached her for help, and she enthusiastically supported my idea, gave me guidance, and promptly referred me to Amea Wilbur. Amea, also at UFV, jumped on board and invited Zahida Rahemtulla, who is her colleague from Pacific Immigrant Resources Society. Zahida began recruiting writers while Amea reached out to her networks for newcomers interested in telling their stories. And Kerry Johnson, a colleague from the English Language Services Department at UFV, recommended one of her advanced students and encouraged her to write a chapter.

As coeditors for this book, Amea, Zahida, and Kerry contributed endless volunteer hours to its development, supported the writers, and offered their own writing, editing, and research expertise.

Paula Mannington, program manager of English Language Services at Abbotsford's Archway Community Services, and a long-time friend and colleague, provided a list of employees at Archway whom she thought would wish to contribute to the book. Her enthusiasm for this project is boundless.

With so many people wanting to contribute to this book, we needed spaces where we could hold writing workshops. Burnaby Neighbourhood House donated space for our first writing workshop, and UFV provided classroom space for a second in-person workshop for contributors residing in the Fraser Valley. We'd also like to thank Sanjay Joshi, general manager at Staples, who kindly donated supplies for both workshops. Starbucks supplied coffee for the UFV workshop.

The UFV event was our last in-person workshop before the COVID-19 pandemic struck and required us to move online for the next year and a half. Authors Aislinn Hunter, Ava Homa, and Carmen Aguirre provided interactive online writing workshops for our newcomers: listening, sharing tips, and offering encouragement.

A long list of people encouraged us and donated generously to our GoFundMe campaign. The monies raised helped make publication of this book possible.

We'd also like to thank Paula Mannington, who recommended our book project to Alison Gutrath, former supervisor at Archway Diversity Education. Alison, along with the Fraser Valley Human Dignity Coalition, provided a $300 honorarium to seven of the writers, who were employees at Archway or UFV students.

The University of British Columbia Centre for Migration Studies sponsored a podcast to support *Geographies of the Heart,* and our thanks go to its creators: Douglas Ober, former director of the centre, Emily Amburgey for her expert editing, and podcast host Hamoudi Saleh Baratta. Thanks also to Malena Mokhovikova who developed our website, Stories for Newcomers to Canada, where readers can see the amazing newcomers who have contributed their life-writing to *Geographies of the Heart.* To listen to the podcast, go to https://migration.ubc.ca/programs-initiatives/podcast/; and the website can be found at https://sntc.squarespace.com/.

And to Nadine Pedersen, editor for Purich Books at UBC Press, whose unflagging enthusiasm, support, and care for the writers helped us bring this collection to readers – many thanks.

RAYMONDE TICKNER

Geographies of the Heart

Introduction

The arts are an invitation to listen, with all our senses, to experiences
and voices often ignored, giving an opportunity to deepen that true
democratic spirit and enliven a dynamic and pluralistic public space
with unheard voices.

> – Shauna Butterwick and Carole Roy, "View of Introduction to
> Finding Voice and Listening: The Potential of Community and
> Arts-Based Adult Education and Research," *The Canadian
> Journal for the Study of Adult Education* 30, 2 (2018):1–9

IN HER FAMOUS 2009 TED Talk, "The Danger of a Single Story," Nigerian
novelist Chimamanda Ngozi Adichie warns that if individuals hear only
a single story about another individual or country, we risk a critical
misunderstanding.[1] She also cautions that in hearing about a people,
place, or situation from a single point of view, there is a risk of accepting
that viewpoint as the whole truth. Similarly, Caroline Lenette, a leading
interdisciplinary researcher whose work focuses on participatory methods
and social justice research with refugees, argues that "single stories can
not only turn into dominant stereotypes but represent narratives in
unfinished forms, because they exclude diversity of experiences and
the intersectionality of individuals' issues."[2]

This book sets out to challenge ideas of the singularity – of what
it means to be a newcomer in Canada. Through a narrative life story
approach, *Geographies of the Heart: Stories from Newcomers to Canada*
highlights the diversity and complexity of what brings individuals

and families to Canada and their experiences of living on these lands. Stories can help us better understand experiences of migration and post-migration, and extend media representations. They create opportunities for readers to explore identity, investigate ideas, and inspire a shift from a single narrative.

The contributors intentionally chose to use the word "newcomer" to include the experiences of both immigrants and refugees, and to be inclusive of the many diverse reasons for coming to Canada.

Contributors came to Canada seeking asylum, escaping war, fleeing economic hardship, and seeking better lives for themselves and their families, sometimes without a choice, and sometimes with choice. Some were professionals in their countries of origin – educators, journalists, scientists. Others were students, activists, or migrated as children to Canada. For several contributors, this is the first time they have spoken or written about their migration story. All of them seek to share their lived experience with other newcomers, settlers, and Indigenous peoples here in Canada, to help others understand the diversity of what it is like to be a newcomer to these lands.

Why Read About the Experiences of Newcomers to Canada?

According to current statistics from the United Nations Refugee Agency (UNHCR), as of the end of 2022, an unprecedented 108.4 million people around the world have been forcibly displaced from their homes as refugees and asylum seekers, have been internally displaced, or are in need of international protection.[3] Among the forcibly displaced, nearly 36.5 million are children.[4] There are also millions of stateless people who have been denied a nationality and access to basic rights such as education, healthcare, employment, and freedom of movement.

Canada currently boasts one of the highest per-capita immigration rates in the world.[5] According to the 2021 Canadian Census, immigrants currently represent 23 percent of Canada's total population.[6] According to the 2021 Census, from 2016 to 2021, 218,430 new refugees were admitted to Canada as permanent residents.[7] Many immigrants to Canada come from Asia and Africa, and the majority of refugees come from Syria, Eritrea, Pakistan, Iraq, Ukraine, and Afghanistan.[8] Most recently, since the Taliban took over in August 2021, Canada has accepted more than thirty thousand

Afghans to the country.[9] Additionally, more than 153,493 Ukrainian refugees have arrived in Canada under the Canada-Ukraine Authorization for Emergency Travel (CUAET) measures, which help Ukrainians and their family members in coming to Canada as quickly as possible.[10]

Newcomers arrive in Canada from many different backgrounds and for many different reasons. They cross borders hoping for new beginnings, and upon arrival, start the ongoing process of reconstructing their lives. Despite the wealth of knowledge, work, and lived experiences newcomers bring, they are not always welcomed or valued in their communities, places of work, or even classrooms, often being dismissed out of hand, ignored, or feared. As well, newcomers may experience deskilling as part of their immigration to Canada,[11] since the non-recognition of immigrants' prior credentials and experience has long been seen as one of Canada's "most outstanding social policy issue[s]."[12]

Canada is a relatively young country, and the vast majority of Canadians who are not Indigenous nor migrants themselves can trace their ancestry to immigrants. Because of this history and the diversity of its population, Canada is one of the most multicultural countries in the world. For many Canadians, its multiculturalism is a source of pride. Even though multiculturalism is one of the ways in which Canada defines itself as a nation, in an article published in the *Canadian Review of Sociology*, race and labour scholar Maureen Kihika pointed out that Canada's multiculturalist policy "reinforces socio-economic boundaries of belonging and unbelonging, by marketing ideals of a post-racial society."[13]

The concept of multiculturalism itself is also highly contested because of Canada's long history of racism – including the genocide of Indigenous peoples and immigration policies that included the Chinese Head Tax and the Chinese Immigration Act, as well as Canada's ongoing exclusionary approach to refugees as evidenced by the government's refusal to take in Jewish refugees fleeing Nazi persecution in the 1930s. There was also the internment of Japanese Canadians during the Second World War, Bill 21, and the ongoing systemic barriers faced on a daily basis by Indigenous, Black, and racialized Canadians.

Some newcomers, as expressed by some contributors to this collection, feel that most Canadians are accepting and welcoming. They are surprised by polls that suggest that public narratives about newcomers have become increasingly negative, indicating that only a "thin veneer of tolerance" exists in Canada.[14] However, there is mounting evidence that Canada is part of the rising tide of nationalism and xenophobia currently sweeping the globe. A 2020 research study found that Canadians are among the most active in online right-wing extremism globally.[15] The increasing clamour of racist and anti-immigration discourse in Canada and worldwide underlines the importance of promoting values that affirm diverse voices. Cognizant that discourse regarding Canadian multiculturalism serves in part as an idealized view and "legitimating myth" that often camouflages discrimination, inequity, and injustice, Canadians continue to interrogate it domestically through different lenses that range from identity politics to the politics of recognition in which recognition of cultural diversity paves the way toward "revaluing disrespected identities and changing dominant patterns of representation and communication that marginalize certain groups."[16]

> *Canada is part of the rising tide of nationalism and xenophobia currently sweeping the globe.*

On an international front, Canada's image as a humanitarian country also often contrasts with realities on the ground and must similarly be interrogated. The legacy and ongoing effects of western imperialism in the Global South mean that Canada has played and continues to play a role in global displacement.

Root causes of displacement, however, are often overlooked in media and scholarship. As migration and social policy researcher Themrise Khan observes in a piece for the London School of Economics blog:

> The causes or drivers of migration from South to North, and more so, the socio-economic impact they are having on the South, have been vastly understudied by Western scholars and practitioners. In Western scholarship, the focus remains on how receiving countries in the West have been and are dealing with the influx of migrants. In turn, such scholarship influences migration and immigration policies in receiving countries.[17]

Since the paradigms through which we perceive forced migration have a direct impact on public policy, it is important to understand Canada's role in displacement within a wider context and a longer trajectory. In recent years, for example, Canadian forces have been part of militarized missions in Afghanistan, Libya, Sudan, Mali, and Iraq.[18] Canada also plays a covert role in international warfare through its sales of arms and ammunition. A recent and ongoing example is Canada's sale of arms to Saudi Arabia in its prolonged bombing campaigns and blockade against Yemen. Canada's weapons transfers are frequently used to commit or facilitate violations of international humanitarian law, and Canada itself has been directly accused of violating international law via these deals.[19] In 2019, Canada sold weapons amounting to almost $4 billion. Many of the parties Canada sold weapons to in the Middle East and North Africa have been charged with violating humanitarian law.[20]

Canada's involvement in global free trade and capitalistic enterprises has also contributed to displacement. The opening of markets to powerful multinational foreign firms has weakened states throughout the Global South, undermining local businesses and markets who are unable to compete. Canadian mining companies and the resource extraction industry often contribute to forced migration, with Indigenous peoples often being the most affected.[21] In 2019, the Conversation published a piece about the extensive role of Canadian mining in the displacement of migrants and the destruction of communities in Central America.[22]

Canada has also played a large role in the increasing number of climate refugees. As a member of the G8, Canada finds itself among seven other nations who collectively are responsible for 85 percent of the world's total emissions.[23] According to the United Nations High Commissioner for Refugees, since 2008 an average of 21.5 million people annually have been forcibly displaced by climate-related events: floods, storms, wildfires, and extreme temperatures.[24] And by 2050, there could be 1.2 billion climate refugees.[25] While many of these issues can seem far removed and abstract, they often contribute to the reasons newcomers end up migrating to Canada.

According to the 2021 Canadian Census, one in every four people counted were or had been a landed immigrant or permanent resident in Canada.[26] Therefore, it is likely anyone working in a helping profession will find themselves working directly with immigrants and refugees. This book was written to help foster understanding of the realities encountered by newcomers to Canada and the forces that brought them to these lands.

It intends to facilitate discussion and exploration that prepares the way for working toward a more equitable society, bridging the classroom with public and local communities.

Currently, narratives written by newcomers to Canada exist in the form of novels, memoirs, and articles within the media landscape, including: *Finding Refuge in Canada: Narratives of Dislocation*, edited by George Melnyk and Christina Parker (2021); *The Good Immigrant*, edited by Chimene Suleyman and Nikesh Shukla (2019); *Putting Family First: Migration and Integration in Canada*, edited by Harald Bauder (2019); *Refugees in America: Stories of Courage, Resilience and Hope in Their Own Words*, by Lee T. Bycel (2019); *Homes*, by Abu Bakr al Rabeeah with Winnie Yeung (2018); *Intolerable*, by Kamal Al-Solaylee (2015); *The Illegal*, by Lawrence Hill (2009); and *A Family Matter: Citizenship, Conjugal Relations and Canadian Immigration Policy*, by Megan Gaucher (2018), to name just a few.

These books have much to offer readers. There is, however, a dearth of non-fiction stories that can be adapted to the classroom for those wishing to work with or understand newcomer populations in the Canadian context. Furthermore, many existing narratives are written by professional writers who occupy middle- to upper-class backgrounds and have often lived in Canada for many years before finally putting pen to paper. In contrast, the contributors to this book come from all different walks of life, and many of the authors have lived in Canada for fewer than ten years.

Thus, this book provides a way to rethink and engage deeply with newcomers through their own experiences. Each chapter provides a different perspective on the experiences of immigrants and refugees. The stories in this volume shed light on the processes of deskilling, discrimination, and resilience required to deal with challenges and day-to-day life in a new country.

How This Book Came to Be

This book arose out of numerous conversations between teachers, students, friends, co-workers, and strangers. In 2019, the first conversation took place between one of the editors, Raymonde Tickner, and one of the contributors, Muhi Bakini, about the latter's journey to Canada as a former refugee from Sudan. Muhi had been a student in the TESL program at the University of the Fraser Valley. Muhi shared the following about the beginnings of the book:

As someone who taught English as a Foreign Language (EFL) to refugees in Egypt and Israel before coming myself to Canada as a refugee, I was overwhelmed by the requirements to enter a classroom again as an ESL instructor in Canada. When I met my teacher Raymonde, we started a conversation leading to the inception of this book. I was at the happiest of times then – I had just received a BA and TESL certificate from UFV, and I was teaching ESL. I felt as if I had reinvented myself. I wondered how other newcomers were experiencing Canada. I wanted to write my story to encourage newcomers, who may be overwhelmed by all that is required to rebuild their future here in Canada, that it is possible to achieve their dreams. I also wanted to write my story to honour the kindness I have experienced on my own journey as a refugee.

This interaction led to many more conversations and the inception of this project, as Raymonde and Muhi continued to think about what experiences have been for other newcomers. Many of the storytellers included here are people the editors worked with or had known prior to this project, through educational initiatives, working in the non-profit sector, or being in the same friend networks.

The result of this original impetus is a book written by a group of twenty-four people who worked together for over two years to workshop, write, and edit the stories you now hold in your hands. By reading this book, readers will understand the backgrounds of the people who created it. As well, it is of interest to be aware of the process through which it came into being. With this in mind, and to be reflexive about the many positionalities underlying this project, the following pages offer a brief summary of who we are.

There is a long history of the curation of voices of racialized and Indigenous peoples.

In undertaking this work, the editors recognized the power differences that can exist between editors and storytellers in the writing process. There is a long history of the curation of voices of racialized and Indigenous peoples that is troubling in its development, content, aesthetics, and circulation.[27] The editors see their work here as dialogical work – an attempt to mitigate and unsettle the power relationship by developing a relational approach to our work and encouraging solidarity.

Solidarity and allyship can be complex processes; however, through trauma-informed methods, the editors centred community-based consensus building to promote horizontal relationships and prevent harm. There are multiple ways to define solidarity, but in this book the editors used a framework that is informed by adult education, which includes thinking about social solidarity as the "interdependence between people in a society, which makes them feel that they can improve the lives of others."[28] Social solidarity has a deep history in community-based adult education, and can be fostered through reciprocal dialogue and learning exchanges.

Backgrounds of Contributors

The contributors to this anthology range from twenty years old to their late fifties, and are from fourteen countries. They have lived in Canada for different lengths of time – some arrived as young people or children. The most recent member of the group arrived in Canada in 2014, while some have lived in Canada for over twenty-five years. A few of the writers worked as journalists before arriving in Canada. For most, however, contributing to this book was the first time they had engaged in personal life-writing.

Many of the writers now work in the community to support other recently arrived migrants and their families. They include early childhood educators; two TESL instructors; a university professor working in migration studies; settlement workers; an Equity, Diversity, and Inclusion coordinator; a newcomer women's creative writing coordinator; and post-secondary students.

The editors – Raymonde Tickner, Amea Wilbur, Zahida Rahemtulla, and Kerry Johnson – each have years of experience working with newcomers. They are from different generations and backgrounds. Three are descended from European ancestry and one from South Asian ancestry. Their families came to Canada as refugees and economic migrants, fleeing famine or religious persecution. They range in age from thirty to seventy-five. They have different professional backgrounds in academia, as English language instructors, adult educators, community developers, and those working in the arts, including storytelling. All are at different stages of their teaching careers. They are all settlers on this land called Canada and are working to decolonize their practices and processes as adult educators through indigenizing their curriculums, building relations, working in restorative justice, actively working on reconciliation, and reflecting on their positions and social locations.[29]

Process and Scope

The editors met with the writers individually and as a group over the course of two years, beginning in February 2020. During Covid, this work was accomplished over Zoom. The group started organically, open to anyone who wished to write, meet other newcomers, and become part of a community. The process was self-selective, which we hoped would provide a more welcoming, less hierarchical structure. In this same vein, the writers also worked as peer editors, providing feedback to one another throughout the process. Over time, professional writers were introduced to the group, and guest coaches were invited including Ava Homa, Carmen Aguirre, and Aislinn Hunter.

It was important to the writers and editors that this book represent diverse migration experiences. This approach to diverse stories and reasons for migrating allowed for a deeper understanding of the different pathways through which people come to Canada and their settlement processes. Although there are many excellent books written by and about newcomers, what makes this book unique is that it offers a diverse range of perspectives, including stories of both forced and non-forced displacement. This allows for a more nuanced understanding of the forces that bring people to this land – by offering diverse and wide-ranging perspectives, much can be learned about what brought us here. Many of the writers in the group found they also learned from being in a diverse group. As Shanga Karim explained:

> I have never thought that I would share my stories and journeys in Canada. Writing my daily new experiences and facing all the new things Canadian culture made me find a hidden skill, which is creativity to write. Even though I struggled a lot from not being myself, losing my career, friends, and family, I could find courage and sweetness in all the bitters that I tasted in my new chapter of life. Listening to my new friends here and their life experience shocked me about how can be our live experiences so different? Why? How? I mean why? There are many untold stories that I think we can tell. It's not just my stories.

Whilst seeking to provide wide-ranging and varied experiences of migration, it is important to note that there are some limitations in the scope of this volume. Since contributors often learned of the project via word-of-mouth while participating in settlement programs and community networks, there are limits in the types of migration experiences covered in the volume. This book isn't a quantitative summary of migrants' journeys. It's a snapshot of experiences held by a small number of people (eighteen to be exact). So, while this anthology offers insights into some individuals' stories, these certainly do not represent all migrants' experiences. Notably for example, Temporary Foreign Workers (TFWs), who inhabit spaces that are often different from other migrants, may not have access to the same supports and community networks that other newcomers use to find out about initiatives such as this one. Since the population of TFWs in Canada is significant, (777,000 as of 2021),[30] we felt it important to recognize this omission.

Additionally, due in part to privacy and safety reasons, we don't have stories by undocumented migrants in this volume. Although there are no accurate figures representing the number or composition of the undocumented migrant population in Canada, estimates range between 20,000 and 500,000 persons. They form a significant portion of Canada's population, and their experiences as newcomers and interactions with Canadian systems and authorities often diverge greatly from the experiences of other migrants. Since this is a population that already faces marginalization and exclusion when it comes to discussions of migration, funding, and support for newcomers, we felt it important to highlight this limitation.

Although we welcomed and encouraged peoples of diverse sexual orientations, classes, and abilities to join the group, there are limitations in this regard as well, which impact and intersect with the positionality of being a migrant. With this in mind, we hope that readers will engage with the stories in this volume with an understanding that the lived experiences in this book are but small pieces of a much larger, ever-changing, and complex picture of Canada's migration landscape.

As readers engage with these lived experiences and narratives, it is important to be cognizant of context and the complex histories that contribute to global displacement. In the writing workshops and community meetings, editors and visiting authors stressed that stories need not follow the arc of showing gratitude or painting the country as a benevolent place, given Canada's complicit and complex role in displacement. However, several writers did express gratitude, explaining that such feelings for one's host country can co-exist alongside gratitude for being alive, for living without fear, imprisonment, death, or in protracted refugee situation.

The editors were committed to a trauma-informed approach to their work with the writers, viewing their stories and experiences through a strengths-based framework that recognizes the need to be responsive to the impact of trauma and the importance of creating a safe environment.

An empathetic, trusting, and collaborative approach to the writing and editing process was encouraged by the editors, who met both individually and collectively over a year-and-a-half to promote the well-being of the contributors through check-ins, community building, and a sense of purpose. The contributors themselves set the pace for the writing and individual coaching sessions. The writing was not intented to be therapeutic, yet many of the contributors noted that sharing their stories was beneficial, healing, and created a sense of community. The stories were often rooted in painful experiences, and as such, we all recognized that many of the contributors had experienced trauma and violence. It was, therefore, critical that as a community we all respected not moving into territory or stories the writers were not ready to share.

To preserve authenticity and to respect personal style and tone, the editing team did minimal editing to the stories, focusing primarily on organization and clarity of expression. Thus, a reader may encounter uncommon phrasing, word choices, or uncommon syntax.

It is worth noting that these stories were written during the peak of a global pandemic that impacted racialized low-income people and newcomers disproportionately.[31] It was also a time when many Canadians found themselves having conversations about systemic racism and injustice precipitated by the Black Lives Matter and Indigenous rights movements. For many Canadians it was a time of changing perceptions and reckoning with our colonial past, figuring out how to move forward with respect and reciprocity. The movement that continues around indigenizing and integrating equity, diversity, and inclusion in post-secondary and other institutions responds to this time of reflection and change.

Geographies of forced migration and colonial domination often overlap. Despite their distinct histories and geographies, and different positions, refugees, immigrants, and Indigenous peoples often have experiences of displacement in common. There is much work being done in recent times to explore the relationship between reconciliation and immigration.[32] Many conversations relating to colonization took place in our writing workshops over the two years of this project. Over that time, announcements regarding residential schools – in particular, the graves of 215 children discovered at the Kamloops Indian Residential School just four hours north of us – were in the news. These developments figured prominently in one of our workshop discussions, as the editors and writers discussed the legacy of colonialism and genocide in Canada. This also opened up a conversation about connections to other displaced people, including the Kurds, with contributors Shanga Karim, Deea Badri, and Diary Marif. In their stories, writers like Sofia Noori and Taslim Damji touch on the complex relationship between displacement, settlement, and Indigenous relations.

With this collection, the writers and volume editors are also responding to these calls for change. Educators and those working within social services can be, and often are, tasked with identifying the changes needed to build more equitable, empathetic, and diverse communities and societies. For those engaged in teaching and learning in adult education, education, the social services, settlement, immigration, and migration studies, as well as other helping professions, this book provides a narrative pedagogical approach to understanding the lived experiences of newcomers through the written text.[33]

Mapping the Terrain

The contributors recounted their stories of coming to Canada across a consistent theme: journeys toward reimagining oneself. The contributors and editors further organized the stories under four specific sub-themes. Part 1: Stories of Risk and Exile includes five stories written by former journalists and activists from Eritrea, Kurdistan, and Sudan who had to flee their countries due to their work. Part 2: Stories of Change and Exploration highlights those who came to Canada to build a new life, be it for education, safety, freedom, personal development, or better lives for their children. In Part 3: Stories of Belonging and Exclusion, immigrants describe the challenges of living in Canada as a newcomer, post-settlement, through systemic exclusion and barriers encountered in education, healthcare, and the Canadian workplace. Part 4: Stories of Displacement brings together tales of forced displacement from Sudan, South Sudan, Kosovo, Syria,

Afghanistan, and Russia, allowing for a deeper understanding of the range of experiences that fall under the broad heading of "forced displacement."

The stories in this book provide new perspectives and can help raise awareness for readers and other newcomers, who may see their own experiences reflected within. They do not provide simple answers to the complexities of migration and settlement. They are not intended to do so. The goals of this compilation are to stimulate dialogue in this important area of study; to prompt educators, service providers, and the general readership to expand their knowledge and understanding of the experiences of newcomers to Canada; and for readers to appreciate a diversity of experience – for there is always more than a "single story."

Notes

1 Chimamanda Ngozi Adichie, "The Danger of a Single Story," filmed July 2009 at Oxford, UK, video, 18:33, https://www.ted.com/talks/chimamanda_ngozi_adichie_the_danger_of_a_single_story?language=en0.

2 Caroline Lenette, *Arts-Based Methods in Refugee Research: Creating Sanctuary,* (Singapore: Springer, 2019), 235.

3 The United Nations High Commissioner for Refugees (UNHCR), "Refugee Data Finder," 2023, https://www.unhcr.org/refugee-statistics/#:~:text=At% 20the%20end%20of%202022%2C%20of%20the%20108.4%20million%20 forcibly,below%2018%20years%20of%20age.&text=Between%202018%20and %202022%2C%20an,born%20as%20refugees%20per%20year.

4 Ibid.

5 Lucille Proulx and Michelle Winkel, "Art Therapy with Families," in *Multicultural Family Art Therapy,* ed. Christine Kerr (New York: Routledge, 2015), 22.

6 Statistics Canada, "Immigration, place of birth, and citizenship – 2021 Census promotional material," last updated on December 13, 2022, https://www.statcan.gc.ca/en/census/census-engagement/community-supporter/immigration.

7 Ibid.

8 Ibid.

9 CBC, "More than 300 Afghans Arrive in Canada as Ottawa Inches Closer to 40,000 Resettlement Goal," April 13, 2023, https://www.cbc.ca/news/politics/afghan-resettlement-over-30000-1.6808123.

10 Government of Canada, Immigration, Refugees and Citizenship Canada, "Canada-Ukraine Authorization for Emergency Travel: Key Figures," August 29, 2023, https://www.canada.ca/en/immigration-refugees-citizenship/services/immigrate-canada/ukraine-measures/key-figures.html.

11 Abdul-Bari Abdul-Karim, "Deskilling of Internationally-Educated Immigrants: Critical Evaluation of the Processes in the Foreign Credential Recognition in

Canada," July 21, 2018, https://isaconf.confex.com/isaconf/wc2018/webprogram/Paper92114.html.

12 Shibao Guo, "Difference, Deficiency, and Devaluation: Tracing the Roots of Non-Recognition of Foreign Credentials for Immigrant Professionals in Canada," in *Canadian Journal for the Study of Adult Education* 22, 1 (2009): 37–52.

13 Maureen Kihika, "'Good Intentions' that 'Do Harm': Canada's State Multi-culturalism Policy in the Case of Black Canadians," in *Canadian Review of Sociology/Revue Canadienne De Sociologie* 59, 4 (2022): 436–50.

14 Angela Johnston, "Majority of Canadians against Accepting More Refugees, Poll Suggests," *CBC News,* last updated July 3, 2019, https://www.cbc.ca/news/canada/manitoba/refugees-tolerance-1.5192769.

15 Thomas Daigle, "Canadians among Most Active in Online Right-Wing Extremism, Research Finds," *CBC News,* last updated June 19, 2020, https://www.cbc.ca/news/science/canadian-right-wing-extremism-online-1.5617710.

16 Sarah Song, "Majority Norms, Multiculturalism, and Gender Equality," *American Political Science Review,* 99, 4 (2005): 473–1489.

17 Themrise Khan, "The Global South Must Create a Reverse Narrative on Migration – Soon," *Social Policy,* March 2, 2020, https://blogs.lse.ac.uk/socialpolicy/2020/03/02/the-global-south-must-create-a-reverse-narrative-on-migration-soon/.

18 Alison Bodine and Tamara Hansen, "Imperialist Made Crisis of Migrants and Refugees," *Common Dreams,* July 23, 2019, https://www.commondreams.org/views/2019/07/23/imperialist-made-crisis-migrants-and-refugees.

19 "Canada Violating Int'l Law by Selling Arms to Saudis: Report," *Al Jazeera,* August 11, 2021, https://www.aljazeera.com/news/2021/8/11/canada-violating-intl-law-by-selling-arms-to-saudis-report.

20 Kelsey Gallagher, "Analyzing Canada's 2019 Exports of Military Goods," *The Ploughshares Monitor* 41, 3 (2020), https://www.ploughshares.ca/reports/analyzing-canadas-2019-exports-of-military-goods-report.

21 Canadian Council for Refugees, "Canadian Companies Must be Held Account-able for Contributing to Forced Displacement," media release, August 23, 2019, https://ccrweb.ca/en/media/canadian-companies-accountability-forced-displacement.

22 Tyler Morgenstern, "The Role of Canadian Mining in the Plight of Central American Migrants," *The Conversation,* August 15, 2019, https://theconversation.com/the-role-of-canadian-mining-in-the-plight-of-central-american-migrants-120724.

23 Sarah Lazare, "Colonizing the Atmosphere: How Rich, Western Nations Drive the Climate Crisis," *In These Times,* September 14, 2020, https://inthesetimes.com/article/climate-change-wealthy-western-nations-global-north-south-fires-west.

24 United Nations High Commission for Refugees.

25 Sean McAllister, "There Could be 1.2 Billion Climate Refugees by 2050: Here's What You Need to Know," *Zurich Magazine*, June 23, 2023, https://www.zurich.com/en/media/magazine/2022/there-could-be-1-2-billion-climate-refugees-by-2050-here-s-what-you-need-to-know.

26 Statistics Canada, "Immigration, place of birth, and citizenship – 2021 Census promotional material."

27 Elena Gonzales, *Exhibitions for Social Justice* (London: Routledge, 2019), 154.

28 Chinmayee Mishra and Navaneeta Rath, "Social Solidarity during a Pandemic: Through and beyond Durkheimian Lens," *Social Sciences & Humanities Open* 2, 1 (2020): 2, https://doi.org/10.1016/j.ssaho.2020.100079.

29 Cindy Hanson and JoAnn Jaffe, "Decolonizing Adult Education," in *The Handbook of Adult and Continuing Education*, ed. Tonette S. Rocco, M. Cecil Smith, Robert C. Mizzi, Lisa R. Merriweather, and Joshua D. Hawley, 341–49 (New York: Routledge, 2023); and Verna J. Kirkness and Ray Barnhardt, "First Nations and Higher Education: The Four R's – Respect, Relevance, Reciprocity, Responsibility," in *Knowledge across Cultures: A Contribution to Dialogue among Civilizations,* ed. Ruth Hayoe and Julia Pan, 1–15 (Hong Kong: Hong Kong University Press, 2001).

30 Statistics Canada, "Immigration as a Source of Labour Supply," *The Daily,* last modified June 22, 2022, https://www150.statcan.gc.ca/n1/daily-quotidien/220622/dq220622c-eng.htm.

31 Public Health Agency of Canada, "CPHO Sunday Edition: The Impact of COVID-19 on Racialized Communities," statement, February 21, 2021, https://www.canada.ca/en/public-health/news/2021/02/cpho-sunday-edition-the-impact-of-covid-19-on-racialized-communities.html.

32 Soma Chatterjee, "Teaching Immigration for Reconciliation: A Pedagogical Commitment with a Difference," *Intersectionalities* 6, 1 (2018): 1–15.

33 Carolyn M. Clark and Marsha Rossiter, "Narrative Learning in Adulthood," *New Directions for Adult and Continuing Education* 2008, 119 (2008): 61–70.

PART 1

Stories of Risk and Exile

1

"Passport, Please"

Akberet Beyene

1) Everyone has the right to freedom of movement and residence within the borders of each State.
2) Everyone has the right to leave any country including his own, and to return to his country.

> – The United Nations Universal Declaration of Human Rights, 1948, Article 13

FOR TWENTY-TWO YEARS I was a journalist in Eritrea, a beautiful country in East Africa, repeatedly rated worst in the world for press censorship. While many of my colleagues had vanished or languished in prisons, I was able to hang onto my job at the national TV station, run by the dictatorship's Ministry of Information. However, the time came when I, too, was placed under house arrest for a year, and my passport was confiscated. No reason was given. My life was threatened, and I had to make a most difficult decision – to flee my beloved country, leaving my family behind.

The night before my departure, I was worried. I had been caring for my aging parents for years. I had mixed feelings and was questioning if I had made the right decision, or if it was all just an egocentric, selfish act. I lay in my bed, restlessly tormented and without answers. That night, the longest ever, crept on. I kept rolling and turning, unable to find a comfortable position, knowing that my mom and dad in another room were also restless. Slowly the darkness started to make room for emerging daylight. I lay there, waiting for the sun's rays to hit my bed, before getting up to face the day.

During the few last hours before my departure, I went through my wardrobe and chose what to wear to best camouflage my appearance. It reminded me of good times, back when I was actively working as a TV reporter. Every morning I had to dress according to the specific job of the day. One day I had to record interviews in the studio, the next I had to travel in working clothes to all corners in Eritrea to report on construction sites, newly built hospitals, or school-opening celebrations.

Now I had to be invisible. I decided to dress in my mom's traditional clothes, so I wouldn't be recognized making my way out of the neighbourhood where I was born and had grown up. My tired eyes were itching and red from lack of sleep. It was time to start the long journey into the unknown – to face my reality, to face my fear. I had no papers to cross borders, which was my biggest problem. A rush of pain washed over me. I closed my eyes. I recalled how proud I was when I got my first Eritrean passport, after the long thirty-year war for independence with Ethiopia. Before that, Eritreans were known as Ethiopians for over sixty years – without the consensus of its people. For us, a passport was more than just a piece of identification; it was a symbol of the enormous sacrifice it took to reclaim our Eritrean identity.

Our passport has a dromedary camel on the cover, our beast of burden, used in the long war to transport supplies that were essential for our success.

Hundreds of thousands of lives were lost. Little did we know at the time that our freedom was to be stolen again, this time by a brutal dictator, Isaias Afwerki. He had fought along so many of those who lost their lives, then he betrayed us all. My eyes welled up with tears, which had often happened during my house arrest. But this time was different. My papa and mamma were here – helpless with tears, speaking to me deeply and wordlessly. It was beyond them to protect me from this overpowering and cruel enemy. Hands on their old worn faces, they wept and gave me their last loving hugs.

I left my home unnoticed. Now I was a fugitive. It was eight thirty on a Saturday morning and the roads were crowded with people coming to the markets. Ali, a person whom I had not met in person and had only communicated with through a middle-man, had chosen this day based on his experience with helping others escape from the guards. Plenty of people came from all corners of the country to exchange goods. Compared to regular days, traffic was heavy and all transportation was crowded.

Even though I had undertaken all possible preparations to protect myself, I was shaking. It felt like every sound around me was calling my name. As if every face was watching me. I approached the first checkpoint with a heavy breath in my throat. Eritrean soldiers had shoot-to-kill orders for those attempting to flee the country. A soldier was concentrating on the young men in front of the line-up where I was standing, awaiting my turn. I presumed they were looking for illegal goods that black market dealers imported untaxed from Sudan. Eritreans tried to buy goods like sugar and coffee on the black market because they were in short supply in Eritrea. Every family had a coupon for receiving them from government-owned supply points. Fortunately, the soldiers paid no attention to women dressed in traditional clothing going in the opposite direction of the market or city, of which I was one.

Seeing vehicles crowding the roads and people everywhere about their business, I thought: the plan was working. I had to cross the congested security checkpoints where Eritrean soldiers inspected every vehicle and all public transportation. Miraculously, I made it through.

Ali was going to meet me after my last five-hour trip with the public bus. It was dark and late when I reached Teseney, a small village near Sudan's border. Stars dotted the endless darkness. Generally, in the low-lands of Eritrea, evenings are everyone's favourite time of day. The sun retreats and the heat leaves; the winds blow gently, like a sighing man.

Right after I left the bus, scared, I started looking left and right for Ali. For a moment I panicked, not seeing or recognizing him. What if ... my mind went, and more tears came. Fortunately, Ali surprised me by coming up from behind. I wouldn't have trusted him if I hadn't seen him barefoot, holding his plastic sandals in his hand. This was our pre-arranged signal – we had never met before. It was easy for him to identify me. Despite the crowd in the bus station, I was the only barefoot person carrying plastic sandals in my hand.

I had almost forgotten the long day spent sitting uncomfortably on a small overcrowded bus. My back was hurting. I worried about this stranger who was going to help me for the rest of my journey, the most dangerous route by foot. I hesitated for a moment, staring at him. I didn't have any option but to trust the sign we had agreed upon to recognize each other. I let out a deep breath and forced a smile when he got closer to me.

He appeared generous and extroverted. He approached me as if he had known me for a long time. I summoned my courage and took a few steps forward before I allowed myself to be at ease. I didn't know what to expect. Ali tried to reassure me. He looked around to see if anyone was watching, then hurried toward me. As if hugging me, Ali whispered in my left ear, "You don't have a passport, right?" I nodded. Ali backed away and looked around again before signalling with his right hand to follow him.

In a worn small hut was a woman in her early forties, feeding a baby. She didn't notice us as we entered, not until Ali called her name. As soon as she saw us, she placed her baby in a bed, and without a word she offered me some food and a blanket where I would lie down for a couple of hours. I needed to rest before we started the hard part of my trip, getting across the border to Sudan.

> Sometimes I swear I could smell water, but it was just my imagination.

At dawn, while the whole world seemed wrapped in a deep sleep, we started the long march. I remember that after two or three hours, I heard the chirping of morning birds. It felt as if they were assuring me that everything would be fine. While walking in silence, I couldn't help but admire the vast beauty of the desert at dawn.

The trip through the lowlands of Eritrea was long and arduous, the vast arid plains never-ending. With the sun burning down mercilessly during the day, it looked as if the earth was connected to the sky, the steam in the distance resembling a boiling pot. Normally it takes a day by car. We walked for four days. It felt like an eternity. My body suffered from hunger and thirst, but I had no desire for food. Sometimes I swear I could smell water, but it was just my imagination. I would have offered a million dollars for a sip.

After some time, we made it to Sudanese territory. I did not realize that we had crossed the border until Ali told me. The people who lived around here knew how to move without getting surprised by border guards.

Finally, I reached my next destination – a coffee shop in Sudan. It was a relief to know it was over, at least for this stretch. I had made it out of Eritrea. I felt exhilarated when the waiter of the café handed me a large oil can full of fresh drinking water, all for me, nobody to share it with. We had made the trip with a mere three litres of water. We drank only if our legs weren't able to take another step. "No more than three or four sips," I was told again and again. This big oil can was so generous, I was in heaven.

From now on, I knew I needed that document, the "passport." How else could I leave? But I did not have one, nor did I have any other identification on me. I needed to find a place to stay. I couldn't stay in a hotel – without such a document, I couldn't register. As I sat with Ali, I saw two people coming toward us. Ali immediately approached them. After a short exchange he returned to inform me that his custody of me was over. He would go back to where he came from, and I now had to trust his two friends and follow their orders. I was full of mixed feelings, including fear and despair, but I surrendered. It was far beyond my abilities to endure all of this. I got up, limping, my feet blistered and bleeding from the long journey. I spent the next night in Kassala, a small village on the Sudanese border.

The night wasn't pleasant. Ali's two friends had left. My whole body was aching, my soles still bleeding. I lay on my back, on a sloping bed made of iron, and struggled not to touch the dirty smelly sheets. I couldn't close my eyes despite being extremely tired. All night I wondered how I was going to get out of Sudan without a passport. No matter how long I thought, no answers came. At the end of the night, I was more tired mentally than physically. The next morning, a person brought me food and water and told me not to leave the place for any reason until the passport matter was settled. Sudanese officers could round up people at any moment.

The sun had been lingering for a while when I finally left my bed. I hardly was able to straighten my sore back, but the worst part was having to stand on my wounded feet. The night before I had tried to soak them in a pail of water and salt, not having any bandages or treatment, but it didn't help. I couldn't put my plastic sandals on, my feet had swollen up during the night. Somehow the daylight lifted my spirits. I paced around the room anxiously. I heard kids playing and people talking in Arabic. From a distance, I could hear the sounds of the morning prayer from a nearby mosque.

After two days I left for Khartoum. I was still not able to take any public transportation or get on a plane without a passport. As a result, I paid all the money I had left to travel in the back of a pickup truck, crammed onto wooden benches with nine other travellers.

Though it was early morning, the sun was already burning. I looked reluctantly in the direction the old pickup truck was headed as we went down an empty hill. We were crossing a scene of utter desperation, with refugee tents and ragged shelters strung out as far as my eye could see. It looked as though the entire population of Eritrea was camped there.

As we travelled on, the air became dusty. The landscape was barren and there were no trees to offer protection from the scorching sun. Lost in my thoughts, I cursed the dictatorship in Eritrea that had caused all this suffering. A group of soldiers in green uniforms appeared suddenly with machine guns and ammunition belts slung across their shoulders. I was full of fear – my heart was beating fast, sweat ran down my back. Would they check for papers? I do not know why, but I announced to the group of strangers I was with that I didn't have a passport. They gave me a scared look but didn't say anything. I felt helpless. I immediately regretted sharing my secret. The driver of the pickup slowed as he approached the military checkpoint. Fortunately, they didn't stop us; they saluted and waved us through. They must have been looking for something or someone else. Hours passed before I felt calm again.

My ordeal with this document called a passport was just the beginning. As I realized many years later, this trip to Khartoum marked the first time that I felt such high anxiety – a feeling that would become familiar as time wore on. I stayed in Khartoum for three long months, never leaving the tiny straw-covered tin hut where fellow Eritreans offered me shelter and hospitality. The darkness in the hut mirrored the sadness in my heart. My days here were all the same. I slept, ate very little, and rested. Not once did I leave my little den, though I was desperate to. Thinking back, I am amazed now that in all those days I did not take a single step outside. Without a passport, a single miss-step could have compromised all the sacrifices I had made.

During those three months many unsuccessful attempts were made to arrange for a fake passport, so I could leave Sudan. My close relatives and siblings – all of whom were refugees around the world in Europe, America, and Asia – tried all possible ways to get me out of Sudan. Nothing worked. I was beginning to lose hope.

At last, one afternoon I received a telephone call from my younger sister in Europe. I listened carefully. She told me that she had found a solution, and that I would get a message soon. I didn't press her for more details, I knew my loved ones were as worried as I was. I decided to be patient and trust. Patience, one of my strongest attributes, has carried me during the hardest times in my life.

Sure enough, a few days later I received mail from my sister. I rushed to open it, full of expectation. I couldn't believe my eyes at what I saw. It was a passport! I opened it and realized that she had sent me her own passport. I didn't know what to feel. What if I got caught and wound up putting her life in danger as well? I wanted to talk to her right away, and after a few tries, I was able to get through. My beloved sister wasn't going to listen to any of my "ifs" or "buts." She already made her decision. "I couldn't live with myself if something bad happened to you unless I tried everything in my hand," she said.

A few hours later, I held a ticket for the first plane scheduled out. My quarantine was going to end with the blink of an eye, just because I had this document called a passport now. But would it work? The anxiety returned.

I left behind some little things I had brought with me, things that connected me to my home, like my mom's dress, which I departed in on that first day of my journey. I felt protected when I held it, traces of my mother's scent giving me comfort on dark days. Whenever I felt melancholic, desperate, or nostalgic, I opened the plastic bag where I kept the dress and inhaled deeply. This time I took two pairs of pants and a few donated T-shirts for another journey into the unknown.

I got in a taxi and headed to the airport. Though I had lived in Khartoum for three months, I didn't have a clue what the big city looked like. My eyes got blurry from the hot sun. There were so many people everywhere, it was overwhelming. I felt like I was going to a different planet. I tried not to show my unstable state of mind to the taxi driver. We reached the Khartoum airport. The driver wished me good luck. My legs felt weak when I stepped out of the taxi. He saw how weak I was and, growing concerned, called another traveller my way and begged her to help me.

I debated whether to go with the woman, but I didn't have time to worry. I couldn't delay. I followed the woman by looking down at her feet. She asked me if I had ever travelled on an airplane. I wish I could have explained more. Instead, I answered her question with a weak smile.

We found the check-in and got into the queue. I started trembling. I felt a tightness in my stomach, and my voice was beginning to crack. My turn arrived. "Passport, please?" asked a scary voice from behind the counter. I collected myself and handed over my sister's passport. I held my breath, watching his eyes as he examined the passport. He closed my passport and checked my ticket. My heart was pounding like crazy. I closed my eyes and heard the voice pronounce, "Thank you Ma'am. Go this way to find your gate." I couldn't believe what I had heard. Without turning my face or saying a word, I followed his direction. I wish I could describe the incredible relief I felt at that moment.

My gate was the last. Lots of people were about, dressed elegantly, happily chatting loudly. I felt completely out of place. My clothes were wet from sweat, hot weather, and fear. They announced the boarding gate. I noticed all travellers had their tickets and passports in hand. Mine was hidden – I'd put everything back in my handbag right after check-in, as if everybody would know I had an illegal document. When it was my turn, I held my passport tightly inside my bag. As I waited, I started searching for the lady I met at the entrance. Maybe she was here? I found her, and she smiled and ran toward me, talking as if we were friends. I looked at her while I handed my passport to the agent as casually as I could, looking at him only from my periphery while still chatting with the lady. He returned the passport and let me through. I was lucky again. I almost ran onto the airplane. I found my seat, fastened my belt, and waited impatiently for the door to close and for the plane to move. I must have fallen fast asleep from exhaustion – I didn't notice anything until the plane landed in Germany and the stewardess touched my back, waking me up from my deep sleep.

Now in Germany, I prayed hard that my sister's passport would continue its magic. We did not look that much alike, but I had been able to book a ticket on a plane and cross all Sudanese checkpoints at the Khartoum airport with it. Now I had to face the German ones. The familiar feeling of high anxiety and fear returned. My heart was hammering so hard, I felt like it would come out of my chest. I clutched my chest, felt blood rushing through my face – if I were a white person, I probably would have looked red. Sweat was everywhere again, unbearable. Angels must have been watching me, though, because again I made it through.

Next thing I knew, I was on a plane to Canada, a ten-hour flight. Unlike the previous trip, I didn't close my eyes once. My thoughts couldn't rest, revisiting happy and sad memories from my entire life. Remembering it all made it feel real.

It was about 3:30 p.m. when I arrived on a grey winter day in Vancouver. I was numb. In a way I felt safe, being so far away from danger. I almost didn't care what happened now. I had made it this far, felt that I had triumphed over all adversities. But, of course, everything was still uncertain. Now I had to make it through the last gates. I kept walking to the security gate. The officer politely said, "Your passport, please?" I couldn't believe it. Again. "Next in line, please," he said as he pointed at me.

I hesitated, and a person behind me said, "Please, your passport!" I went to the gate and handed the customs officer my sister's passport. He gave it a quiet look and then asked me to follow him to a separate small room. He shut the door behind me and then started checking my handbag, each piece, then the inside and outside of my bag. He still was holding my passport, but I noticed that he never looked at it again. I don't know why. Maybe he was amused to find such an empty bag, with only a few not-so-costly things inside. Thanks to American films I had watched back home, I felt like I knew what was going on – maybe he was looking for something illegal, like drugs. Finally, he let me go, but I was not sure if he meant it. I just stood there until a second order confirmed what I had heard. I was free to leave.

I left the airport without looking back. I was almost running. Once I was out on the street, my body started shivering. I was dressed very lightly, in a summer dress that I had worn since I boarded the plane in Khartoum. I was freezing. I hadn't predicted this moment. I'd made it through every obstacle. But now what? I didn't have a clue where to go, whom to ask for help. I was lost. I saw plenty of people rushing about their business, cars everywhere. Life was going on for everybody, like it always does. I had left everything behind – me, my family, everyone I loved, and everything I loved. How could I explain that to any of these people here? I felt so alone. Indeed, nobody knows or even cares, I said to myself.

Realizing that the hard part was behind me now, I made up my mind and approached a taxi, to ask for help. It is odd how sometimes Samaritans arrive at just the right time, as if guided by guardian angels. I confided to the driver that I was a lost bird and needed to find some place to stay. He was surprised when I couldn't even supply him with an address to deliver me to in Vancouver. I said, "Anywhere in downtown."

I knew this phrase from American films. Also, I confessed that I couldn't pay him, at least not right away. But one day I would, when I was able to stand on my feet. He drove me downtown. I threw away my sister's passport.

During my first week in Vancouver, I tried to find some normalcy again. I had found shelter in a refugee home. I had lost a lot of weight over the past three months, and I started suffering from trauma and a sleep disorder.

Uncertainty invaded my life. I knew I wouldn't be at peace until I resolved my passport issue. After two weeks I made my way to the Canadian Immigration office. I told them my entire story and applied for asylum. I received a paper certifying my refugee claimant status – a document that verified who I was. With it I was able to open a bank account and receive some financial assistance.

It took another two long years until I finally had my hearing and got my refugee status approved. There had been countless sleepless nights to get all the information I needed to support and prove my case. Luckily, I had so many well-meaning people on my side who helped me with all the translations and documents, supporting me with love and kindness. Sometimes I was so overwhelmed, all I could do was cry on their shoulder. The support and care I received made it so I could move forward with hope and strength. I am forever grateful to those wonderful souls who appeared in my life, and I am so proud to call them friends to this day.

Eventually, the day came that I received my Permanent Resident card – my first Canadian ID. I was completely thrilled. Now I could apply for a Travel Document, which is issued to refugees under the United Nations Geneva Convention in lieu of a passport. After another year or two, I finally received this. It looked just like a passport, but it was blue. I was so happy. I could now travel without problems. I wanted to see my mom, and to thank my sister for her help.

After I had saved money, I decided to book a ticket to Germany. My mother was going to travel to Germany as well, so I could meet her there. I was so excited.

I arrived at the check-in at Vancouver International Airport with my blue document in hand. I could not wait to embrace my mother.

"Passport please," the agent said.

Enthusiastically I handed over my blue document. Immediately I could feel something was wrong. The agent kept looking at it, as if he had never seen anything like it before. "What is this?"

I said it was a legal travel document for refugees, like a passport. The agent left to talk to somebody then returned and informed me that I could not travel with this document. I tried to reason with them, insisting it was legal, that it was a legal document accepted in Germany. I showed him the relevant information from the German Government website. Nobody would listen. I was not allowed to board.

I was heartbroken. Here I had a travel document that took me two years to get, and still I couldn't travel. I phoned my family and informed them I could not come, at least not on that flight, but that I would try again. After days of phone calls with the airline, they finally were forced to admit their mistake, and I was able to book another flight.

But this was not the end of it. Every time I've crossed the US border, I've heard, "Passport, please," then handed over my blue document before being taken aside. Interrogated. Held for two hours, waiting. Then forced to pay extra fees. Apply for a visa. There was always something. It just wouldn't end. This blue document didn't mean anything. Worse, when customs officials saw it, it showed them immediately that I was a refugee. To them it meant that I must be a terrorist or something. The way I was treated felt like harassment. Regardless of how stigmatized I felt, I learned how to remain calm in these situations.

To me it always felt like when I had my sister's passport in hand. I developed a phobia. I dreaded hearing those words "Passport please" – it triggered anxiety every time. I stopped trying to go to the US.

I tried to travel once more with my blue refugee passport before I gave up on it altogether. I had planned to participate in a very important conference in Geneva, Switzerland, to discuss Eritrean human rights abuses.

Without obstacles I was able to board in Vancouver. We were scheduled to make one stopover in London before arriving in Geneva. Everything had gone well. I arrived in London without any problems. Having two hours to myself, I relaxed and strolled through the many stores at the London airport. Then it was time to check in at the Swiss Air gate.

"Passport, please."

Once again, while all others boarded without incident, I had to step to the side where my document was under severe examination. I sighed, waiting for the officers to finish looking for the "hair in the egg."

Finally: "Sorry, I can't let you pass."

I couldn't believe what I'd heard. Again? Really? They said it as if nothing had happened. I tried to explain that I had travelled to Europe with this document before, that the Vancouver agents had said it was okay when I boarded. My words didn't matter. They sent me back directly on the next airplane to Ottawa, Canada. By the time I finally got home, defeated and wounded, I had spent more than forty-eight hours on airplanes. I made the hard decision not to travel again until I had my very own passport.

The agony finally ended on June 6, 2019, when I proudly got my first Canadian Passport, a few months after becoming a Canadian citizen.

A huge weight had suddenly been lifted. I was overwhelmed. Freedom at last. I finally had an official identity again.

I arranged travel to meet my mother.

"Passport, please."

Sure. "Here it is," I said happily.

2

Beyond the Mountain

Deea Badri

THE BELL WILL RING in a minute for the next stop.

Loud voices were coming from throughout the bus: "Touch the door! Touch the door!"

I looked back from where I was, sitting in front of the door at the back of the number nine bus headed to Vancouver Community College. Usually buses in Vancouver are really crowded in the early morning. Some are sitting, many are standing. That morning, a couple was laughing and kissing each other. An old lady was sleeping in her seat. Maybe it was too early for her to be awake.

I heard many different languages and tones on the bus. Some people were shouting, some were whispering, and some were speaking normally.

Since coming to Canada, I've learned about a lot of countries in the world and how to recognize different accents. Canada is a multicultural country where people come from everywhere to start a new life.

I looked back. There was a young Asian lady with black hair, white skin, and black eyes. She looked nervous and embarrassed while waiting for the door to open.

Two loud voices sounded at the same time: "Touch the door! Push the door!"

No one cared except me and the young lady who desperately wanted to get off the bus.

One of the voices was the bus driver, saying, "Please, young lady. You have to touch the door. Then the door will open for you, or come to the front door to get off."

But the young lady remained standing still.

From the expression on her face, she looked like she did not understand a word of English, or did not know how a bus door opens in Vancouver. I think she was waiting for the bus driver to open the door, because in other cities the bus drivers open the doors.

Another loud angry voice, this time from a homeless guy who had taken the disabled seat at the front of the bus for himself. No one was sitting near him because of how he smelled. He had two big plastic bags filled with cans.

He was ranting, "You are in Canada! You must speak English. Otherwise, go back to your country."

Suddenly the bus went quiet. All the eyes turned to look at the white guy with long blond hair, blue eyes, dirty clothes, and dirty sandals. It was hard to recognize the colour of his socks because the dirt covered everything. The other passengers gave him angry looks. Some of them were distressed – they were either new to Vancouver or they could not speak English. People felt uncomfortable, threatened, and unsafe.

Suddenly, this loud man remembered that no matter what, he is a white Canadian who speaks good English, and he has the power to talk. I am an immigrant, and I don't talk the same way he talks.

"Yes, all of you must speak English! You are in the best country in the world. Hey, you, pointing, where are you from? All of you crazy people come to my country to take my money! Our money!"

He continued ranting. He directly looked at me – maybe because I was close enough to him, maybe because of my angry eyes or the colour of my skin – and gave me a silly smile and said, "You came here as a refugee from Iraq, Syria, mmm, you look like a Latino, too. Whatever. You take our money."

Go back to your country.

I stood up and opened the door for the young lady without saying anything. She ran out. Maybe she was late for her English class, or maybe she was a tourist and needed to catch the Hop-on Hop-off tour bus.

I looked at the homeless man and did not say anything, but I had a vast hidden feeling to express or say something. He did not let me alone; he started talking. He was chatty.

"Let's have a conversation. We are so friendly here in Vancouver."

I looked at him again and took a long deep breath, to regulate my mood and manage my anger.

"Where are you from? Are you from a country where a man can beat you? Look at you, here you are wearing shorts, so attractive! And walking around freely." He spoke as if his eyes were touching me.

"Next stop is VCC, Clarke Street." I got up and ran to catch my stop. He was still talking, parroting, "Have a good day, gorgeous."

I entered Vancouver Community College (VCC), heading to my English class, but what happened on the bus made me sad. I went first to the cafeteria to get my morning coffee.

"Large dark as usual," said the barista with a smile.

"Yes, please," I answered sullenly.

"Are you okay?"

"Not a good day for me."

I sat down outside the cafeteria to have my coffee before class and to reflect on what had happened on the bus. It made me realize how a small incident can stay with you and affect your entire day.

Suddenly I found myself talking to my mom in my head.

"Mom, I wish you were still alive. I wish we could leave everything behind and go back to our home, to live our simple life. Mom, life here is so difficult if you cannot speak English or are a new immigrant from third world countries. Especially someone like us who do not have a country to be proud of like everyone else. I am sick of telling everyone where I came from, Mama."

Today was my first day of English class. The teacher asked everyone to stand up and show their country on the map at the front of the room.

"Who's going to volunteer first to show us their country?" asked the teacher.

The class was silent. No one answered.

The teacher asked me, "Hey, Deea, how about you? You were a journalist, right? You should go first."

While I was looking at the teacher and thinking, "Why me, I do not have a country to show everyone," a voice brought me back to my class.

"She's from Iraq," said one of my classmates.

In my mind, I was screaming "NO! I'm Kurdish!"

And so, I started my long historical story about Kurds. "We are the biggest nation in the world without our own country. They cut us like a cake into four pieces: Iraq, Syria, Iran, and Turkey."

Before I finished talking, some of my classmates interrupted me:

"Not true!" said the one from Iran.

"That's a crazy story," said the classmate from Turkey.

I was surprised, because I had many friends from Turkey and Iran, and they believed in our independency.

"Your time is over," said the teacher.

We are the biggest nation in the world without our own country.

Another student got up and went to the map to show their country, and I went back to my seat and started talking to my mom again as I retreated into my shell.

I thought, "Mom, look how tired I am. I came to Canada to live freely, to be able live on my own and to express my feeling, to live in a country where I can walk around late at night without fear, to find tolerant listeners who will listen to my suppressed inner voices. To see empathetic things and be beyond the mountain. As the old proverb says, 'Kurds have no friends but the mountains,' so I came to see what is beyond! There are so many obstacles in this new world, but I must fight and find a way in this new start."

3

Saddam, the Fallen God

Diary Marif

EVERY DAY, AS A CHILD, I was taught, "God created us; he watches over us everywhere. He is the biggest and the most powerful, but he is also the most merciful."

Every day my mother asked me, "Did you pray five times today? To have a better life in this world and the next world, you must worship God."

I would typically respond, "Okay, I will pray, Mom, if you remind me no one is bigger than God?"

Shockingly she would severely warn me that it was *kefir* (infidel) and I should repent. However, in my child mind, Saddam Hussein was bigger than God. In order to have a better and safer life, we needed to consider him a god.

The merciful God I was taught about, I never felt his power. Instead I saw Saddam Hussein's power from everywhere. Children always judge things depending on their visibility and tangibility. And Saddam was everywhere: on TV, his pictures were everywhere, in every size. His massive picture in the *brayati* – brotherhood – camp hung on the entrance gate of our local market, which I often passed. The camp's neighbourhood school, where I was supposed to be studying, also had a huge picture of Saddam. He was on the second page of all my school books. He controlled everything in the country. No one dared tear his pictures because his easy reaction would be killing many people.

We never had a television in our house and would visit my uncle Rahim's to watch cartoons. When we switched on the TV, we saw a man with a huge moustache, smiling while saluting at the same time. No one smiled back at the man on the screen. This scenario was always followed by several repeats of past war videos depicting the Iraqi Army with the same man. He totally controlled and monopolized the media. There were no alternatives or foreign sources of information. No one told me who he was, and I never asked. When I was around eight, I understood this man on the screen was Saddam. He was everywhere.

His picture was on the walls of his loyalists' houses, in all administrative offices within and outside of government. Many of his sculptures and statues were scattered throughout various parts of Baghdad and in many other cities. His speeches were frequently aired on TV and on the radio. The newspapers constantly put his picture on the front page, where he was consistently quoted. Even several streets and public places were named after him. He spent millions of dollars creating an illusion by portraying himself as a great national leader, a successful diplomat in politics, a brilliant military survivor, an Arab tribal sheikh, and the ultimate father of the nation. Saddam became a feared and revered god to many.

> *I saw Saddam Hussein's power from everywhere.*

After many years, I realized he was a god, but he was *Ahriman,* the Zoroastrian evil god. Instead of uniting the nation, this fear instead brought distrust and division. Saddam made the country like a stacked-blood lake. Some families spied on each other, in both public and private places. Friends betrayed friendships. Parents did not trust their children to tell them some secret. Children, like my siblings and I, were afraid to reveal their views of Saddam to their parents. My mother, like many other mothers, often advised my siblings and me not to say anything against him because she feared he could hear us wherever we were.

"You must shut up your mouth. If you hate him, his men will come to kill us."

I felt the birds would deliver our words to him, that they would kidnap us within one second. I hated the spy birds, those who delivered my words and my ideas to Saddam.

Saddam Hussein, the former Iraqi president, ruled the country by fire and iron. In 1979, the first year he came to power, he ruined my paternal and maternal grandparents' houses in our village Bardabal in Sulaymaniyah province, known by locals as Slemani. It was just one year before my parents got married. They could no longer enjoy their lives in their beloved village. Saddam not only destroyed my parents' house but also five thousand more villages close to Iranian borders, forcing villagers to live in camps. My parents got married and had four children in Shanadari camp in East of Slemani. I was the third born.

I was a child of war, born in this environment of warfare that Saddam had created. It was the middle of his eight-year war with Iran (1980–88). This was the period of widespread instability. My family moved from one place to another because we lived in the epicentre of the war. My parents were constantly looking for safe shelter, to protect us. As a result, they remain uncertain of where and when I was born. According to my Iraqi passport, I was born on November 17, 1984. There are several reasons why this is not my actual birthday. First, my parents could not approach government offices because they were occupied by military personnel. Additionally, the Kurds tried to hide the males' identities to avoid them being forced to join the Iraqi army. Also, the Iraqi government did not favour recording newly born Kurds as they wanted to hide the real number of the Kurdish population.

As if to further deepen my doubt, my cousins would often joke that my parents were not my real parents. They claimed I was abandoned by my real parents when I was a toddler because they did not have enough food for me. This was a very common scenario during the wars. Years later, I asked my parents when and where I was born, but they were not sure. They only remembered that I was born during the Iraq-Iran war.

My mother told me, "You were five months old when the Iraqi Ba'ath party murdered Abdulkareem." Abdulkareem was her middle brother.

But my Uncle Hussein told me a different story of my birth, and he is well known for his excellent memory. He said, "You were born one day after Abdulkareem died."

My parents were constantly looking for safe shelter, to protect us.

However, my father remembered that I was one year and four months old when my mother's second brother, Hassan, died stepping on an Iranian-made landmine near the border. They only remembered that I was born sometime during the war and between the deaths of my uncles. Every year, on November 17, when people wish me a happy birthday, it brings me no joy.

This past, the era of instability, poverty, brutality, and fear, which was the darkest and the most painful in the history of the country, had driven my life. There were no silver linings – just darkness. Sirens, air raids, and bombing were the first sounds that I remembered hearing. I started playing with cannonballs among ruins instead of playing at a kindergarten playground. One particular day I fell down into a destroyed three-metre deep sewer and slit the left side of my face. Years later, I was told that my mother had frantically looked for me while crying hysterically. She found me unconscious at the bottom of this hole. I had been severely hurt when I fell and I had a deep gash that needed to get stitched. Later the stitches left a scar that looked like a scorpion, which earned me the nickname "Scorpion."

With a fresh scar on my face, I clearly remember the Iraqi airplanes bombing our settlement area of Shanadari in 1988. I distinctly recall my mom screaming and pushing me below our house, through a tiny filthy underground room with a dirt floor. I think it was about two metres high and just three to four metres wide and long with only a strip of light from the door. I did not understand then why we stayed for such a long time in that tiny and uncomfortably hot room. I thought it was a game of hide and seek. I even enjoyed seeing other people. I didn't realize we were hiding so the helicopters couldn't find us.

There were many people around us all squashed up like sardines, anxiously listening for the terrifying sounds of bombs blasting around the neighbourhood. I remember once the humming sound of a car passing by and loudly hitting a bump in the road, which caused someone to mistakenly exclaim that the helicopters were coming. A few minutes later, a helicopter passed. It flew close. The ground shook like there was an earthquake.

Everyone repeatedly screamed, "*Ya Allah!*" asking God to protect them.

My mom put my younger sister, Snoor, on her lap and held me close to her. I jealously tried to sit on my mother's lap by displacing my sister. My mother reminded me, "Your sister is a baby and you should be patient until we go home."

The only reason I calmed down was the gentle soothing whispers from my mom, declaring, "I love you more than anyone. I promise you can have cookies later."

"Okay," I said, convinced to be patient.

She patted my recent scars softly. Her hand was sweaty, but I felt safe and loved by her sweaty hand. I could not see her face in the darkness, but I still remember the soothing deep scent of the dianthus flower that she traditionally wore to decorate her chest. I felt safe. I would slowly touch her front pocket for cookies. I found a small solid item there and smelled it. It was a piece of dough. I did not know how long it had been there, but I put it in my mouth and sucked it.

Many women prayed to God, children cried, and the elderly suffered terribly due to the heat and lack of fresh air. They coughed, and their voices changed.

After around one hour a man cautiously opened the narrow, shabby wooden door. He shushed everyone, squinted, peeked out, and then went out to check. He came back and reported, "The helicopters are not there anymore."

He opened the door, and everyone ducked down and hurriedly went out. We all went to our separate homes. Unlike some houses, ours was still standing. Exhausted, breathless, with dust-covered faces like wounded soldiers. The streets were foggy, empty, and grey. Once in a while a car passed leaving a thick trail of dust behind it. Ruined sidewalks. Trees along the ruined sidewalks all shrivelled and dried up. The colours of people's front doors were rusty and fatigued resembling our tired faces.

This same scenario happened many times. I usually did not like to go to the scary room underground, and I did not know why we kept going there. It became a part of our daily life. It did not only happen in our area; it was also part of the lives of the majority of people in Kurdistan.

We were demoralized. Men had no desire to shave. They wore dirty old clothes. Women were not putting henna on their hair anymore. They mostly resorted to wearing black clothing like they were in mourning, like my mother since she lost her brothers and cousins in the middle of the 1980s. My mother, like many other mothers, advised us to play nearby, in case the planes returned to bomb our settlement. There were many times in the heart of the war when I questioned our survival. My parents said they prayed to God and brought written prayers into the underground hideout. My paternal grandmother, on the other hand, had a piece of *shakha fyl*, or elephant horn, which she believed would protect us. I saw the elephant horn many times during the war and during other life challenges and other difficulties.

My grandmother said, "This is a holy piece. It will keep us safe."

And when the planes and military came around, my grandmother took it out from the piece of green cloth she normally kept it in and kissed it and instructed my siblings to do the same.

I put it between my hands and deeply kissed it without understanding why it was holy and how it could protect us from bombs! I have never asked my parents about the horn or any other superstitions they traditionally practiced and believed in.

Many had their own underground places in which to hide and protect themselves during the war. The security and lives of so many depended on these underground shelters for avoiding air raids, bombs, and military harassment. Later, I realized why we all had to go underground to hide from the bombings. I wanted details and asked my parents, "Where was this place we went to? When did we go there?"

My father replied, "During the eight-year war, we moved to many places and spent many days and nights in different underground places. It was impossible to keep track of time and place."

Other times, I did not need my parents to guide me underground during the bombings. I went there directly and found them there among many others. I was terrified of the sound of the helicopter. I didn't want to go to dark rooms or live in a basement. I hated the military uniform. Since then, I am still traumatized by underground places, and I am very uncomfortable in basements.

Barbarity and brutality became obvious features of the country as people, including children, turned against each other. One cold grey day in the fall of 1989, without any particular reason, I was severely injured on my head by a wild boy just as I strolled out of our home. I was only five, but I remember that day vividly like it was yesterday. Despite only a gentle wind blowing, the electric wires outside appeared to be humming rather loudly. A notorious boy from the neighbourhood savagely threw a block of cement with nails in it from an adjacent building, two storeys up. It hit me hard on my forehead and I immediately passed out and started bleeding profusely. I did not know what had happened until hours later, when I found myself on my mother's lap. Tears were rolling down her cheeks. I do not know who picked me up off the ground and what they did for me. At that time, we had recently moved to a suburb village of Slemani City. We had escaped there during the war and stayed for several months. The families there had to take care of their children, to protect them from strangers. My injured head was hurting, but there were no doctors or medicine. My mother put a fried egg on the wound and tied it with a rope, which she untied again after several days. Although she often said that the wound would heal, it left two parallel scar lines that will remain with me forever.

After a generation of severe trauma, the Kurdish people finally rose up against Saddam in 1991. There was finally a light at the end of the tunnel. Saddam withdrew his army from northern Iraq, which is currently called Kurdistan. Saddam, however, continued to rule the rest of Iraq. When the Kurdistan region gained semi-autonomy and formed its own government in 1992, I was so excited. My family, relatives, and neighbours all celebrated. My paternal grandmother danced tirelessly – she was like a gilded bird that had finally escaped from a dark cage. In fact, I had never seen her in such a good mood. She was so excited and happy. Her feeling was so infectious, and many women in the neighbourhood also danced and expressed their joy. I danced with her, too. I was extremely happy, but I was also overwhelmed because I was only six and still did not understand much of what was going on. In retrospect, when I now think about that moment, I understand more about that joy the women expressed so freely. Like my grandmother, these women's sons, grandsons, and relatives were at war. Many had died. My mother, however, was depressed because she was still mourning the death of her two brothers after six years. That night, she did not dance. She laughed and cried while praying. Boys ran in the streets, cheering and launching beautiful arrays of fireworks to celebrate. Adults stole guns from Saddam's abandoned military base and shot into the sky. In fact, everybody celebrated everywhere in the country. In contrast, the Iraqi regime imposed severe internal sanctions against the Kurdish population as a response to their aspiration for freedom and self-governance. Again, Saddam still had his hands on our throat. Though he never came back to Kurdistan, the dire scars of his political action still remain.

People were full of hope and expectation to return to their villages. They hoped their miserable lives would be converted into better lives. They had high expectations of the Kurdish government, to rebuild the remnants of their destroyed villages. Despite difficulties, in 1992, at the age of eight, I enrolled in school. I missed two years of studies during the war. In the 1990s and early 2000s, Kurdish parties reminded us every day of Saddam's cruelty and atrocities. What was most unfortunate were the dreams and hopes that never came to fruition due to many Kurdish leaders forming militias, which then looted the nation's wealth and sold it to Iran. At the same time, they went on to follow in Saddam's footsteps by continuing to rule by nepotism. Also, the culture of controlling the media and freedom of expression continued to prevail. After Saddam was overthrown in 2003, I was older and more aware of the mounting political injustice and atrocities that had been committed, which led me to openly criticize the political system.

Once I started talking about the Kurdish militia's ferociousness, my father tried to shut me up. The main problem between us was my career. When I decided to start writing in 2006, particularly against corruption, my parents warned me against doing so.

"The political parties will kill you, just like Saddam did to journalists."

My father urged me, "Stop criticizing. Join the party I support. Then you will have a better and safer life. You have two choices. Join the party or leave! I swear, if they kidnap and torture you, I will never support you! I will deny you!"

"I know you love me, but I refuse your demands, father. I will make a different life elsewhere to protect my dignity and stability." And I left home.

He repeatedly expressed his fears that the authorities in power would one day kidnap and kill me. He knew about the parties' brutality better than I did, but I stubbornly stuck to what I believed in and continued to write. Although most politicians had fought hard against Saddam Hussein, they ironically, and quickly, stepped into line to become the new Saddam. The Kurdish militias and parties reinforced Saddam's dictatorship style and not democracy, as they had promised. Masoud Barzani, president of the Kurdistan Democratic Party (KDP) since 1979, and his friend Jalal Talabani (1933–2017) former Iraqi president and general secretary of the Patriot Union of Kurdistan (PUK), were Saddam's biggest critics and also tirelessly fought against him. Yet they adopted his horrific political leadership style.

The new regimes killed and tortured their opponents as well as terrorized people in prisons, to silence them in the same style that Saddam did. When their supporters told me the torture stories, I panicked. I put myself in the shoes of people who had been tortured. I empathized with their pain. Similar to Saddam, these leaders also put their sons, brothers, cousins, and relatives in high-security positions. The new regimes used secret intelligence spies, just like Saddam did, to spread fear among the people. On several occasions, the different political parties sent spies to test me and other critics, to gauge my allegiance. Their intention was to incite me to talk negatively about their parties with the motive of later using this information against me. I was always cautious about what I said, especially from 2006 to 2010, during my years at the University of Duhok.

Talabani's and Barzani's pictures replaced Saddam's everywhere. Another similarity between these Kurdish leaders and Saddam was how they masterminded the seeds of hatred between Kurds and Arab people. The brutality of these leaders reminded us of the dark days of Saddam's dictatorship. We hoped to find strategies to cope with our trauma, but these new political regimes controlled all governmental and private organizations – just like Saddam.

Kurdish militias also used Saddam's tactics to kidnap and beat people into submission. They attacked innocent people for demanding their basic rights. They assassinated and jailed journalists and writers who dared to criticize their political system. Over the next several years, Kurdish people continued to suffer, but this time they suffered at the hands of Kurdish political parties who claimed they would bring justice, equality, and democracy. Thus, because there was a civil war between the Kurdish parties, and because Saddam's party had imposed severe restrictions, many Kurdish people, like my father and I, had no other job options except to work at the borders as marginalized people, jeopardizing our lives just to survive as kolbars, or porters. A kolbar is someone who takes items across the Iran-Iraq borders, usually on their backs. My father and I put ourselves at great risk working as kolbars in the mid-'90s, when I was only eleven.

Evidence of Saddam's tragic use of lethal weapons remained. It was like he intentionally left a reminder of himself everywhere you looked. Landmines from his regimes continued to cause endless loss of lives. In 1991, an exodus of Kurdish refugees from neighbouring Turkey and Iran returned to Iraq as empty-handed as they had left. They used the remains of Saddam's lethal weaponry to build themselves temporary shelters. Men collected Saddam's plastic items for heating wood stoves. I followed my father to help him. He warned me against touching plastics that still had gun powder in them.

He said, "You might lose your hands or eyes, or even die from the gun powder."

I found one piece of plastic, but I forgot his warning and removed the powder and kept the plastic. Nothing happened to me, but in 1991, two of my cousins put gun powder into a bottle and burned it, and their faces got burned. Luckily, they didn't die, but for months they had to stay at home.

And in 1996, another cousin went out to eat berries. He found guns in a stream and checked them. I was eating berries when I heard an explosion. I fell down. He cried out. I ran home. My cousin's face and the rest of his body were burned. For years the marks covered his body.

Barbed wire that had previously been used in war zones was converted into fences for cows and sheep. My father made food storage from pieces of military vehicles, as did other villagers. Men found guns and used them for protection. My father found two Kalashnikov rifles and dangled them in a corner of the tiny room where our family slept. These guns had been used to kill people during Saddam's reign of terror. Every night before he slept, my father put one of them next to himself. Whenever I heard the sound of a gun cocking, it took me back to the dark days.

Gradually I gained courage and asked my parents, "Please buy me a plastic gun, and teach me how to use it like a real gun."

Girls and women planted beautiful flowers within empty guns shells as if to erase their ugliness. People used cannon tubes as pipes to channel spring water. We children played marble games with weapon shells, and we made games from the shells of mines and other types of guns. We put weapon shells as goalposts for soccer. My mother used a huge wooden box from Saddam's military remains as a cupboard for my siblings. I kept my books in a military box. My father put his shaving items in a green military plastic sack. The remains of such lethal weapons of war, which we once hated, became crucial parts for rebuilding our lives. Ironically, in so many ways, Saddam was still part of our lives.

Saddam's ominous presence somehow continued to linger. To so many, this only reinforced the belief that he was a god. For whatever purpose, Saddam's pictures still remained in school books. On the second pages of these school books, under his portrait was written "The Honorable President of Iraq, Saddam Hussein, May God bless him." I often thought that Saddam should be the one blessing God. That was part of not only my thinking but also that of most of my generation.

One of my friends often said, "God cannot kill a man, but Saddam killed five thousand Kurdish people in one minute."

The evil dictator jailed and murdered thousands of innocent citizens, and he executed and slaughtered uncountable numbers of Shiite and Sunni Muslims, Yazidis, Christians, and other ethnic minorities. When I used to hang out with my friends, we did not talk about our childhood memories.

We talked about wars, clashes, and the abilities of Saddam and his regime. Everyone exaggerated his abilities and shared stories.

Someone said, "Saddam could hide among tree branches; he could go into the ears of a cow."

I believed his shoes were bigger than God's. His handkerchief was bigger than our house carpets. His slingshot was larger than the old oak tree in my village. His cigarette was taller than a rocket tube. The stories about Saddam made us more vulnerable and frightened. We were not only afraid of his photos; we were scared of people who even looked like him. Most children did not admire Saddam, but our family, friends, and the Iraqi regime created an atmosphere wherein we acknowledged rumours about his ruthlessness.

In March 2003, US-led military forces commenced the invasion of Iraq. I never thought they would defeat Saddam, since I always imagined he was invincible. His propaganda minister lied about the ability and capacity of the Iraqi army. When the war started, I was nineteen and very vigilant about gaining information about the war. We still had no TV, but I went to my relatives for updates. After three weeks, on April 9, the US forces arrived in the capital of Baghdad, and they toppled Saddam's iron statue. I remember being so shocked because for the very first time, I and many others realized that Saddam was a mere human being like us and not God!

After he was overtaken, most citizens throughout the country celebrated. They spread out on the streets and hugged each other. I participated in several political parties as we happily, and with much relief, celebrated the end of Saddam's era. The Kurdish parties claimed they'd played a vital role in destroying Saddam, but this was not entirely true. Once again, we hoped for a better life as Iraqi politicians and the US spread propaganda of a democratic life where everyone was equal and safe. In 2006, the US finally killed Saddam's brutal sons, and later that same year, Saddam himself was captured and hanged.

Although Saddam was destroyed, his political leadership and adopted cultural practices remain. It is now 2023, two decades since Saddam was defeated. I learned from this experience that when people do not make their voices heard, when they do not collectively fight for their rights, they can create a Saddam in any corner of the globe. They pave the road to create dictators. But the memories of these events have traumatized me and given me nightmares that have for years led me to sleepwalk. My thoughts, feelings, memories, and aspirations were never those of an average child. In my village, among my people as a child and young adult, my voice was not heard. I have also learned that somewhere along the way came the realization that my pain is also strength. My past traumatic experiences have created in me a strong sense of justice and equality that has dared me to stand and write against any tyranny in my country, to prevent the emergence of other dictators like Saddam. I have continued to write since coming to Canada in September 2017.

4

What the Poppies Know

Shanga Karim

"IT'S TIME TO GO HOME, we all have to go home, home again!" My dad said that very loudly and kissed me while he put me down from his back and put more stuff inside the *buxcha* on his back. You could barely see him because of the colourful big tied blanket that we called a buxcha, which was full of clothes, bread, and some food. The surface of it, covered with big and small bubbles, made it look like there was someone hidden inside. This was where I sat during our four-day walk in March 1991.

After the Allied forces expelled Saddam Hussein's army from Kuwait in February 1991, the courageous people of Kurdistan rose up against the tyrannical rule of the Ba'ath regime in four key Kurdish cities: Hawler, Sulaymaniyah, Kirkuk, and Duhok. However, as the United States failed to topple Saddam's regime completely prior to withdrawing its forces, he swiftly regained strength and cracked down on the Kurdish uprising. Fearing a repeat of past atrocities, such as the chemical attack carried out against our people on March 16, 1988, the people of southern Kurdistan made the difficult decision to flee. Millions of people abandoned their homes and, in a matter of hours, undertook perilous journeys to the mountains and the borders of Eastern Kurdistan (Iran) and Northern Kurdistan (Turkey).

One evening, the distant rumble of approaching military vehicles caused panic to ripple through our own city of Sulaymaniyah – the dreaded Republican Guard, loyal to Saddam Hussein, was drawing near. My father, as with other men who had suffered under the regime, knew that it was time to flee. He had heard stories of atrocities committed by

Saddam's forces, and he could not bear the thought of his family suffering the same fate. Since that evening, when we were told to run from Saddam, I had been sitting on one of the buxcha's bubbles. From my position, I could smell gun smoke mixed with the scents of the coming spring, and I could see a long line of dark heads, people who looked like worker ants that leave their nest to find food, leaving behind a pheromone trail so they don't lose each other or their way through the rough terrain. It's the same picture to me, and for the same purpose – except that the ants might have had a plan for where to go. We didn't have a plan, and we didn't know where we might find another nest. That was frustrating for me as a five-year-old girl.

I remember talking to myself while I was on dad's shoulders. Isn't it fun to be a loved child, to see all these crowds from above? To see the longest line of united people without seeing the line's end? Tiny me, on the shoulders of a tired dad, with my favourite flowery dress and pink pyjamas and my old maroon shiny shoes – you could still see a bit of shine where they were not covered by dust. I was having fun with all the up-and-down movements. I was beside my chubby almost four-year-old sister, who was on our only brother's shoulders. We were arguing about who's really older, or higher. I think we wanted to have fun rather than see our parents' tired pale faces or the fear in their eyes.

Starting a fight in the sky, I said, "I am older than you, and higher than you!"

She tried to convince me that she is older. "I am older than you, you know why? I am number ten of the eleven sisters, but you are number nine!" She stuck out her tongue to tease me.

I put my fingers toward my mom's belly and said, "How do you know that this one is a number eleven girl?"

She answered, "I know, mommy can just have girls, as the neighbours say." I think she forgot that she was talking from our brother's shoulders.

All eight of my other sisters surrounded us, walking slowly and very closely, and some of them smiled as they listened to our fight about our birth order.

"I am hungry," I said to myself. I touched my dad's buxcha, looking for something that could make my little heart happy. For a second, I thought it was full of dates. Now, I was thinking of putting one of those dates to my mouth, so delicious, but not sure which type of dates were in my dad's buxcha. I may not like one or two kinds of the two hundred varieties of dates that we have in this world. Which kind of dates are there? "Are they the hard ones? Oh, I hope not! Are they the acidic yellow ones? Or the soft juicy ones from Iraq that I die for?"

"We are going home again. Wow, can we have a home again?" The loud voice and reaction of one of my sisters interrupted me as I was imagining taking out the hard seed of a date.

Suddenly she screamed and said, "We don't have a home, we never had a home, and we will not have one ever, they ruined everything, everything we had, not just home, our land, our culture, and even our identity and our names! The Ba'ath regime did whatever they wanted, whatever they liked, and now they want us to go home after we fled through all the treacherous mountains to find a life that we never had since they took away everything." She continued, "Dad! do you believe them? Do you even believe our government when they say they really care about us and want us to go home to a safe life? Which home do they talk about? Do they take this big responsibility? We haven't done anything, why do we have to pay this price?"

Who is going to take all these children's dead bodies to our home?!

She looked at her surroundings, her curly hair and sad face, and signalled with her hand. "Just look, look at this woman who died because she could not get milk to her infant. Look at this child whose family had to throw her away because they could no longer hold her with their empty stomachs and their bloody bare feet. Look at this man who doesn't have any clothes and doesn't care that he is naked because he wants his children to stay warm. Who is going to take all these children's dead bodies to our home?! No one, because we do not have anything called a home. We are homeless and would rather be homeless Kurdish than be forced to speak Arabic and lose our language."

I was still playing with the imaginary date seed in my mouth, thinking back to a few nights ago when my dad decided that we needed to leave. It was a normal evening, dark and quiet on our narrow avenue. The smells of Kurdish foods came to my nose: rice, and the spicy, yummy smell of *yaprax*. I could also smell fried onions. I wanted to run and put a piece of bread in it and eat it. I love eating bread with burnt oil. The smell of the oil spread in the air, along with that of the *Niskena* soup from the neighbours in the corner. I could see the steam from small houses with grey *azbez* – asphalt-shingled roofs.

All the neighbours brought warm dishes to each other's houses, each one on a plate with a different Middle Eastern pattern. They always cooked extra to share with other neighbours, but when we gave back the plate, it was never empty. You could never see the design on the plate. It was always filled with warm food to share.

Suddenly, this peace changed to the sounds of people running, yelling, shouting, and spreading news that we had to leave. Everyone came out from their homes. Some were shocked. Some ran to collect their belongings, while children were still yelling and playing hide-and-seek. I closed my eyes and started saying loudly, "One, two, three, four, five, six, seven, eight," trying to reach ten. But before getting there, I opened my right eye to hear what my little friend's mom was saying to my mom in a loud voice: "We must leave. Saddam will attack us shortly with chemicals, just like he did to Halabja city. All our Kurdish soldiers have left. We don't hear any news from them to tell us, 'Please don't move or leave, we are here to save you.'"

> *We do not have anything called a home.*
> *We are homeless.*

I heard another person say, "Our city is empty, everyone is running and fleeing, no one defends us, we have to run." Another terrified voice, a neighbour man shouting, "Saddam will kill anyone he can reach, he doesn't care about anything."

These voices were mixed with those of the Kurdish leader on the radio, telling his people to leave their homes. That became a real hide-and-seek game for me and my friends. I noticed that I really could not see my friends anymore, as everyone was trying to conceal themselves, to run and put as many clothes in their bags, to save everything they could because they didn't know what they would need.

The voices coming from all the radios became one loud voice that said, "Move and leave the city."

It was a big decision by the leader of one of the dominant Kurdish parties at that time. People were so disappointed when they heard that. Word spread so quickly that no *peshmerga* – our military forces – were left in the city!

That is how we decided to leave, along with one of our close neighbours, as one family of seventeen people: fourteen in my family, three in our neighbour's family. Then, we started our journey.

While we prepared to leave, one of my sisters shouted, "We are not ready because Lana is not here!"

"Lana!" my dad said. "Where is she? Why is she not here?" He was counting us and noticed that number five of the girls was indeed missing!

"Na top u na tayara, darman nakat lam shara." Lana was shouting these Kurdish words very distinctly – words that appeared on protesters' signs, which surrounded her. "No weapon, no helicopter, can take us away from this city." Then she said, "I am here!" She yelled at my family and ran forward, away from the protesters. "Let me grab my stuff, I wanted to protest and support my people." She wanted to be brave and stay in the city, but she knew it was time to leave. She had always wanted to be some- one, a girl with her thoughts, with her voice, making her own decisions. But when she realized that it was 12:00 a.m. and the number of protesters was getting smaller and smaller, she returned. She grabbed her backpack and put in her sketchbook, which had some Kurdistan mountain drawings, along with her old grey pencil, two books, and a few articles of clothing to take with her on an unknown journey.

Lana could not trust very easily. In our culture, when there is a negotiation between families, men always have the power. They are expected to solve problems, but sometimes they make things worse. My family was a little different as there were eleven daughters and one son. Women had power in my family just by sheer numbers. Lana always expressed her own thoughts and opinions, which was not so easy for girls her age in our society. She was the strongest of all the girls in my family and still is to this day.

"DATES, DATES, DATESSSSS," I yelled silently in my mind. My mouth wanted so badly for some sweetness that I thought about it for three days of walking. I pouted to get my dad's attention. I looked at my dad's face, the circles beneath his eyes growing darker with each long night spent staying up and watching over his family. On his face, I could see fear, the uncertainty of leading us all without knowing the right direction. He knew that he didn't have any power except for his belief as always in his God. I think his relationship with God was because of himself, not the written pieces in the Quran, as he never could read a word of the holy book, nor could he read and write his own name. How could he understand all 604 pages of the Quran?

Dad was trying to tighten his *jamana*, winding and winding it three times around the small hat on top of his head until it was tight enough. My eyes fixed on all the dust that had accumulated over our long journey, now released from his hat as he wound it around his head. My dad's jamana was so grey with dust that it was hard to recognize its original shape and colour. The hat, with its triangle shapes, symbolizes strength, bravery, and fighting for fairness. Kurdish peshmerga always wear that hat during conflicts to show their strength and to show their pride in being Kurdish soldiers.

The dust did not stay on only his hat. His dusty split lip spoke to how long those lips had not been wet. His yellow skin was a strong witness to not getting enough nutrition, and his eyes, one honey and the other brown, showed how much strain he was under. Those eyes were half closed, and it looked like he was feeling sleepy, but the big responsibility on the owner of those eyes did not allow them to take a rest. There was no time to rest. When they were open, they were looking after all the other eyes, saying that we were going to be okay. They were seeking water or a good place to take a short rest after hours and hours of walking at the same time. I witnessed many disasters by the side of the road; many died from disease, a lot of older folk didn't make it even half way, and many people – including young children – went missing.

Luckily, I was holding my dad's hand. I was still waiting for him to get just one date, but fear reminded me to hold his hand tighter. My eyes moved to his coarse dry hands, to look at all the lines, the witnesses of his hard work spent feeding, educating, and supporting all his children. I wanted to really feel the coarseness and the dryness. I wish I had brought the *waazany* to put on his hands, to make them softer. I miss being at home and putting this cream on his hands.

"Aww my back, I cannot stand anymore, please take me somewhere to sit before the baby comes out." My mom's face was swollen, and her eyes were smaller than usual, her cheeks redder, which made her more beautiful, with her round belly in her traditional Kurdish dress, a *jli kurdi*. She tucked the bottom of her long delicate dress in her wide Kurdish pants and tightened her belly to support the baby. My dad suddenly moved my hand away and took all the stuff off his shoulders so he could hold my mom's hand and help her find a comfortable place to sit on one of his backpacks. He spread his *mraxane*, a traditional Kurdish man's jacket, on my mom's shoulders to keep her warm.

When mom sat, I could sit in front of that beautiful round perfect belly to smell her for a brief time. I was so close that I could feel my youngest sister kicking from inside my mom's bump, as if she was in a hurry to come out. How about having your birthday at this time, in the middle of a thousand fleeing people? I hoped that she knew how many children had been left and separated from their parents, that had died because of not having food, warm clothes, and shelter to stay in. I wish we could decide when and how to be born and be welcomed to this planet. I whispered in her small ears, above my mom's thin peach-and-orange Kurdish dress with little dark flowers on it, to tell her, "I wish I could come back to stay with you and play, I am tired of walking in this muddy, wintry, unpleasant weather, and of being outside and not eating anything for a few days."

No home. No food. No direction.

That was the most silent moment I can remember, when everyone stopped talking and moving because they were afraid that she was going to have a baby now! My dad, with tearful eyes that washed the dust from his face, tried to tell my mom, "We won't do anything and won't go anywhere until we are sure about your situation and your comfort, my darling."

This picture of my mom made my sister recognize that we were in the same situation as all other families who couldn't carry their infants anymore. But it was not just our unborn child; it was our mom that we could not do anything for. No home. No food. No direction.

My sister ran to my dad and hugged him, crying, her voice strained. She exclaimed regret about what she had said about not going home again, that she doesn't mean to hurt. She was just not sure about her family's future and safety, whether to leave forever or return to Kurdistan. She wasn't sure where there could be a real home, for us? For all Kurdish people? She was afraid of seeing those big brown boots and scary army uniforms again. And then she said, "It is better to die because of having no home, with my empty stomach and my bloody feet, than to be killed and have our home taken by their brutal soldiers, who buried us alive during the Anfal campaign, and massacred us with chemical weapons at Halabja."

My oldest sister, Kwestan, held my distressed sister and said, "Why do you hurt yourself like that? We all have the same feelings, but the best way is to decide and follow the government instructions even if it's not true. We do not have any more choices; we cannot all go to stay in refugee camps! Who will give us asylum? Which country can be our real home? They all have a big border. But we have each other still, we don't want to lose each other."

They both started crying very silently and embraced each other.

Unexpectedly, I found myself in the sky when one of my sisters held me up. From above, I could see their messy hair and hear their scary crying mingled with laughter. I could not understand why we were squeezed together while we were all so tired, especially with the smell of our unwashed bodies.

At the same time, my sisters' feelings and empathy for each other evoked the pleasant green smell of their hopes and dreams, like the scent of the red spring flowers that had accompanied us throughout our journey, giving us hope in this grey, dusty place where currents created by helicopters overhead raised and covered us with dust. That same air moved the red flowers slightly toward the deceased as if to express their sympathy to these unknown dead victims. The flowers wanted to tell them, "How strong we people are, and that's why we are here."

"We know what you suffered, we know that more than the world, where everyone uses words like 'humanity,' and everyone wants to stop all these wars." Yet the flowers continue to return every spring, when people need to cross borders seeking asylum, where the sea becomes home for Kurdish refugees before arriving at their dream homes in Europe.

We were close to the border to Iran, which was opened to Kurdish refugees after the displaced people heard their leader, Jalal Talabani, say, "We all can go home again." That is why my dad had to decide whether we should keep walking or stay in the refugee camps in Kurdistan–Iran, where many other Kurdish people were, or leave for European countries as many already had.

I could taste the flavour that I had craved throughout the journey. My dad called me and said, "I am so sorry for the delay, Shana *gyan*. Here are some dates. Eat them and enjoy the sweetness. It took me so long to find them for you from some other people."

"My two dates!" I yelled. I was so excited! "Thank you, Daddy!" Without waiting, I put them in my mouth.

"Be careful with the seeds, please," he said.

I answered by turning my head upside down with a full mouth of juicy dates and small hard seeds, which I did not care about – I wanted to eat all of it. How lucky I was to get these sweets.

My dad hugged me and continued, "How do you find a sweet moment in your tough times, not just food?"

"These dates will give you the power to be able to go back all the way from the Iranian border to Kurdistan alone with your mom. We will ask the soldiers to find some space in someone's car to take you home, Sulaymaniyah!"

"I want to hear your story when we are reunited again, how my little daughter arrived home and took care of her mom and the baby." Those words prepared Mom, my baby sister who was still inside her belly, and I to go home alone. That is how we separated from the rest of the family.

The moment when I tasted those dates was the moment that I learned that even in the toughest time in our lives, we can still enjoy the tiny, sweet things, the small joys, and find courage to go forward. From the taste of those dates, after our long trek, I realized that we could find home anywhere.

Since 1991, we have been displaced because of Saddam and our own Kurdish government. Our people continue to seek a home, and peace. There is not a year that the seas don't find Kurdish children, whose small broken boat sinks while their families risk a safer life. And that's how the poppies have many stories of us Kurdish people.

My heart feels so heavy, and the air is stuck in my chest while mixed sweet and tart memories return from when I was five years old. Here I am, sitting on a bench in a beautiful park, during my second journey to Canada in 2015, thinking about the memories that I still live with and write about in my diary. Writing them down encourages me to tell the world about all the stateless Kurdish people everywhere. To tell the next generation of Kurdish children who don't know where their families came from and what they suffered or why. To explain why they accepted being refugees rather than living in their beautiful Kurdistan.

As I look around me at the trees and their colourful leaves of red and yellow, with some orange and green ones on the ground, my eyes go to the back of the bench I am sitting on. I read:

IN MEMORY OF OLIVIA BROWN 06/02/1946 – 01/11/2015
BELOVED SISTER, MOM AND WIFE. CLOTHE YOURSELVES IN
LOVE, WHICH BINDS EVERYTHING TOGETHER IN PERFECT
HARMONY.

I wonder if Olivia knows that her name can serve all of us even after her death. It is not just about Olivia and how much she was loved. It is about people of all ages who visit this park and become tired after a long walk around the lake, all the different humans with assorted skin colours and different names who all came from different countries, cultures, and beliefs. It is for all these people who have found security, love, and hope by sitting on this bench after leaving their birth homes for different reasons. I wonder about migrants and refugees: Do they feel a sense of belonging here? Do they experience love and acceptance? Do they fit into their new environment? Do they feel welcome, or do they grapple with loneliness and exclusion? How do they contribute to their new community? In what ways do they seek to become an integral part of their new surroundings, and how do they integrate with the differences?

I remember to write something in my notes on the cracked phone that came with me from Kurdistan to Canada. This phone, which contains many untold stories, is so important in my new chapter of life here. With a split screen that sometimes makes it so I can't recognize the words, it allows me to transfer the endless stories from my childhood to the cellphone's memory. It also translates all the Kurdish words in my memory to English words in the phone's memory – her memory. For me, it's not just a phone to make or answer calls. She (the phone) is a listener and co-writer, one who will listen to all my challenges and adventures. She understands how to be a storyteller because she has a story of her own, just like everyone else. Though her story is a bitter one.

How many untold stories could be written on this phone that was so difficult to get? When I arrived here as an asylum seeker, I began working as soon as I received my work permit. My initial role was as a labourer in a screen company, where I measured large mesh materials used in window production. I was thrilled to have the opportunity, even though it wasn't in my profession of journalism, and it taught me that gaining Canadian experience isn't solely about the field you work in; it's about how you adapt and contribute to any Canadian workplace. After a few months my husband joined the company as an accountant. This allowed us to work together, though my focus was on learning the intricacies of inch measurement for window materials and operating aluminum cutting machines. It was a headache to use inches instead of centimetres and all the different ways to measure in English; however, throughout the eleven months I spent at the screen company, my mind was working and thinking differently every single day.

A journalist at heart, I found my thoughts wandering to my dreams of being a writer and crafting stories. I realized I needed to buy a better phone to facilitate these endeavours, so my husband and I went to buy one. We had all the papers and documents from the Canadian government, which allowed us to stay in this land. Surely we would be allowed to buy a phone.

The sales person was so nice at first. He showed us all the beautiful different versions of phones, iPhones, and iPads. He seemed so empathetic, and I thought that he understood our situation more than others. He seemed like he might have come to this country in a similar way.

When it was time to make the payment, he requested our IDs. We presented our refugee documents, hoping they would suffice; however, he seemed unaware of their significance. After a brief conversation with his manager, he said, "I'm sorry, but I can't sell a phone with only these papers."

We were speechless, uncertain of whether we were in the right or wrong. The man's lack of understanding regarding newcomers in Canada made us feel like outsiders. He didn't know how much we needed the phone to talk with our family and show them how beautiful our life was here! He destroyed those feelings, that picture, and my positive view of Canada. It felt as though he didn't view us as individuals who could be trusted with a phone, despite all the effort we had put into obtaining the necessary bank information and documents.

Now I have the words and power to say that he was wrong. If he could read the stories that I have written on my phone, he would never treat us the way he did. If he could read the story of that day when we were buying the phone, he would never put anyone in a situation where they feel that they don't belong and don't count.

I want to tell him, "We came here to make a new life; we were working full time that day we came and asked you for a smartphone."

He was so wrong to judge us. He was wrong to decide by our nationality. He was wrong to decide by our age. He made me feel that I shouldn't be here. He made me feel as if there was a sign on their door that said, "This store cannot sell anything to refugees."

I will never forget the moment we came out of the store with our useless papers. I had never felt so rejected in my life. I faced two different challenges as a person who'd fled to safety between borders, but I had never been rejected from any of these big countries until we were rejected just for not having a phone, for being here and making our home here. I felt that every other store would say the same, and that we would not be able to get our supplies. Happily, though, a neighbouring company accepted our papers. I hope when people like that salesperson read the story of my phone, they will change the way they think and understand our pain.

"Go back to writing," I told myself.

But which story should I tell? The taste of the dates between the Iraq and Iran border? Or the new taste of blackberries? As a child or as a young woman? Should I write about leaving behind my broken doll when we fled from Sulaymaniyah? Or being rejected in a phone store in Canada? My story? Or my people's story?

In English or in Kurdish? To my Kurdish readers or my Canadian readers? How am I going to tell this story, and who is going to read it? Will my son read it? Will he read it in Kurdish or English? Should I write about my life in Kurdistan when I was fighting for women who suffered from lack of respect in society and were killed because of love? Or should I write about here, in Canada, where the first man I saw was my lawyer? How he never listened to me during the immigration process? Perhaps I should write about the kind and honest Canadian people who provide me with countless reasons to feel a sense of belonging? These are individuals who truly listen to every word I say and are eager to comprehend everything I share. They have become a new family for me and we've built a strong foundation of trust between us.

A text tone that sounds like *ti, ti tin* stops me from asking so many questions. I see a name on the top of my screen: Jody Kuhn. I opened the text: "Hey Shanga, how are you today? Can I come for a patio visit with a Starbucks drink?"

What could be better than this? Having a visit from the kindest person I know in the middle of the COVID-19 pandemic while everything is shutting down, and it is even harder for those who are far away from their families and have limited connections.

I see Jody in front of our patio in a beautiful maroon dress. My eyes go to her shiny silver cross pendant. I always tell her how I love her style.

Seeing Jody always brings not just joy to me. She is a reminder of all the positive thoughts I need every day. She reminds me how to take care of myself and love myself the way I am, and to not forget about others around me. Day by day, I feel more loved and listened to by Jody.

This is not just a friendship. It is hard to explain how our relationship since 2015 has influenced my life and changed my entire perspective. Jody is an angel. She feeds my soul and reads my mind even though the lack of common language and the differences in culture between us are still there. But that makes us closer, and we understand each other more deeply. There were days when I was having a rough time, but after meeting and speaking with Jody, my perspective completely shifted. Even though she wasn't aware of what was bothering me, our discussions would bring me a tremendous sense of gratitude and peace and I would suddenly remember to appreciate and love my day.

I taste so much sweetness from Jody's love and from the caramel Frappuccino I am sipping as we sit two metres away from each other, chatting together, laughing, crying, and discussing events going on around the world. This friendship gives me hope to live better, her hugs give me a sense of a sister's hug, and her love makes me feel at home inside myself.

After all the beginning and searching for a new version of herself in a new country, that tiny five-year-old girl with curly fluffy hair who sought safety and shelter with her family finds another taste of sweetness from her lovely friendship with Jody. Now in her new home, Canada, she is settling in rather than fleeing.

5

The Power of Perseverance

Muhialdin Bakini

MY STORY BEGINS with me as a young lad born in 1981, the seventh of eight
children, near Khartoum, Sudan's capital. My parents were farmers, and as
a preschooler, I was charged with the task of shepherding our cattle. I led
them to green pastures and pools of fresh water every morning. This might
sound like an easy-enough job, but I wasn't very good at it! Instead, once
I was out of sight from my father, I became easily distracted with the
abundance of fruits, nuts, and the roots of trees. Although I do not recall
having the luxury of dreaming, my father might have had a different
perspective. In my distracted state, the cattle I was supposedly tending
would break into other villagers' farms, eating and destroying their crops.
This neglect got me into trouble with my father and the affected farmers;
however, this seeming catastrophe had a positive outcome, for I was
able to start school at the age of six in Khartoum. My mother, who had
separated from my father when I was five, managed to convince him that
this option would be better for me than staying on the farm.

Mom was self-employed in Khartoum, making and selling traditional
sorghum wine. She found out about the Christian school I began attending
from her customers, some of whom were teaching there. Even some of our
tribesmen taught there, an important fact that helped my father decide he
could spare me as his cattle herder in favour of my older brother,
Dafa-Allah.

In 1987, less than six months after I moved to Khartoum, the first civil
war broke out in the Nuba Mountains. A few days before I left my father's
home, a handful of gun-toting individuals in military uniforms came to

our village. They claimed they were looking for items stolen from a local market in the inner-city of Abri. At the central bus station in Abri, as my mother and I left to return to Khartoum, I saw those soldiers again. I asked my mom who they were and why they were in the Nuba Mountains. She had no answers. Later, I realized that a significant number of the Nuba people, including young boys, had joined the Sudan People's Liberation Movement (SPLM). There, in Abri, I heard my very first gunshot. At that moment, I sensed something ominous would soon hit my ancestral land.

As I am writing this, guns are still being fired over Kadugli, the capital of the Nuba Mountains. From when I left in 1987 until now, the Nuba people, the most ancient indigenous peoples in Sudan, have been continuously targeted by the governments there. I felt lucky back then to escape the war, but now, as I hear what is still happening, I feel powerless to stop it.

These negative political realities led to decisions that ultimately worked out for me and my family, leading to the materialization of my dream of emigrating to Canada.

Sudan is a multinational and multicultural country. People who identify as Black and African constitute the majority. Animism, Christianity, and Islam are the major religions in the country. Upon its independence from colonial Britain in 1956, Sudan insisted on becoming an exclusively Arab, Islamic country. In order to command conformity to the state's religion and culture, the central government in Khartoum embarked on brutal campaigns of cultural marginalization, enslavement, Arabism, forced conversions, and genocide. These acts of violence were initially directed toward dark-skinned, non-Muslim Africans living in South Sudan, the Nuba Mountains – my home region – and the Southern Blue Nile. Later, the national government and their self-professed Arab and Muslim supporters in Northern Sudan also targeted Black Muslims in Darfur and Eastern Sudan.

What's in a Name?

As Christians and Nubians, my parents considered assimilation into the dominant culture. They decided that sparing me trouble in school and society at large outweighed potential risks. To avoid the stigmas attached to our Nubian names, my parents assigned me an Arabic name. I became Muhi-al-Din, in addition to my Nubian name, Kacho. The word "Muhi" means "life-giver," "al" means "the," and "Din" means "religion." Thus, my name literally means "the life-giver of the religion." This name imposed on me an Arab/Muslim identity, which would prove, eventually, to be problematic, since I am an African and a Christian. This is not an inconsequential declaration to make in Sudan, where minority identities are governed by power asymmetries.

Failure: Backdoor to Success?

My mom and step-dad invested considerably in my education, but what I needed was direction and greater self-awareness. I spent my entire pre-university year unsure what I wanted to be or do.

Failure brought clarity. In 2000, I took a university entrance exam and failed. That was the crucible in which my aimless way of living finally melted. I emerged from that humiliating defeat with a strategic intent, invigorated with a burning passion for education, and transformed myself into a self-directed learner. The following year, in 2001, after nine months of studies at home without a teacher or tutor, I passed my exams with high marks and was admitted into the University of Juba in Khartoum, where I studied Developmental Communications.

At the University of Juba, I became involved with the Juba University Bible Study Association (JUBSA). The association organized campus conferences on interfaith communication, comparative theology, and social justice. These events created a culture that encouraged interfaith dialogues and increased religious tolerance and openness.

My active participation in these events aroused the ire of university security personnel of the then-ruling National Congress Party (NCP). I was repeatedly warned and threatened to cease my activities with JUBSA. As I continued ignoring their threats, they baselessly began accusing me of being a convert, citing my name as proof of that. Apostasy, a severe crime in Sudan, is punishable by death. Fearing for my life, I had to discontinue my education, just one year from completion. In July 2004, I left Sudan for Egypt with my wife, Huwaida, and our daughter, Mercy.

Unfortunately, such harassment is not the only factor forcing the marginalized people of Sudan out of their own country. The economic, political, legal, and cultural institutions of the country are all structured in a way to push them to the margins and, ultimately, outside the country's borders. Arabism and Islamism in Sudan are tools used to weaken marginalized peoples. They were designed to colonize, enslave, and eventually eradicate Africans in general, and Christians and animists in particular.

A Dream Deferred

In 2004, Huwaida, Mercy, and I fled Sudan as refugees. Upon arrival in Egypt, we discovered that the United Nations High Commissioner for Refugees (UNHCR) had unfortunately slowed down the resettlement process for Sudanese refugees as the South Sudanese revolutionaries and the government were engaging in peace talks, which culminated in the Comprehensive Peace Agreement (CPA). Nevertheless, I submitted my claim to UNHCR's office and waited, in vain, for three and a half years.

During my first three months in Egypt, I worked at the Egyptian Belgium Company for Elevators and Aluminum serving tea and bringing lunch and cigarettes from nearby restaurants and stores in Roxy, Cairo. Later, I found employment at a restaurant with a Sudanese fellow. I worked for him for about four months, while teaching EFL to a few Sudanese adults awaiting resettlement. During this time, Huwaida and I celebrated the birth of Joy, our second daughter.

Luckily, for many refugees in Egypt, the Australian Embassy started accepting asylum claims from seekers with an Australian sponsor. This initiative was a beacon of hope amidst a prolonged period of despair. The opening of the resettlement window increased my employability, but most importantly, it provided me with a rare opportunity to serve the community. People who wrote their claims in Arabic brought them to me for translation into English before submitting them to the Protection Visa Office.

Apart from language ability, the process of preparing a refugee claim is a demanding one. It is based on assumptions that refugees know the relevant contextual factors that have shaped their experience. For many, incidents of persecution, to which refugees are subjected, are triggered by factors tens, if not hundreds of years in the making. For example, during an interview, a would-be refugee might mention that a security interrogator referred to him as an infidel, *kafir*, or unbeliever. The immigration officer might ask why the interrogator had called him such names. He might simply say, "I do not know." The interviewer could then interpret his response as being untrustworthy. But the precise answer lies beyond an average asylum seeker. In many of the marginalized regions in Sudan, conversions to Islam were achieved through intimidating processes. Verbal abuse was the least-extreme measure taken to force conversion. Thus, I had the opportunity to help refugees synthesize their claims, translate them into English, and interpret for them during the Refugee Status Determination (RSD) interviews.

The Australian government's initiative, though sorely needed and genuinely helpful, was a proverbial drop in a huge bucket of needs. Many families, including my own, could not make it to the interview stages. Compounding the situation for refugees, Egyptian public schools refused to admit Sudanese kids. As I was helping adult refugees acquire English skills, two other community members, Haroun and John, responded to the children's educational needs. They approached me with the idea of aligning our efforts to serve the community better. We agreed on a plan, drafted a proposal, and submitted it to the Evangelical International Church (EIC) in Cairo, asking for financial assistance to open schools for refugee kids.

Our proposal was approved promptly. We rented two buildings, one for kindergarteners and the other for elementary school students, with an adult education program in the evenings. I became the school principal, John my assistant, and Haroun the finance person. With the funds from EIC, we hired teachers, cooks, and security. Several leaders in the refugee community followed our lead, reached out to other Christian and humanitarian organizations, and asked for funds to support adult and childhood education.

However, none of us was a trained teacher. We reached out again to EIC, requesting teacher training. Many of the refugee schools were linked with retired Canadian teachers who volunteered to come to Egypt to assist with our professional development under the auspices of Cambridge Teachers' Training. After two semesters, our training ended due to financial hardship.

Nonetheless, through the teachers' program, I managed to make one of the most lasting professional, personal, and family friendships of my life. I came to know Dr. Dean and his wife, Glenni Tweedle. They became my field supervisors and eventually privately sponsored my family to come to Canada. Luckily for me, I was completing two programs at the same time: the teachers' training and translation certification, which helped me contribute to my community.

In December 2005, a number of Sudanese organized a sit-in in front of the UNHCR's office in Cairo, to attempt to apply pressure to resume resettlement. The CPA neither brought about peace nor addressed the root causes of conflicts in the Nuba Mountains, Southern Blue Nile, and Darfur. On December 30, 2005, the Egyptian police, allegedly with a green light from the Sudanese security authority, mounted a brutal intervention, breaking up the demonstration, wounding many and killing several refugees.

Promised Land

The nightmare of that attack precipitated a dangerous new reality. Egyptian security began targeting community activists. News of arbitrary arrests, detention, and the disappearances of active members circulated within the refugee community. As someone directly involved in community activities, my security was compromised. Consequently, aided by the Bedouins, nomadic Arab tribes in Egypt, I was smuggled into Israel through the Sinai desert. I had to leave my family behind as it was too expensive to get a family of four smuggled. I took the venture in the hope that I would find employment and save enough money to have my family join me. Wages in Israel at the time were significantly higher than composite jobs in Egypt.

My journey into Israel was hardly hopeful. The decision to illegally cross the perilous Israeli-Egyptian border was driven partly by frustrations over an indefinite waiting period imposed by the UNHCR to grant me a hearing through RSD, and the personal risks of staying in Egypt. In brief, I weighed three undesirable alternatives: returning to Sudan, staying in Egypt, and crossing illegally into Israel. This narrowed the alternative to two: clinging to a negative certainty or venturing into the unknown.

I harboured prejudices against Israel before I moved there. Sudan has been in a hostile relationship with Israel for more than four decades. Such enduring animosity toward Israel stems primarily from Sudan's identification as an Arab-Islamic state, standing up for its occupied sister nation of Palestine. These sentiments culminated in Sudan joining the Arab coalition, which fought against Israel in the Arab-Israeli war 1973.

Though I find it noble to fight injustice and support a nation's right to self-determination and independence, in particular those under occupation and colonization, I have always found the Sudanese government's self-righteous attitudes perplexing. They act as if they are treating their people differently than how the Palestinians are being treated. This is the danger of any state that shrinks its national commitment to one religion. It risks becoming a destructive tool in the hands of religious extremists and ethnic entrepreneurs who use religion and culture to pursue self-serving agendas.

Like many marginalized Sudanese, I resented seeing the Sudanese governments neglecting and persecuting minorities while extending a helping hand to people elsewhere. Unfortunately, Israel thought Sudan's hostile official position was shared by all Sudanese nationals. This perhaps explains the many policies hostile to Sudanese refugees in Israel, including imprisonment, arbitrary detention, and deportation.

> *I have always found the Sudanese government's self-righteous attitudes perplexing.*

Fortunately for me, unlike other Sudanese refugees who entered Israel between 2006 and 2007 and were held in detention for a year or more, I was kept at the border camp for less than twenty-four hours when I entered in January 2008. When released, I quickly found employment as a dishwasher at the Sheraton Hotel in Tel Aviv. Workers in Israel receive their monthly salaries on the tenth of each month. After the first fifteen days of work, I calculated that I would be receiving about $1,000 US – enough to pay the Bedouin smugglers to bring my family into the country. I had no expenses other than my cellphone bill. I ate and showered at the hotel and slept at a shelter.

I ran into Marwan and Naser, both friends and former adult students of mine from Egypt. My eagerness to bring my family to Israel made it challenging for me to "wait it out" until payday to transfer money to my wife. I asked these two friends to lend me a thousand US dollars. They each agreed to loan me five hundred. I promised to pay them back on payday. I sent the money to Huwaida in Egypt.

Lonely Man

When Huwaida and our daughters tried to cross into Israel in late February 2008, they were arrested by Egyptian border guards and imprisoned in the el-Arish women's prison. I found out about their arrest a month after it happened. The Bedouin smugglers I'd hired had no definite information about whether they had entered Israel – they had coordinated their crossing into Israel with another smuggler. I trusted Abdo, the Bedouin smuggler, who had helped me infiltrate into Israel. He took care to make sure I made it safely. He even gave me a used cellphone with an Israeli line to call him once I made it. I could not be angry at him; I knew deep down that something else had gone horribly wrong.

My daughters spent about ten months in various prisons before they were released into the care of my oldest brother, Mustafa, who was in Egypt. My three-year-old daughter, Joy, became calcium deficient and could not walk properly due to the over-crowdedness and malnutrition in prison. Huwaida was confined for an extra three months and spent those thirteen months alternating between six different prisons before being released.

I almost lost my sanity during those painful months. I started blaming myself and regretting not waiting longer. "If only" I had hired the right Bedouin and weighed out all other counterfactuals. Yet my reality remained unchanged: I was a lonely man. I missed my family. This episode in my history came to be the crucible that would define and shape me both mentally and spiritually. Two pre-existing conditions helped turn this devastating experience into a transformative one.

First, the Biblical story of Job, a man who lost everything but remained patient, spoke to me. I realized that my trial was not unique, and that I could choose to experience it as a victim or a victor. Choosing to experience this test as a victor opened up the supply, resources, and grace I needed. Though the experience was emotionally challenging, I held my head above water and chose to "hold fast to dreams" and be a victor.

Second, I was able to reconnect with my God-sent angels: Dean and Glenni Tweedle. Dean and Glenni had returned to Egypt for a second time when the EIC in Cairo salvaged the program. Surprised by my absence from the program, they asked as to my whereabouts. A former colleague, Abram, told them I had crossed into Israel and that my wife and daughters had just left to join me. He gave them my cellphone number.

In mid-March 2008, during my coffee break, my phone rang. A familiar voice said: "Hello, is that Muhialdin?"

"Yes."

"This is Dean and Glenni Tweedle, from Cambridge Teachers."

I knew right away they were my beacon of hope. It happened that Dean and Glenni were planning to spend part of their vacation in Israel, so we scheduled a time to meet in Tel Aviv.

Lasting Friendship

Dean and Glenni and I enjoyed reconnecting and met regularly after my shifts to catch up on each other's lives. We sometimes went to local restaurants or to Levinsky Park. Oblivious to what lay ahead, I enthusiastically shared my thoughts on Job's story. During the first two days spent meeting with them, I had thought my family was somewhere in detention centers in Israel. Women with kids were not released unless the authorities knew beforehand where they would stay. The Bedouin I'd hired also kept me under the false impression that my family had successfully crossed into Israel. I kept regular contact with humanitarian organizations. At our third meeting, I told Dean and Glenni that Huwaida and the girls had not made it into Israel; Egyptian border patrol had arrested them.

Now, my theoretical understanding of the book of Job met my ugly reality. As I spoke with Dean and Glenni, I could not hold myself together. I burst into tears. They comforted, encouraged, and prayed for me. I vividly remember Glenni hugging me and singing "God Will Make a Way When There Seems to be no Way," and how comforted I felt. This was a regular practice that earned her the title of Mommy.

As Dean and Glenni were preparing to return to Canada, Dr. Ward Wilson, their friend, arrived in Israel with his family. Dean and Glenni shared my story, and they expressed an interest in meeting me. It was over coffee with Dr. Wilson's family that one of the most memorable conversations of my life occurred. It instilled in me the habit of seeing things not as they are, but rather as what they could be.

His son, Andrew, said, "When [not if] you come to Canada, come to visit us."

His wife, Carmen, said, "Don't be shy; God has put you in our path. Ask for anything."

Dr. Wilson said, "Canada has everything. Tell me what you want."

Their words transformed my perspective. Before encountering them, scarcity was the prism through which I saw everything. Here, I met people who viewed things through a lens of abundance. Empowered by my new mindset, I put forward two requests: to reconnect with my family and to come to Canada.

Dr. Wilson pulled out two business cards and told me to enquire about the process at the Canadian Embassy, and to let him know as soon as I learned something. Dean and Glenni were going back to Egypt, and they would see if there was anything they could learn or do about Huwaida's circumstances. Due to my family's prolonged imprisonment, I temporarily set aside my goal of immigrating to Canada. The pause that punctuated and delayed the achievement of my goal to immigrate to Canada allowed me to consciously own my goals, utilize any means available, and involve others in achieving them.

Things were tough for my wife after her release from prison. She was free, but we were separated. In the first few days after her release, she expressed strong displeasure with my choice of crossing into Israel. I couldn't blame her. Spending thirteen long months in a nasty Egyptian prison doesn't put one in good humour. Fortunately, we had two conciliatory dreams still alive: our family reunification and Canadian emigration. We both initially decided it would be more sensible and safer if I illegally crossed the border back to Egypt and started planning. However, remembering how unsuccessful male crossers were captured and treated cruelly by the Egyptian border guards, Huwaida changed her mind. She told me how those men were severely tortured and then deported back to their countries of origin.

Accounts from these tortured men caused Huwaida to summon an act of incredible courage. I was astonished when she told me she would give the border crossing a second try. I was perplexed by my family's arrest the first time they attempted to cross the Egyptian/Israeli border. My own experience crossing into Israel, in comparison to other refugees, had been fraught with fewer misadventures. Besides, in Israel, I saw some families that had been successfully reunited. These two experiences made me entertain the possibility of joining my family in Egypt and re-crossing back with them into Israel.

Family Reunion

Huwaida's daring break from the mental shackles of imprisonment birthed in us both a renewed faith in our future, in our shared vision, and in the strength of our desires. But we knew we had to approach the crossing very carefully. I hired Mohamed, a Bedouin with a solid reputation for successfully smuggling families into Israel. I agreed to pay him $2,000 USD and decided to pay for the expenses for every day he chose to keep my family at his place, sparing them a dangerous crossing. I arranged for him to keep the $2,000 and return my family safely to Cairo if the border crossing became permanently dangerous.

Seeing how much I cared about my family and knowing that I would not let them be a burden to him, he promised to honour our agreement and deliver them to me in Israel. I trusted him. Mohamed kept my family with him for almost two months as the borders became increasingly dangerous.

In September 2009, after more than a year and a half of separation, I received a call from Huwaida saying she was calling from a border camp in Israel.

"We made it!" she said.

I could not believe what I'd just heard. She gave me the name of the camp, and I reported their case to the Hotline for Migrant Workers (HMW), a humanitarian organization working in the service of refugees and asylum seekers. They helped in issuing me a permit to visit them in the camp, located about three hours by bus from Tel Aviv. I have no words to describe my feelings on that bus ride. All I wanted was to see Huwaida and the kids, and to hug them.

I was among the first visitors to arrive. Families expecting a visitation were taken from their rooms and put in a separate area. Visitors queued outside the camp, awaiting their turn to be let in for a maximum of twenty minutes. As soon as I entered, my oldest daughter, Mercy, screamed, "Baba!" All my fear vanished suddenly. My identity as a father was conferred back on me. The hardest thing I faced during our separation was returning to an empty home every evening, without Huwaida's smiles and Mercy and Joy's warm reception. As insignificant as this may seem, these little things significantly transform a house into a home. My family looked healthy, which gave me relief. Two months later, Huwaida and the kids were released, and we were reunited. This marked the achievement of the first of our two goals.

Dream Delayed

Being able to reconnect with my family and being afraid of losing them again made me temporarily forget my second goal of immigrating to Canada. Then, another storm arose. Yet again, we had to "hold fast to our dreams."

In 2010, the Israeli immigration authority instituted racist policies to drive refugees out. They also made the renewal of work permit visas a cumbersome process. The purpose of such policies was "to make life miserable for African infiltrators," and thus force them to leave the country independently. The creation of an organization claiming to be working to "voluntarily" resettle African refugees back to African countries such as Rwanda and Uganda coincided with these events. The policies seemed to have brought about outcomes to the liking of the Israeli authorities. A sizable number of refugees agreed to return to Africa, to conditions similar to those they had escaped.

I had eked out a living by teaching English as a foreign language to refugees, so such policies meant losing my employment, as students became unable to attend classes or pay for them. Huwaida could not retain a permanent job. This additional pressure on the part of the immigration officials reawakened my dream of immigrating to Canada.

"Now it is time to reconnect with the Tweedles," I said to myself.

Dr. Tweedle is the most compassionate person I know. Nobody else can so quickly and genuinely sense the things I feel. Thus, as measures taken by the Israeli immigration police became unbearable, I emailed him, explained my situation, and asked him to help us. He reached out to Dr. Ward Wilson and the Mennonite Community Church in Abbotsford, British Columbia.

In less than a month, I submitted my application to the Ministry of Citizenship and Immigration Canada (CIC). After two and a half years, the Canadian Embassy in Tel Aviv finalized our immigration. In February 2012, we passed our resettlement interview. A few months before departing Tel Aviv for Vancouver, Dean and Glenni's friends, Dr. Harold Faw and his wife, arrived in Tel Aviv for vacation. Dean and Glenni had arranged for us all to meet at the Sheraton Hotel in Tel Aviv. Harold was a professor at Trinity Western University (TWU). When he asked me what I wanted to do in Canada, I told him I wanted to complete my education, and his offer to facilitate that reassured me.

Reinventing of Self

One evening, in a noisy crowded Sudanese Club in Tel Aviv, I shared a cup of coffee with friends. This Sudanese Club, which I had helped to establish, had become an important education and leisure hub. It was a thriving centre where virtually all refugees who frequented it knew each other. And I was leaving this community and the self I had become here. I was profoundly overwhelmed with thoughts of my pending departure.

Maawiya, a former student of mine, was wondering aloud about my future in my soon-to-be new home. He was concerned yet happy for me, for I was about to leave a country whose officials once said they would not allow it to be an outlet through which African migrants found a way to the Western world. I was among the luckiest few to have used that very outlet.

"Teacher, what kind of job are you going to have once you arrive in Canada?" asked Maawiya.

I remember telling myself that my students must have been thinking of me as someone capable of doing only one thing professionally: teaching English as a foreign language. "How limiting!" I thought. I was silent until our talkative interlocutor, Marwaan, whom I had taught in Egypt, jumped in with an answer to the question.

"He will be teaching English to Canadians! What is so difficult about that?" he enquired.

I admired his confidence in the ability of a non-native English speaker to teach English to native Canadians. Confidence enabled Marwaan to answer the question, but I needed clarity.

From my experience, it is imperative to keep goals clear and measurable within one of three areas: the pursuit of higher education, the acquisition of vocational and professional skills, and the improvement of personal finances. For me, a successful immigration experience means advancement in at least one of these areas. Otherwise, everything remains vague and elusive. Thus, I was clear about what I wanted to do in Canada.

Maawiya's question later became the driving force behind my journey toward self-reinvention. Upon hearing it, I felt a little uncomfortable. The human spirit naturally hates to be limited, confined, or constrained. On the flipside, I had to wrestle with the reality of how to be valuable and useful in Canada. Maawiya's query prompted me to consider what parts of my identity, capability, and skills needed to be transformed or improved for me to adapt to Canada and its specific needs. Thus, reinventing oneself becomes important, not just for personal fulfillment but also to make positive impacts on and meaningful contributions to others. Newcomers have tremendous potential to thrive in new contexts if they reinvent themselves in a way that makes such contributions possible.

My goal to acquire higher education helped me to realize this potential. When I arrived in Canada in May 2012, my wife needed to improve her English. I found a job at a turkey plant and started putting in an extra four hours of overtime to buy a car for the family. Huwaida attended ESL classes at Abbotsford Community Services. A year later, as her English improved, we both enrolled in the University of the Fraser Valley. She began upgrading, and I took TESL and political science courses. Academic writing was particularly challenging for me. Fortunately, Professor Harold Faw, a patient and gentle friend, helped me tremendously. Harold proofread and provided comments on my papers without altering my writing, and he has created a safe space for me to experiment with the language. He has helped me learn how to write by engaging directly in writing, not learning about writing in academic classes.

My clear goal enabled me to graduate from both programs with distinction, named twice to the Dean's list of Distinguished Students, nominated as a student speaker in the 2018 convocation ceremony, and currently featured on UFV's Political Science Department website as one of the department's most academically successful students.

Upon graduation, I taught ESL at the Universal Learning Institute in Coquitlam. In 2019, I got a scholarship to complete a master's degree in Public Policy at the University of British Columbia. I attribute my academic success to persistence, clarity, and maintaining relationships with those who align with my purposes.

In June 2021, I graduated with a master's degree, and I am now employed as Diversity Education and Resources Supervisor—also known as the DEAR program—with Abbotsford's Archway Community Services (ACS), which provide education, resources, and support on diversity, anti-racism, hate, and bigotry. In addition to supervising and supporting the DEAR team, in my role as supervisor I develop programs and ensure their effective implementation in meeting the DEAR program's goals and objectives.

Working with ACS has provided me with the opportunity to engage diverse clients in a multi-stakeholder framework. Working with a diverse range of clients within and outside the city of Abbotsford, such as businesses, schools, and service providers, has afforded me the opportunity to utilize the skills I developed in the MPPGA program. I envision myself directly involved in designing policies and programs for DEAR and instituting policies for multiple departments with ACS in the future.

Newcomer's Dream

Remember my conversation with Maawiya and Marwan at the Sudanese Club in Tel Aviv? Maawiya thought it would be challenging for me to reinvent myself in Canada, but Marwan was confident I would replicate my success. They were both right. After almost six years, I rebuilt my career and walked into a classroom as an ESL teacher. Reinventing myself and reaching my goal of teaching again was challenging and rewarding and required several reinventions. I worked as a poultry meat boner, a sanitation worker, and a family financial advisor, learning such skills simply to survive and support my family.

PART 2

Stories of Change and Exploration

6

Decolonizing Forced Displacement

Sofia Noori

"YOUR GREAT GRANDDADDY and his brother were killed for treason."

During my childhood I was told many stories about my ancestors, mostly by my mother and her mother, often around bedtime. The stories I enjoyed were about the fights for Afghan sovereignty and freedom. Rarely did these tales put me to sleep. Instead I stayed awake and alert, absorbing the characteristics of these tragic heroes and the geographic details of where they lived and taught, and where they were arrested and displaced. Our relationship to the land was important to these women, and they described it in great detail.

My maternal grandmother was the only grandparent I met. Bibi – a term of endearment for grandmothers – was a highly respected elder. She was Nuristani, and originated from an Indigenous community in north-eastern Afghanistan. Upon her arrival, family, friends, and neighbours poured into our home in Etobicoke, to pay their respects and to listen to her wisdom. I called them all aunts and uncles. I could not believe how many people she called "my child." Every night she had a story to tell. I did not want to hear fairy tales, and Bibi had none to offer. Bibi often started with a hook: "Your great granddaddy and his brother were killed for treason ..."

Their crime was trying to convince the learned and religious elite of Kabul to protest the proposed British declaration for peace. The British attacked Afghanistan in 1878 from British India. This invasion from the British colony next door was not the first, and history proves it was not the last. The Afghan monarchy wanted to end the war so, the following year, a treaty was signed between the Emir and the British to settle the border disputes. In return for an end to their aggression, the British Empire would have indirect influence in the central Asian country, curbing Tzarist Russia's imperial ambitions. The treaty also stipulated that ethnic Pashtuns on the eastern border would be divided, with half their territory belonging to British India. Rebellions against the Afghan Emirs continued because most of the local ethnic groups did not want to accept British Imperial rule of any kind, and certainly not in exchange for territory. My mother's paternal grandfather and his brother refused the terms of the declaration proposed by the British and were gaining support from influential locals through their teaching circles. The two men were arrested and taken from their homes in Kabul, leaving behind their young wives and little children. Reports from palace guards revealed that my great-grandfather was executed in a prison in Kandahar and his brother died in the palace's prison. Their bodies were never returned to their families.

Many nights, my grandmother described the majestic mountains, rivers, valleys, and springs of Kantiwa, Nuristan. She caused a lot of havoc as a child. Her father was the local chief and often scolded her. When she was six years old, she pitted two bulls against one another. This was a very disrespectful thing to do for a people whose lives depended entirely on their animals. She knew how to capture my attention: "The waves from the river roared and jumped so high as I ran across the shaky bridge, I thought the waves would swallow me for what I did to the bulls. If my father did not catch me, surely the waves would."

Once the Afghan monarchy reached an agreement for peace with the British Crown, their attention turned to national reconciliation. Bibi's ancestors lived at the southern slopes of the Hindu Kush valley, where the people adhered to shamanist and animist beliefs – the "land of disbelievers," or Kafiristan, is what it was called. This Indigenous community had managed to hold onto its cultural and traditional ways even though surrounding tribes had adopted Islam centuries earlier. The fight to maintain Indigenous traditions continued, despite foreign interferences and exchanges. At long last, in the late 1800s, Bibi's ancestors were overrun militarily by the Emir at the time, Abdul Rahman Khan, and forced to adopt Islamic principles. Chiefs who refused were killed. Others, like my mother's maternal grandfather, negotiated treaty agreements; they accepted Islam with the understanding that the Nuristani continue to have self-governance and complete control over their territories.

The stories my mother told were gorier than Bibi's. My brothers enjoyed the "scary stories series" that she told us at bedtime. She would say, "Afghanistan has such a mystical history. Once upon a time, it was ruled by vampires. Tonight, I'll tell you the tale of Taraki, who sucked the blood of thousands in a single night."

In 1978 there was a brutal and bloody coup at the palace in Kabul. The monarchy was replaced by a communist group, led by Taraki. The following year, two of my uncles were arrested by military officers in front of their families. One left behind a young wife and four children. The other was a seventeen-year-old teacher candidate. They were accused of being part of the resistance, participating in activities against the communist ruling party. My uncles were never again seen by their families. Their brothers went into hiding until there was no alternative but to leave the country. It would be decades before brothers saw sisters and children saw their mothers. In 2013, a "Death List" was published online with both my uncles' names on it.

My parents and their siblings lived as refugees in Pakistan, some in camps, while seeking asylum in several different countries. My parents and their four children, all under the age of four, ended up in Tkarón:to, on one of the last days of 1988. We lived in North Etobicoke, the original home of Mississaugas of the Credit First Nation.

Colonial Education in Tkarón:to

My family's history as being Indigenous and anti-imperialist translated into language and beliefs that did not exist in my experiences outside the house. We were not allowed to speak English at home. While my grandmother was the only person who spoke Nuristani, my parents made sure to teach us Dari and Pashto, the two official languages of Afghanistan. We were reminded almost daily by my father that, "if you lose your language, you will lose your connection to your ancestors, historical accounts and connection to the land." As refugees, my parents really believed that we would one day return to Afghanistan. That our settlement in Canada was temporary, and as guests we had to respect the land, its laws, and its people.

It would be decades before brothers saw sisters and children saw their mothers.

Unfortunately, we did not know the original inhabitants of the territory we resided on. More often than not, the definitions and challenges of refugees are addressed in political circles of migration and citizenship, while the displacement of Indigenous Peoples is taken up by a completely separate set of conversations and offices. The Indigenous Peoples of Canada have been internally displaced through various legal and political manoeuvres originating in settler colonialism. The silencing of colonial history and its reverberations has come to a head in my life story here in Canada.

Growing up on the northern edge of Tkarón:to in the 1990s, I received what I like to call a "colonial education." Our teachers were mostly white, from Scottish, Irish, and English backgrounds. They made school fun. There was hardly any academic rigor or high expectations. There was only one Black teacher, who was originally from Trinidad. He was my grade five teacher. He taught us passages from the Bible every Friday. Our books were written and illustrated mostly by western Europeans and Americans. We took great pride in reading literature written by Canadian writers, but again, they were white, as were the main characters. The children at my elementary school were mostly poor. Their parents worked multiple jobs and were hardly around. They mostly originated from the Caribbean and Latin American nations, and a smaller number were from war-torn nations like Afghanistan, Iraq, and Somalia. There was also a small number of very poor white families, who generally kept to themselves.

In elementary school, I did not learn about Indigenous Canadian history or culture. In fact, I remember children playing "cowboys and Indians," and making sounds that mocked Indigenous languages. These games were never challenged by teachers; they jumped in and played along. For Halloween, my kindergarten teacher encouraged us to wear traditional clothes. I remember my mother was horrified seeing children dressed as animals, robots, and cops – she wondered what kind of traditional clothes these were. She misunderstood the pagan celebration of the dead as a celebration of heritage. I recall seeing many children dressed in traditional Indigenous clothing, called "Indian" clothes. Obviously, this further confused my mother who understood traditional Indian clothing as saris, lenghas, and shalwars. The culture shock and the misappropriation of Indigenous clothing really bothered her. High-ranking chiefs, or khans, of Afghanistan are also embellished with specific gowns and headdresses. As a descendant of chiefs herself, she simply could not tolerate the disrespect she was witnessing. This degree of insult resulted in her never allowing us to attend classes during Halloween festivities at school.

In middle school, like most tweens I yearned to fit in. I was the only girl wearing a hijab. I felt out of place and like an outcast. I was called "Indian," "smelly," "stupid," "poor," "dirty." Once popular, outgoing, and outspoken, I became increasingly quiet and isolated, without a single peer to call my friend. I eventually stopped caring about the people around me and started rummaging through my schoolbooks for connections. I wanted to learn about anything that was non-European – about people I could relate to. This drew my attention to Indigenous stories and their beautiful illustrations, which I found in our school readers. During silent reading time, I got lost in Raven Tales and poems. In grade 7, I learned about the Indigenous peoples of both Ontario and Québec from a textbook. I memorized how the Iroquois First Nations were amazing farmers who helped the British establish trade routes. The Iroquois taught them about the land, how to stay warm, hunt, and maintain trading routes for fur. The Huron and the Algonquin helped the French in similar ways.

As children we were made to believe that Indigenous people stayed there, in the past – in history books. That they no longer lived among us. Nor were we taught that our school was situated on the lands of the Mississaugas of the Credit. They are Anishinaabe, allies to the Algonquin.[1] I walked through and passed their fishing grounds at the Humber River daily on my way to and from school. This one connection would have lifted the ink from the history book's pages. Instead, I learned that Indigenous peoples were killed in various ways including wars between the English and the French over the fur trade, and through viral infections like smallpox and syphilis, inflicted upon them by early white settlers. After these lessons, the focus turned to Confederation and the creation of Canada as a nation-state. The atmosphere of morbidity around Indigenous peoples and their culture continued through my public education.

In my grade 10 history class, I once again saw Indigenous people referenced. This time, there was a short paragraph about residential schools in our textbook. The teacher did not have a lesson planned to discuss the matter. I read the passage over and over again on my own, but I did not understand why Indigenous children were sent away to these boarding schools. I found it confusing because my father had to get special permission for me to attend schools outside our postal code, yet Indigenous children were forcibly displaced and sent to these far-away schools.

By high school, I had learned that the best way to succeed academically was to keep my head down, do my work, and achieve high marks. While I did not conform via my dress or my beliefs, I did conform to the rules; I did not question or raise my voice when I did not understand something. Instead, I stored these curious issues in the back of my mind and discussed them at home.

When asked about residential schools, my parents did not know anything about them. Our conversation soon turned to various colonial systems of oppression. My parents connected various international forms of imperialism and the denial of rights to Indigenous people across the world – if the British and French could force the displacement of Indigenous people worldwide, then it was not unimaginable that the government would also control where their children went to school, what resources they had access to, and with whom they interacted. While my parents' knowledge as to the specifics of Indigenous peoples' conditions in Canada was limited, their own histories of attempted colonization and land annexation in Afghanistan gave me a sensitivity to colonial systems of oppression.

During my undergraduate studies at the University of Toronto (U of T), I took history courses each year to balance out my heavy science load. In one first-year course, "Ten Days that Shook the World," our professor encouraged us to take a class on Indigenous Canadian languages. He explained that these classes were an attempt to revive Indigenous cultures. The assumption was that there were not enough Indigenous people to speak these languages, therefore the languages were dying. This reinforced a theme set forth in my elementary colonial education: many Indigenous people had died and now their languages were also becoming extinct. My parents' reasons for and insistence on learning Dari and Pashto became apparent to me. Bibi's language and the stories she told of home were transmitted verbally. The danger of living in a foreign land is the loss of language, which can easily translate to a loss of connection to history and to meaningful cultural creation. Bibi spoke to us in Dari, the language of Kabul, not her native land. None of her children or grandchildren speak Nuristani. After her passing, how do we connect with those still living in that remote area of the southern Hindu Kush? How can we know about their lives and heritage? In a strange way, when I heard my professor talk about the loss of Indigenous languages in Tkarón:to, I saw into my future and what might happen to my Indigenous connection.

From my personal experience, having received a colonial education in Tkarón:to, I realize that public educational practices serve a national political history by repressing or brushing over Indigenous agency. Assimilationist curriculum and pedagogy was not limited to residential schools. My public schooling shows that colonial themes were taught well into the early 2000s, and to non-Indigenous students as well. This formal history allowed for the once-displaced Europeans to define borders and stipulate land use and restrictions placed on Indigenous peoples. Settler colonial ideology is not simply racial assumptions about the inferiority of Indigenous bodies, but, more saliently, the spatial absence of Indigenous peoples in participating and partaking in the creation of

> *The danger of living in a foreign land is the loss of language.*

curriculum, especially in places in which they continue to reside and have strong historical ties to. It took twenty years for me to have a more truthful account of Canada's history.

Decolonizing Our Refugee Stories

Following the terrorist attacks on US soil on September 11, 2001, the Canadian military entered Afghanistan as part of a joint coalition of forty-two countries known as the International Security Assistance Force (ISAF). In the years that followed, we watched as millions of Afghans from remote areas like Nuristan were displaced, their homes raided, their lands used to build army bases and their villages bombarded by the occupying forces. To be frank, since my Bibi's passing, my connection to Nuristan is obsolete. As her population dwindles due to war and displacement, her people are again omitted. From Canada we watched and heard what was happening through national broadcasts where the story of Afghanistan was reinterpreted and told through the lens of mainstream media. Canadians were convinced that these acts of war were necessary for establishing a democratic system, women's rights, and other freedoms. The colonial legacy is very clear: divide, conquer, write a history of erasure.

In the summer of 2008, as part of the Truth and Reconciliation Commission (TRC), Prime Minister Stephen Harper apologized for the role the Canadian government played in the residential school system, admitting to the cultural genocide of Indigenous peoples. From Harper's speech I learned exactly how multiple ruling federal parties had sustained an education system that forcefully separated children from "the influence of their homes, families, traditions and cultures ... to assimilate them into the dominant culture."[2] He admitted that lawmakers presumed "Aboriginal cultures and spiritual beliefs were inferior and unequal" to their European Christian ways. Then he said, "Indeed, some sought, as it was infamously said, 'to kill the Indian in the child.'" He went on to describe the various forms of physical, sexual, mental, and emotional abuse that were inflicted upon the children in those schools by various church groups who had complete control and oversight. I still feel nauseated and tearful – they deliberately wanted to erase Indigenous peoples from Canada, the United States, Australia, and New Zealand. I saw Indigenous survivors and leaders on the Parliament floor; Indigenous people were not extinct, they continued to fight and push against each point of occupation, often returning to the state with their grievances and holding the government accountable for their colonial wrongdoings. This event challenged the narrative of erasure. I was witnessing a chapter of Indigenous peoples' fight for sovereignty and freedom in real-time.

The colonial legacy is very clear: divide, conquer, write a history of erasure.

It was during my master's at U of T that I started to develop the vocabulary for the xenophobia, institutional racism, and microaggressions that I had personally experienced in my life. The things people said to me growing up that I thought were just mean, were learned prejudices. In fact, the list of adjectives I was called were also derogatory comments about Indigenous people. I used to think that ignorance was the reason people were rude to me during my childhood, but I realized bullies were informed by a history of colonization where people who did not look like them were seen as less-than. I also learned that Indigenous people have been dealing with settler colonialism for three hundred years. There is a stratification of races in settler societies. My name, skin tone, and citizenship gave me privileges that I did not consider previously. I started to understand that an entirely different set of laws govern Indigenous Canadian lives: the *Indian Act*. I was horrified by the intrusiveness and brutality of settler colonialism. I was learning a lot – or should I say, unlearning a lot – and filling in the gaps that my earlier colonial education had created. All those questions at the back of my mind took immediate thought and deep contemplation. Much of Canada's history, I learned, was not in the past but continuing in the present moment.

Over time, I realized that my family's story shares an interesting inter-connectedness with the Indigenous peoples of Canada whom I listened to, as part of the TRC stories. There is the sense of multiple losses that comes from that initial uprooting experience: the emotional connection to a stable sense of home, language, and culture is gone; by being displaced due to imperialist projects, we are forced to submit to and abide by laws and practices that are not culturally sensitive to us; there is the loss of control over the appropriation and representation of our clothes, symbols, stories, and other forms of cultural production and expression; and the loss of citizenship means a loss of political voice and the ability to legally advocate for one's people. There are spaces that further dehumanize displaced people and extend feelings of loss to their ability to move, seek care, and other vital protective conditions (even those stipulated by international human rights). Spaces that constitute such situations include but are not limited to refugee camps, border tent towns, irregular border point crossings, residential schools, reservations, and holding centres. The overwhelming sense of loss held by both refugees and Indigenous people is an outcome of colonial ambitions, practices, and legacies. In the case of Afghanistan, with the British, the Soviets, and even the Americans and their forty-two-nation coalition, decolonization necessitated violent wars that eventually led to the expulsion of the foreign militaries. In a settler colonial state like Canada, invasion is not an event but an upheld structure.[3]

Over the years, I have found myself bringing home answers to my childhood questions. My mother patiently listens to every word of the stories I tell her. After a particularly difficult explanation of the Sixties Scoop, I noticed her neck and shoulders slouched as she lowered her head. Sitting there silently, I could tell she was in pain. I asked her, "If you knew about all these things that happened to the Native people, would you have still chosen to come to Canada?" Without hesitation, she said, "No." We refugees are benefactors of an oppressive colonial system. My family and I, along with tens of millions of other displaced peoples, have been used by the state and the media as a distraction from the distress of Indigenous peoples in Ontario and across Canada. As Mi'kmaq scholar Bonita Lawrence and Ena Dua stated, "People of color are settlers ... [who] live on land that is appropriated and contested, where Aboriginal peoples are denied nationhood and access to their own lands."[4]

Acknowledging my positionality and the ways in which I benefit from this history is the start to moving toward a more meaningful family story and relationship to Tkarón:to and its original inhabitants. The decolonization of my learning and education is premised on coming to terms with my relationship with the state that has welcomed me, while simultaneously further displacing the original peoples and their rights to their lands. As I navigate this dilemma, I have the added feelings of the guilt and regret held by my parents, who needed a safe haven for their children only to later discover that Indigenous children were denied these same rights. I now understand that part of the ongoing colonial violence emanates from ignorance. To undo and unlearn the ideological framing of colonization means learning about the specific nature of the treaty claims, rights, and responsibilities of the localities in which we reside. For my family's resettlement on the lands of the Mississaugas of the Credit, there is the Toronto Purchase of 1805 (Treaty 13). My family's perspective and deep respect for treaty making helps me read these negotiations between the state and Indigenous peoples with great humility and openness.

I now know that the Crown purchased the grounds on which I grew up for ten shillings.[5] The Mississaugas of the Credit charged the government for misappropriating the treaty, fraudulent federal actions, and an unreasonable sum for the exchange. In 2010, the Government of Canada settled the Toronto Purchase Claim and the Brant Tract Claim for $145 million. At that time, this was the largest settlement in Canadian history.[6] As a refugee, it is important for me to see and understand the process of accountability in a settler-state. Decolonization is an ongoing process that begins with acknowledging the humanity of Indigenous people. The state is slowly coming to some form of reconciliation by engaging in truth-telling.

Indigenous treaties explained by wampum belts provide an avenue for refugees like my mother and I to resolve the internal strife that stems from our responsibility to Indigenous people and to the Crown as new Canadians. The Haudenosaunee describe their relationship with settlers and newcomers through the Two Row Wampum belt. The two rows on the belt "symbolize two paths ... One, a birch bark canoe, will be for the Indian People, their laws, their customs and their ways. The other, a ship, will be for the white people and their laws, their customs and their ways. We shall travel the river together, side by side, but in our own boat. Neither of us will make compulsary [sic] laws or interfere in the internal affairs of the other. Neither of us will try to steer the other's vessel."[7] As the Crown and/or the Canadian state define us as refugees, we enter this unique relationship with Indigenous people, which is based on the respect of each other's laws and ways of life. I was a child when my parents became Canadian citizens through the lieutenant governor's office. Upon reflection, this inauguration was another strong symbol of colonialism in the immigration-citizenship process. In the same way my parents had taught us that we are guests to this land, the Indigenous people have this understanding about immigrants to Turtle Island. Understanding the Two Row Wampum belt helps me decolonize my family story of forced displacement. This is primarily due to my family's history of negotiating and respecting treaties in their full spirit and intent, as informed by Indigenous legal traditions.

Decolonizing Schooling in Tkarón:to

As a multilevel educator, and with siblings in the field as teachers, I find myself in a very unique position. A new tradition in Tkarón:to schools is the announcement of a land acknowledgement right after the singing of "O Canada." At the start of new classes in K-12, I often realize that students do not understand the purpose of a land acknowledgement or its tenets. I spend a substantial amount of time discussing Canada's colonial past. I begin by asking them content-level questions like, "Tell me who are the treaty partners mentioned in the land acknowledgement?" I hate to admit this, but many students are not actively listening. My experience informs me that students are suffering from the internalized myth of erasure. Land acknowledgements must become meaningful to the individual student's life story and their relationship to the original stewards of the land. Unoriginal copy and paste statements are ineffective in my opinion, as I see students in public schools disengaged from the daily announcements. The myth of non-existing or vanishing Indigenous people that I grew up with must be undone.

It is important for me as an educator to provide students with spaces and methods to engage with Indigenous people and their experiences.

Sometimes, this can occur through epistemic or ideological connections between the structural racism that Indigenous people face and the unique kinds of race issues that immigrant families face in Canada or in their native countries. Trips to Indigenous communities and centres and guest-host exchanges inside schools are more beneficial. These engagements must be continuous and ongoing in order to build strong communal relationships between Indigenous and immigrant youth.

As a trained high school science teacher, I look for ways to decolonize the public education system that I now am a part of. I find the curriculum devoid of and virulently opposed to discussion about the discipline's role in oppressing Indigenous people. Most of the time, it is left to the teacher to bridge such gaps by explaining why Indigenous people distrust western medicine, science, and schooling. I reframe various Ontario curriculum objectives by creating Indigenous-centred projects. For example, the weekly "Scientist Spotlight," showcases videos and articles from Indigenous scientists like Dr. Nadine Caron, Senator Lillian Dyck, and Dr. Alika Lafontaine. These brilliant Indigenous scholars are currently doing exceptional work in the fields of medicine and science. Students also write reports that discuss the institutional and personal barriers these people overcame in order to achieve the esteemed positions they hold in their respective fields. According to L'nu Mi'kmaq scholar Marie Battiste, "every child, whether Aboriginal or not, is unique in his or her learning capacities, learning styles, and knowledge bases ... knowledge is not a commodity that can be possessed or controlled by educational institutions, but is a living process to be absorbed and understood."[8] The public school educators in my family are making every effort to guide students away from binary knowledge systems and practices, to open their perspectives to various forms of knowing simultaneously.

Canada is seen as a benevolent state for opening its borders to refugees like my family. My family's story of indigeneity complicates the dichotomous understandings of settler–Indigenous relations and the real and conceptual divide between us. Growing up, I was unaware of the history and continued legacy of state institutions, including schooling and immigration policies, in the oppression and erasure of Indigenous people, their culture, and their rights to their own lands. Through critical reflection and more learning, I know there are points of strong connection between my family's experiences and the Indigenous peoples in Canada: a shared history of loss, displacement, and erasure. In an attempt to decolonize my family's story of forced displacement, I hope nuanced perspectives about newcomer refugee–Indigenous relations emerge from what I shared in this chapter.

Notes

1 Darin P. Wybenga and Kaytee Dalton, *Mississaugas of the New Credit First Nation: Past and Present* (Hagersville, ON: Mississaugas of the New Credit First Nation, 2018), https://mncfn.ca/wp-content/uploads/2018/10/Mississauga softheNewCreditFirstNation-PastPresentBooklets-PROOFv4-1.pdf.
2 Government of Canada, Crown-Indigenous Relations and Northern Affairs Canada, "Statement of Apology to Former Students of Indian Residential Schools," September 15, 2010, https://www.rcaanc-cirnac.gc.ca/eng/110010001 5644/1571589171655.
3 Patrick Wolfe, "Settler Colonialism and the Elimination of the Native," *Journal of Genocide Research* 8, 4 (2006): 387–409.
4 Bonita Lawrence and Enakshi Dua, "Decolonizing Antiracism," *Social Justice* 32, 4 (2005): 134.
5 Mississaugas of the New Credit First Nation, "Toronto Purchase Specific Claim: Arriving at an Agreement," (Hagersville, ON: Mississaugas of the New Credit First Nation, 2017), http://mncfn.ca/wp-content/uploads/2017/04/MNCFN -Toronto-Purchase-Specific-Claim-Arriving-at-an-Agreement.pdf.
6 Ibid.
7 Aparna Bhatia, *We All Belong: Indigenous Laws for Making and Maintaining Relations against the Sovereignty of the State* (PhD diss., University of Toronto, 2018).
8 Marie Battiste, "Indigenous Knowledge and Pedagogy in First Nations Education: A Literature Review with Recommendations," paper, October 31, 2002 (accessed June 11, 2014), https://www.academia.edu/3375155/Indigenous _knowledge_and_pedagogy_in_First_Nations_education_A_literature_review _with_recommendations.

7

A New Form of Colonialism

Nuria Sefchovich

BACK WHEN I DREAMT of who I wanted to be as an adult, I remember
feeling that I was living inside a box. And here I am, thirty-four years later,
sitting in an armchair writing my story and wondering, "Why did I choose
Canada?"

"How I would love to live in Canada!" I used to say when I was twenty.
I didn't have a sense of Canada, just a gut feeling about it. Months later,
some of my closest friends came to Vancouver to study English.

"Come with us," they said.

But I didn't. I had a promising future. I wanted to be independent. I did
not have time for carefree hippie journeys, but a scolding voice in my head
kept saying, "You should go with them."

One or two years later, wanting to live closer to work, I found a tiny
suite in a house owned by an old woman. Every night she chased me down
to invite me to chat while drinking herbal tea. One night she shared how
she ended up single and living in a new country. Her house was huge
and filled with so many kitsch ornaments, but her conversations were
exquisite. I was twenty-one at the time, and I remember thinking that I
wanted to have adventurous stories to tell when I'm sixty, just like her.

One Saturday morning as we were having a chat in the kitchen,
someone suddenly unlocked her main door. She turned to me and said,
"You haven't met the new tenant, have you? He is Canadian, and he is
leaving soon to return to Canada."

I was nervous to meet him, but I felt an unknown excitement – he
would be my first connection to Canada.

Over the next sixteen years, I pushed back that dream of moving to Canada. My job was great, and my marriage met social expectations. However, due to changing circumstances in my country, my daughters were living in a bird cage. Mexico had become an unsafe place to live, a non-sensical world where anyone could be kidnapped or assaulted at any time. I was so far away from being my own version of that elderly woman I met in my early twenties. I was thirty-six, tired, bored, frustrated, and scared.

In January 2014, like a shy little girl trying to get a yes from a parent, I asked my husband, "What if we went to Canada for a year?"

Right away, he said, "No."

A voice inside of me had hoped for that answer as my deepest self was scared of the challenge. But I knew our life needed to change. We agreed to go just for the summertime. And on Sunday, June

People laughing, people dancing, people playing music - people from everywhere.

29, at 10:15 a.m., my family of four landed in Canada. I was excited like never before. I was free, financially independent, married with two girls, and I'd had many professional successes and gained important academic credentials.

The city of Vancouver mesmerized me immediately. Everything worked – the buses were on time, public spaces were accessible for everyone, and each neighbourhood had character: the spicy smells of Chinatown, the silence of little India on Main Street. We could visit the mountains and the beach in one day. There was just so much space. While there, I took care of the printed monthly compass card that each English student held tight as if it were a treasure. I had fallen in love.

People laughing, people dancing, people playing music – people from everywhere, vibrant, commuting via public transport, living without a dress code. People covered in tattoos, people following the rules, people reading here and there, people with disabilities on buses and in parks. People of different social classes everywhere, talking a variety of languages. We all got together at the English school.

"Mom, we want to live here," my daughters told me two weeks after our arrival.

They did not know this was my dream as well. *Maybe this is the time,* I thought to myself.

My husband made the most important statement, "Do what you need to do to bring us here."

I had my daughters and husband on my side. In the end, my husband stayed three weeks, and I spent two months there with my daughters, ten and four years old. On August 31, we went back home; meanwhile, in British Columbia teachers went on strike and parents launched a fundraising website to support them. I left reading that news and was touched by the level of commitment and companionship.

> *People of different social classes everywhere, talking a variety of languages.*

Finding the Right Path

How do I stay in Canada? To start, I found an agency in my country, which provides help to newcomers seeking their dream life in Canada. Through this agency, I learned the easiest steps to live in Canada:

- Go back to college
- Apply for Permanent Residency once finished

Easy right? Who would not choose it? I would be a student in Canada. The best part, the agent working with me would fill out all the forms for me. This service is not cheap. I had to get a specific score in the academic TOEFL test to then receive a letter of acceptance from a Canadian college. I failed this, twice! So, my agent told me to travel to Canada and study in an intensive English course for two months.

"Wow!" I thought. "Let's do it!"

Culturally speaking, in my country it's not accepted that women, specifically mothers, live apart from their family, especially if they're in a different country. I knew that taking this step would be highly judged by my immediate circle, and it was. As a family of four, we said it would be just two months of this and then we would all be in Canada. The separation would be worth it. So it was that we four, for the last time in our lives, slept in the same bed in a hotel in front of an airport. It was the shortest night of my life.

Alone, in Vancouver again, I kept my summer memories from the previous year at the front of my mind. It was October 4, 2015, when I landed in Vancouver to study English. Going to school every day, I saw a city that I did not know, the beauty of the trees as they transitioned to a new season, the leaves changing from green to red to pink.

On the streets, people were silent or sad, dressed in grey, black, and blue clothes. Many locals were wearing just a sweater whereas the rest, including me, were wearing as much clothing as possible. I do not even remember how many umbrellas I bought, broke, and lost. By November, I had experienced cold from the weather, and also the people, the city, myself.

The environment in English schools is particular, for each student has a longer goal of either going to college in Canada or getting a better job in their home country. Back in those days, I remember seeing a group of guys in their early twenties stressed out in a classroom.

When I asked why, someone told me, "It is because they are in the Pathways Program to go to college." That was the first sign I didn't pay attention to, and I should have.

I was thirty-seven. All my classmates were under thirty. I didn't feel like I belonged. One day a twenty-four-year-old girl from Slovakia sat next to me in class. At lunch, this lovely girl took out a container with pasta in it, but she forgot to bring a fork, so I offered her mine. That day we started a friendship, and in time she and her boyfriend became my family. We visited more places where locals go, not just tourist places. We would go out for food and ask for one meal with three spoons.

I was cold and wearing layers and layers and layers – it was to the point where I had immobilized myself, as if there weren't enough layers to keep my heart warm. I missed my family. I looked out through the window of my bedroom. It was raining, and I knew that rain would be the pattern for the following months.

Each day I felt more confident speaking English, and a bit more fluent. I learned that when you do not talk, your listening improves. However, the internal conversation never ends – the self-approval, the self-judgement, the constant questioning and the uncertainty of situations, my physical appearance. Guilt for feeling excited by experiencing moments of freedom where I did not have to be a mother, a wife, a successful leader.

One day I emailed my agent to find out the next steps. Suddenly, sitting down in my bed while reading my agent's response, my mouth got dry. I was ashamed, shaking, mad, desperate.

"Unfortunately, you did not get the English level the college requires. Sorry," he wrote.

I paid him $5,000 plus flight tickets and he lied to me. He lied to us. I sent an email to the English school to find out what happened. I emailed every single person I could think of to ask for answers with the subject, *Can you help me?*

It was Friday, December 27, 2015, 9:00 a.m., and my flight was planned for the next day. Everybody replied kindly, showing empathy. The International Marketing and Recruitment Coordinator at the college got back to me:

> It has come to my attention that you have sent your email separately to multiple people in the International Office as well as the Faculty of Language, Literature, and Performing Arts. Please do not do this in the future as there are only a few people who are equipped to best answer your questions. When emails are sent to multiple people, not only does it cause confusion, it is also very inefficient as there will be multiple people all helping your case at the same time when your questions could easily be answered by one person. If you would like to send emails to more than one person in order to get a faster response, the best thing to do is to "copy" or "cc" people as I have done. I can help clarify a few points for you when I return to the office on Monday.

She was teaching me how to send an email when nobody else was responding to my messages, when I had a flight to catch, when I was heading back home empty-handed. Her boss reacted after I acknowledged her for teaching me the appropriate emailing code, which is the same in my country. Fortunately, she cc'd everybody, so all of them read my response to her.

I called home to ask my family what they thought we should do. My eldest was eleven years old and answered right away, asking, "What happened, Mom?"

I explained. She said, "I will find Dad and change your flight. You confirm the college appointment."

Yes, this tiny lady told her mom what to do. She was not clear with respect to what I was dealing with, but she definitely knew her mother was standing up for herself, and she was fully on board.

At my meeting on Monday, I got "accurate information" from the International Marketing and Recruitment Coordinator: "Your agent always knew you had to study Pathways, which is a four-month academic course. If you get a specific score, you'd get the letter of acceptance."

My husband said, "Let us do it. You are already there."

I replied, "It is four months now. I won't be there for your birthdays, nor your graduations."

My family said, "And we stand up for you; we can do this."

Empowered by them, I followed the new option offered by the college and deposited the fees. "Now you are perfectly in," they said.

Pathways 3 was challenging. In one month I had to write an essay and give a presentation about it, plus practice listening and reading to pass the final test. Understanding the structure of an essay, thesis statement, and topic sentence became a daily cloud storm over my head.

My daughters' birthdays were coming up. What kind of mother was I? I felt guilty about leaving them, yet at the same time this journey was my legacy for them.

One of my skills is remarkable creativity. I was planning a surprise for my little one, whose birthday is on January 29. I bought a tiny cake, an electric candle, and a clown's red nose. Finding a convenient place close by the school with good wifi, I went to FaceTime with my girl. Through the screen I could feel her amusement. She smiled at me. She knew I would do anything to get one smile of hers. I started singing happy birthday to her. When she hung up, I broke into tears – I felt like they had forgotten about me.

That month I did not level up. My essay was great, but I was still two points below the required score. An incredible peer told me there is an English test you can take at the college once every six months. There was hope. I took the incredibly easy test, and I failed it as well! It was time to redo Pathway 3.

My essay this time was about the world happiness index. It's possible that writing about it triggered some increased positivity in me. This time I hit the score I needed and got my letter of acceptance to start college in April. I called my family, and together we cried and celebrated our first victory. I had less than a week to move into a new homestay and get ready for the next step.

The distancing I experienced came in stages. There is a point where you must accept that you left and the impact that your leaving had on others. Just two people had my back from a distance, and they became my pillars. The first was my oldest brother, my spectacular male support. His English is impeccable. One day he said, "Let us keep our interactions in English for you to practice." Every time I was dealing with something, I reached out to him, and despite the distance and the time, he was always there, sending me a book or recommending an inspirational movie.

I will never forget my brother's advice: "We come from an immigrant family, and wherever they landed, they thrived." My family from my father's side is Jewish, and immigration has been a part of our lineage. His words flew through my skin. They brought me hope. He was right: it is in my genes.

The second pillar was my friend of the last twenty-plus years. She was there for each up-and-down, helping me put myself together even when I did not want to. On the day I failed yet another English test, I was devastated, exhausted, frustrated, crying in my tiny room while it rained and rained. My friend called, and I was not able to say a full sentence – my words were stuck on my throat.

I said, "I failed."

Then she asked, "How are you feeling?"

"I feel like I am in the ground."

"Well, where do you want to be right now?"

When she stated that, it felt as if she was giving me permission to rest. "On the floor," I said.

"So, do it, I will be here," she assured me.

I did it, and she stayed there waiting for me to fall asleep.

Volunteering

Months before college started, I was accepted to volunteer at a non-profit. I had the opportunity to contribute my knowledge and experience as part of their communications committee. This particular non-profit supports immigrant and refugee women. It was my first chance to see what women deal with coming into a new country and how challenging it can be to learn a new language when you've experienced trauma. The bravery, silence, and gratitude projected in their looks rendered me speechless. I was touched, and in that moment, I decided I did not have the right to complain about anything. I paid a high price for that decision. The more overwhelmed I was, the more I stayed silent. Those quiet moments marked the beginning of an unknown emotional stage in my life, now defined as depression. At a certain point, nobody notices that a tiny hurt can transform over time into a deep emotional wound that is hard to cure. Regardless of your path to immigrating, the experience of not belonging is part of the system, and it shows up differently for different people. What was next for me was a silent sadness, which announced a profound depression.

My Changing Identity

First day at college, I felt I was changing both physically and mentally. I moved in with a new homestay family. For the first time in Canada, I was part of the family, I was visible and part of the conversation while having dinner. My classes were delightful. At the beginning I thought going to college would be just a part of my immigration process; however, it became the stepping point to building the woman I wanted to be. I discovered my ethnicity, nationality, marital status, cultural background, age, gender, etc., could all be understood by doing an intersectionality analysis – an essay here, an academic article there. It shaped my identity.

The more I discovered myself, the more I drifted away from my husband. We both were living different realities while trying to keep to a picture called "it should be this way." Time passed and I was thirty-seven. My listening, reading, and writing were improving, but I never talked. Why bother if I did not have any friends in Canada? Eventually, I made a good friend at the non-profit who became a tremendous ally. She helped me out with my essays, and we got together once a week. There was something in her that reminded me of who I was. My routine became predictable, I was either at the college or at home, studying, reading, writing. After dinner I usually went for a walk. While walking, I started to have self-conversations in English – they just happened. Doing so allowed me to stop thinking about reality in my language.

My husband surprised me with a visit to celebrate our thirteenth wedding anniversary. I was in class when he texted: "Do you want to have lunch with me?"

I replied, "I would love it."

Then he sent me a picture of the cafeteria at my school. I was shocked! I later learned that my daughters helped him organize this surprise.

We spent four great days together. We didn't know it then, but that was the last time we would be together as a couple.

"You look different," he said while we were walking toward our hotel.

It was raining, as it was in the marriage, but we did not yet recognize it. Well, we knew, but we did not name it. During our walk we had a respectful and empathetic conversation about what we should do while living apart, a conversation about fidelity and loyalty, and we gave each other permission to fail this test.

One day, my sociology professor handed back our midterms. I did not fail, but I disagreed with the way she evaluated one of my answers. It wasn't about the grade; it was about my ideas. Kindly, she accepted my request to speak with her after class.

"Yes, I can see that the content is there, but you did not express it accurately," she concluded.

I felt disappointed, and all my previous thoughts about how I'm not enough flooded back. I avoided taking another class with her until the end of my studies, when hers was the only class needed to complete my certificate. This time she was the same, but I wasn't. Before registering your classes for the following term, you must first get advice from the international students' department. As expected, the advisors were international students themselves – the only difference between me and them is that they worked there. They are seen by the system. However, the rotation of personnel there is confusing for students. One term, one advisor is in charge of your file, and the next everybody is new. Therefore, nobody follows up on anything, and it's very easy for your documents to get lost.

I remember when I booked my appointment. I had planned to take a class with a lab. My advisor told me, "Sorry about this, but you cannot take the lab because we do not have your high school certificate, and you cannot take English because you have not done the English test."

My world was falling apart. Again, I pointed out that I was not told a year ago about needing to provide my high school certificate, nor was I told that another English test was necessary; however, a high school certificate was indeed required. I couldn't enroll in my classes. It's a big deal because when pursuing your Permanent Residency, you must be a full-time student.

Finally, a month later, I passed the English test and submitted my high school certificate. I was sure that the next term everything would be fine and I would be able to register for my classes.

The next term came and, when I went to register for my classes, guess what? You got it. The advisor was new, and the international student department had lost my file. I was mad! I was a client and my path in that college, administratively speaking, was a nightmare. I questioned if this was normal in Canada. I questioned if it was personal or if all the international students got the same disrespectful treatment. I felt mistreated, incomplete, invisible. You have only two years to complete your program in order to get your full-time work permit after graduation. I got it, but I did it without them.

Settling into a New Reality

By the end of June 2016, I was getting ready to welcome my daughters to Vancouver and find a permanent place to live. When you are a mature international student, you do not have any rental history, therefore landlords do not want to rent you a place. After looking for months, my husband sent me a link from Craigslist, and despite my skepticism, it was the best choice. I allowed my inner Demeter, Greek Goddess of harvest and fertility, to assist me in decorating the place. This was my new home and I wanted to get everything ready for my girls. I was counting down the days until I would see them again.

When the day finally came, my legs were shaking. Their flight arrived, but my daughters did not come out. I was worried. My husband was texting me, "What happened? Where are they?"

I asked security many times, until one guy asked me, "Are you sure they got on the plane?"

I gave him the names and descriptions of my daughters. Forty minutes later he came back to me and told me there were two girls who matched their descriptions filling out forms.

"What? How? Let me get in and help them."

Three hours later, standing at the arrivals gate, I heard a sweet voice saying, "Mama, Mama, Mama."

I saw a young lady approaching me. I did not recognize her until she was standing in front of me. "Mom, it's me."

We broke into tears. Her younger sister had fallen asleep, and someone from the airline was carrying her out. We kissed and hugged each other. I had missed ten months of their life, which I would never get back. When I asked my daughter about the delay, she explained to me that nobody helped them fill out the forms or talk to immigration. My brave twelve-year-old took care of this for herself and her six-year-old sister.

The distance between me and my husband increased day by day – helping the girls settle into their new country was my priority now. My husband was supposed to join us in a couple of months. In the meantime, I supported my daughters emotionally and continued to get my assignments done.

Speaking Out and Becoming Visible

My professors always got it. I needed support. The international department offered me a spot as part of the Tuesday coffee led by a counsellor, to talk about our lives or to attend the Free Pizza night on Fridays and meet other international students. International students and mature international students are people in between – visible when paying tuition fees and invisible when we need specific support. Private counselling is not affordable, therefore not accessible for most students. This new country was my choice, but there is a rite of passage that comes with it, similar to a new way of colonialism: the social construction of the foreign students, the exclusion created by college ghettos – Koreans with Koreans, Indians with Indians. You never know who might speak your language. All of this shapes both your reality and your identity.

When Trump won the American election, my little one's classmate chased her, telling her she did not know anything because of her nationality. My eldest had a test graded by her classmate who wrote "reviewed by Trump." Both my girls got spectacular support from their teachers. We are not Americans, but our country has a specific connotation in people's minds, as do we. When a shooting occurred at a mosque in Quebec, it seemed that everyone who was not white could be targeted. I asked my daughters to stop speaking our native language in public. I was scared.

When it was time to register for the next term, I encountered a new advisor. "Well, the classes you would like to take are not available until next year, but you can take any class and get your certificate as an Associate of Arts without the specialization in Gender, Sexuality, and Women's Studies" the advisor said.

"Sorry, I registered a year ago to get a specific certificate. My tuition fees are way higher than the locals and now you are telling me I do not have the right to get the certificate for the program this college promised me." I was desperate, frustrated, and exhausted.

I left the office because my class was about to start, with that same professor I'd struggled with previously. One day she talked to me about my midterm. She acknowledged my answers, saying, "The content and the ideas are there, that is what matters." She saw me.

At the end of that class, my professor asked me why I was distracted. I broke into tears in her office and told her of the depression I was dealing with – my potential divorce, and the pitiful outcome I got while trying to register to get my women's studies certificate. She listened, and I saw in her face her desperation, frustration, and exhaustion. She grabbed my hand and we visited the professor in charge of that program, and then we went to the Registration Office. Incredibly, the girl at the front desk at the moment did not know my "friend" was a professor, so we got no help there. Finally, we discovered an option: If I took history of women in Canada I and II, I would be able to get my degree; however, I was running out of time. My only chance was asking that professor to recognize my academic background studying global history while also studying for my degree in my home country. Fortunately, she trusted me, and I was able to take other classes to complete the program.

As a newcomer to a country, your identity is built in stages: a) international student, b) immigrant, c) immigrant worker. Finally, I was headed in the "right direction." What was next for me was finding a job. I went to the career centre at my college and got valuable insights into how to craft my resume and how to perform in a job interview. I applied for 181 jobs in one year. One day, a friend of mine recommended me for an entry-level admin position at a carpet cleaning company. I applied immediately. The manager met me and told me, "You are ninety-nine percent in, I just need you to meet the owner and the director of operations."

Thirty-six hours later, my appointment was scheduled. We met at McDonald's. The owner was respectful and kind, and said, "Nuria I have a hard time hearing you, I am sorry for asking you to meet here. Why did you choose this place?" he asked the operations guy.

"Well, we are around the neighbourhood," he replied.

Every nice comment the owner said about me was an opportunity for the operations guy to say something negative: "We cannot sponsor you once you apply for your Permanent Residence. What if a client says something about your accent? What was your English score? It would be better for you to work at McDonald's."

I had an answer for each of his questions. The owner was ashamed and questioned his employee about the relevance of his "concerns." "You are overqualified for us, Nuria, but let me think about it," he concluded.

I went back home and told my daughters, who were waiting for me with a big jar of Nutella and three spoons, that it was *a difficult interview*. They understood, and I cried. The manager called me later to say what I already knew.

I do not know if what I experienced was misogyny or xenophobia, but it made me stronger. I returned to my student life – I had an assignment to do for class. I talked to my professor about writing an essay to illustrate how, together, the college's internationalization plan and the immigration process are a new form of colonialism. She not only supported me but also helped me develop a proposal for the VP, to improve service for international students. Somehow, I was creating my future job there. I went to his office to hand in the proposal personally, and then I sent him an email to let him know about it. He never got back to me. To me, this made it seem as though post-secondary institutions in Canada only see international students as a juicy source of funding. Still, I had started building my network at the college, with people on the business side. And in that time, just one guy, one unforgettable guy, looked at me as a human being. "Apply for this particular job and drop my name in your cover letter," he told me. I applied unsuccessfully for ten to fifteen different positions at the school.

Now I contribute in the non-profit sector. I am a life coach and consultant, and a co-host for a collective group called Living in Between Worlds: Conversations for Healing and Belonging. This community was created to offer a safe space to heal the wounds from generations of having to forfeit who we are to be accepted. We support and help each other to realize our fullest potential.

8

Licensed to Drive

Sushila Sharma

"**I'M NOT READY YET.** I can't do it now. I need more practice."

"You won't be perfect at this. You will never be perfect at it. After you get it, your confidence will boost. Things get easier then, trust me. Book the date for the road test."

He stood up from the chair and went to the sink. He came back in a minute.

"I need to learn certain skills. I need to get past my fear of being on the road first. I do not have confidence yet." I stated.

"Sheela, you always look to become perfect, and you have trouble recognizing your own strengths. I had to force you to go for so many tests back home in Nepal, too. You passed all of them. In some, you had excellent results. I know I have to repeat myself for you to do something. Sometimes, I wonder why do you not listen to me."

I left the last bite of my lunch. "Please, this is not like theoretical tests. This is technical. You know, I'm not high tech. I understand what you are saying. You are encouraging me to go for the test. I know a driver's licence will promote me to a full-time job. I understand, a full-time job will lead to many things: paid vacation, benefits, eligibility for buying property and sponsoring our parents to come here, to Canada. I understand our children have a big dream of owning a house in Canada. Various dreams are inter-connected with this one tiny thing. But please, listen to me. I want to get the skills first, then the licence with a photo ID. What if I hit a car? Will the licence save me? Once I have a licence, I have to be on the road, with you beside me and the kids in the back. Please take it seriously. It's not like reading a book and getting passing grades."

But he was not convinced with what I had said. In desperation, he kept reiterating:

> "You listen to me, have little faith on me, how can I misguide you?
> This is not the only thing in life. We have many in our to do list.
> Once you get the licence, we both will have more availability to take
> more shifts at work. There are so many things related to getting a
> driver's licence. Let's get it done."

He helped our five-year-old son finish his lunch. I started doing the dishes.

These are the consistent conversations between me and my husband, with each of the five driving tests I've had. I was nervous each time I was pushed to the testing centre. I had to accept the test I was booked for, no matter where my skill was. I knew I was not ready, but I had to take it to please him.

On my first road test, I did not properly listen to the examiner's instructions and made a lot of mistakes. I guessed the result ahead of time. I just wanted to be at the wheel for forty minutes. More than that, I wanted to go home and sleep. I wondered if I was the only one who was forced to take a driving test like this. My husband had expectations. He wanted me to have a licence. I could see him frowning, sensing that I had failed. As expected, the result did upset him. It was obvious. Since that first test, he'd taken me out on the road for driving practice every Sunday. I followed his instructions as best I could, but to no improvements. I listened to his scolds. I tolerated him blaming me, telling me that I was not attentive. So many tears and frustrations, and so much disappointment hovered around me. I was hard on him. He was hard on me.

But his persistence did not lessen. He wanted to see me succeed quickly. He hired a private instructor who could not teach me either. A slow-paced learner and a quick-paced instructor do not work well together. After I completed a driver's package with that instructor, my husband focused on booking a second road test. Money was paid. I failed this time, too. I didn't have any hope after that. I didn't even know what I should do differently to pass – I received no comments with my result.

Continuing the same conversation, my husband booked me a third test, but I was still not confident. I had to take the test for him, otherwise I would not be a "good wife." A good wife, in Nepali culture, listens to her husband regardless of her own choices, interests, and willingness. Before marriage, she listens to her dad, and after marriage to her husband. Males' decisions are the ultimate in almost all families back home. This is the social structure in which I was born and raised.

I practiced driving with him. During our practice times, we were like two fighters in an action movie. We fought to defend our logic.

The third test also did not favour us.

I almost gave up trying to get my driver's licence. I began to think of myself as a loser or a failure. Once, I posted a sad picture on my Instagram. I received so many caring comments from friends: "What happened to you?" "Are you okay?" "Is everything all right?" "A sad face doesn't look good on you," etc.

Once my dad asked over the phone, "Do you drive in Canada?"

I said, "No Dad, but why?"

He said, "Your sister-in-law drives in America, why not you? Who will take us in the car and show us Vancouver when we are there?"

I assured him, "Okay, Dad, I will take you in my car when you are here."

This conversation panicked me further. My dad wanted me to just be able to drive. I had to juggle between expectations and my actual driving performance. My people expected a simple thing from me, but that was too much. My dad's encouraging attitude was pushing me down in this case. It was producing heart palpitations.

At work, a driver's licence was necessary in my work as a Community Living Counsellor, because I had to drive clients. My job had offered me conditional status in the beginning, requiring I submit my driver's licence by a six-month deadline. Once my manager asked me about the license and I told her I was practicing every day and would take the test soon. Of course, I was practising for my next test, which was coming soon. Deep in my heart, I knew how it was really going. Maybe God, too, knew how it was.

On my fourth road test, I made a traffic violation by touching the bus lane. And I took more than two minutes to parallel park. After this test, I felt like I had woken up and was starting to figure out where my weaknesses were. Now I realized, what I needed was to find the perfect instructor, one who could teach me well. I googled and found one lady instructor. She sounded more expensive, but the voice on the phone felt like someone who could teach me well. I decided to take lessons with her.

I had started to make progress. I decided to take more lessons with her, but there was an issue of finances. My husband would not agree to paying for more lessons So the cost would certainly fall to me. I would have to tolerate so much blame. But I wanted to prove to him that I could obtain the license. I was determined to be prepared the next time I took the test so I took a couple of lessons without telling him. Actually, I took five lessons with this instructor without letting my husband know.

Though my job was casual, I was given enough hours at work and had the money for the lessons, but the account was joint – I shared it with my husband. So I had to steal my own money. I felt guilty, but I had no choice. There was a genuine reason behind it – it was crystal clear that he wanted me to get my licence. At the same time, he had a responsibility to keep his family in a financially safe zone. Every day and night, I could see his shoulders, so heavy with fear and insecurities in this new land. His tone was always anxious. He was taking a big risk in rowing our lifeboat over a vast ocean in poor visibility. I had to carry out the role of a significant other, handling the torch to point him in the right direction for us all. If I told him what I spent for the driving lessons, that would add extra stress on him, which I did not want. I could also understand his double persona – needing to save money and get things done simultaneously. If I didn't understand him, who else would?

I took my fifth road test with a lot of joy, as I had taken more lessons and gained more skill. Nobody forced me to take the test. For the first time, I felt confident. I told the instructor to book the test. I did well on it, fulfilled all the requirements. Yet the result made me feel hopeless again. On the test paper, I saw a tiny remark: "slow speed on Zone 60." The fact was, the road was bumpy, and I had used my brain, as the instructor had taught me to do, to adjust accordingly with the road condition. My anger and frustration did not allow me to stay quiet. I broke my habit of silence. I called the licencing office to re-evaluate my result. I defended myself, saying that I had to be slow because of the road condition. I challenged them to re-pave the roads rather than blaming their student drivers for slow speeds and putting them in unnecessary stress. I told them it was not fair to me.

"I do admit to my previous mistakes, not this one." I started to cry over the phone to a lady at ICBC's customer service, saying that I wasn't ever going to get my driver's licence. Me and my family are too worried about it.

Then I could not talk. So I talked to myself for a bit. My voice inside was so upset.

"It has disrupted everything. It has interrupted my desire to lead a free and independent life in this new land. This failure has shattered my children's dreams and disturbed my husband's emotional securities. With all these failures I have questioned my self-esteem, my dignity, and my independence as well. Without a license, I am dependent on my husband and friends for rides. I want to be independent and able to drive my children, offer rides to friends, and do things on my own. Instead, I feel like a nasty failure.

> *I needed someone to tell me that I had lost nothing.*

Breaking my interior monologue, I unknowingly uttered the following to the lady over the phone: "I feel like I want to kill myself."

With patience, the lady listened to me. "I know you are so upset," she said. "I will share your concern with the manager. Do not worry, Mrs. Sharma. I agree that the result has made you very upset."

She tried to calm me down. Her voice was soft and soothing, and she reassured me that I will get my licence with my next test. I released all my anger and frustrations. Then I stayed quiet, because I had no choice.

I lay down on the couch. I was hungry and tired, and I wished my mom was here. I imagined her wiping my tears, offering me a cup of tea and massaging my head. I needed a shoulder to put my head on. I needed someone to tell me that I had lost nothing. Someone who would assure me I was doing good. It does not matter how many times I had fallen. But it should matter how often I have tried and stood back up after my falls. But my efforts had not mattered at all. I did not have a licence, and that one thing was a shadow over my efforts to integrate.

I had lots of dreams, among which the licence was not a dream at all. I never imagined having a licence and driving a car. I had taken this thing for granted. It was nothing more than a basic need, and as an ambitious woman, I did not make it one of my dreams. It was like tea, coffee, food, sleep – any other thing that I would normally have. These things are not my dreams, not then, not now. Alas, this tiny little thing got me so disturbed, it sidelined all other things that I had been dreaming of.

In the meantime, I heard a loud noise from outside – it was a knock on the outside door. I thought my husband had come early from work. But I was startled to see two RCMP officers standing there.

They abruptly entered my basement suite. Immediately, my head was a whirlpool, and for a moment I could not remember all the questions that the police officers asked. I tried to think positively, that they were there to help me. Why should I fear them? I'm not a criminal, and I have done nothing wrong. Lady officer began to check in my kitchen drawers, making sure there were no weapons.

The lady officer also asked if she could check my body. I promptly said, "Sure."

She looked into my eyes and asked, "Mrs. Sharma, Are you thinking of hurting yourself?"

I said, "No ma'am, how could you say this?"

"You called ICBC, and they said that you were going to hurt yourself."

"Yes, I had expressed my feelings to the ICBC staff, but how could I hurt myself?

I'm a mom of two lovely children. I should be alive for them at least. But to be honest, I'm so upset about the result of the road test today. I have tried it so many times. I failed for no genuine reason this time. That's why I called them to re-evaluate my test." I explained all this to the police officer in one breath.

They checked my rooms and everything, and then asked me, "Do you think you need help with anything today?"

I said, "No, thanks. I have to go pick up my kids from school. I know I'm not okay, but I have no option, sir."

We ended the conversation. They could see my swollen red eyes and nose, but still they left. That night, before I fell asleep, I thanked Canada for having concern about my safety and checking on me.

The following morning, when I went outside for my morning walk, my landlord crossed my path and said," You know the RCMP was here yesterday."

I said, "Yes."

His tone was dubious. "You know, it's not good for us when police-*wale* visit us so often. We have concern about this."

I was suddenly more scared than the previous day. My landlord had the power to evict us from his suite so I tried to convince him: "It's all about me. I did not feel good yesterday, so they came to check on me. It's not a big issue. Mr. Grewal, please, do not worry about it. I'll try my best not to let it happen next time."

Now, I realize, this was not the right answer. But I could not tell him more than this at that time. It was something very personal. It was my issue, not his. Nothing had happened to him because of me or the arrival of cops. I did not pose him any threat or risk. Why cops or anyone come to me or my home was not his concern. Good God, people do not stop prying into others' lives, even in Canada. I had to be upfront about it. But I was not. I do not know what made me so hesitant to respond to him. I had other worries – would Mr. Grewal kick us out of his house? Why was he so worried about his image? He sounded like he was worried about how his neighbour might think of him. Later, I understood his worries and concerns. It took me time to understand that people here are concerned with whether a neighbourhood is peaceful or not when choosing an apartment residence. They worry about the safety of a building, so they concern themselves with their tenants' activities. I did not share this incident with anyone. If I had, they would have called me crazy. I had to conceal it.

I regained my energy once again. Using all my skills, I practised hard, convinced myself with all my positivity, and told my instructor to book a sixth test. Before going in, I went to practise with my husband. It was the worst. We fought about nonsense again. The consequences were disappointments, hatred, anger, and anguish. We both stopped thinking rationally. What did I get? What did he get? Nothing.

We'd lost so many things coming to Canada, not only financial but also our emotional and psychological well-being. The entire journey had been disrupted because of this tiny little thing. No one was there to share these feelings. Once I tried to share with someone in my circle, but I did not feel good about it. Few of them really helped me. Some suggested having patience and taking more lessons. The rest of them did not even care about it. I questioned and answered myself. Do I care about them? No. Do I listen to them? No. Why should they care about me? Like me, they are preoccupied and overwhelmed with so many things in their lives. Who has time to listen to my failure? Who has patience to listen to my tedious story over and over?

I lost hope one day, but the next day I grabbed it so hard. I got ready for the test again, and promised to make it the final one. Otherwise, I thought there was no meaning to living in Canada. I wiped my tears, pushed back my fears, and went for my sixth road test. I hired the same driving instructor to take me to the road test. She boosted my energy and confidence as we drove around the possible test route ahead of test time.

I knew I did very well. Near the end of the test, I realized that I hadn't parked well. Breathing fast, I started to sweat. I politely asked the examiner if I could get a chance to fix it.

He smiled and said, "No, it's good. You did good. You passed!"

I was overjoyed. I asked him again, "Did I pass?"

He confirmed, "Yes, you passed, madam!"

I expressed my happiness to him. "Thank you so much. You are God."

"No, it's not me. You did it all by yourself. You deserved it." He declined my thanks. Then he took me to the office for paperwork. The lady in the office handed me a paper to sign. While filling out the paper, she asked me, "Ma'am, do you have any health issues?"

I said, "No, not at all." And then I added, "You know what? I had so many issues because of this licence. Now, I'm no longer unhealthy."

She laughed at my reply. Other staff laughed, too. I asked the examiner if he had a business card. He handed his card to me.

I told him, "I will show this card to my kids and tell them how nice you are. Probably my family will invite you for a coffee one day."

He uttered, "Awwww," with a sweet smile and left.

My driving instructor was so happy to know that I'd passed the road test. She dropped me off at the nearest SkyTrain station, and from there my husband came to pick me up and drop me off at work. I did not say to him that I had passed, nor did he ask about the result. He might have already suspected that I failed – that or he was waiting for me to talk. I was happy inside, but I was reluctant to share. It seemed like nothing would make us happy again. I wondered if any happy news could bind us together.

In the past, we did not need big achievements to laugh and smile. I remember how happy we were when we got Canadian Permanent Residency. We used to smile with our tiny little triumphs. Why was I so hesitant to share this good news today? Maybe I was too tired of my many failures. We barely talked as he drove. When we reached my work, right as I was about to get out of the car, I threw the yellow temporary licence on his lap.

He said, "What is this?"

I said, "Have a look."

He saw, and he knew that I had passed but still hid his response. Probably he wanted to smile, but he concealed it from me. I also wanted to give him a big hug, but I hid that. Maybe it was not the right time?

I headed in to my workplace. It was April 18, 2018. When I entered my office, the manager gave me another surprise – I had been promoted to a permanent full-time employee. He also reminded me that they had given me full time on the condition that I had to get a driver's licence within two months.

I chimed in with, "Thank you for offering me full time, and you know what, Max, I got my licence today."

"Oh, did you?"

"Yes, I did, Max."

"Okay, double congratulations to you, Sheela! Have fun tonight with your family after work!"

"Of course. I will, Max."

Postscript

We applied for my parents' visa. They came to visit us in June for the first time. We had a lovely reunion after five years apart. I applied for a two-week vacation, which was approved. We all made a trip to beautiful Victoria, BC. At the start of the trip, my dad sat beside me. I told him to fasten his seatbelt. He smiled at me, and I do not know what he recalled in that moment. In my case, my past phone conversations with him were resonating in my ears. That same month, we applied for a mortgage. In our free time, we all gathered on the couch and surfed beautiful houses on the internet. Every weekend we went to an open house. In September, the mortgage was approved. We moved into our own house in October 2018. I started taking the driving licence issue with a bit more seriousness. I encouraged two of my friends to go and take the road test. I took them out to practise a couple of times. They got their licences on time, and I am still getting credit for this.

9

Becoming the Person I Admire

Yuki Yamazaki

IT WAS THE FIRST DAY of the month. The day I was most excited about as a child. It was the day new books were delivered to my house. I was waiting and waiting to hear the noise of the delivery person's motorcycle. Footsteps approaching the building excited me. I often peeked out from the window to see whether it was the delivery person or not. A lot of the time, I was disappointed.

I was a girl who loved reading books, and my parents bought me tons of books throughout my childhood. Whenever we went on a trip, my parents always bought my sister and me a few books, so we could enjoy them on our journey. When we found any books that seemed interesting, they never hesitated to buy them for us. Our travel bags were always full of books and snacks.

They named me Yuki. "Yuki" means "snow" in Japanese. My parents thought I was shining like snow when I was born, and that is why they decided to name me Yuki. In Japanese, we use three different alphabets to write our language. For Japanese names, we use Kanji (Chinese characters) to describe the meaning of people's names not only in their sound but also in their writing. All parents give personal meaning to their children's names, wishing for their children's futures. My name is described as "由記." "由" means "reason" and "freedom," and "記" means "memory" or "record." My parents chose those Kanji characters to describe my name, hoping I would become a memorable woman who does not hesitate to express her feelings and opinions freely.

When I was a child, I lived in Kanazawa, in the central part of Japan's main island, Honshu, on its northwest side. It was not a big city then, although it had many attractive and historical sightseeing places such as old temples and one famous national park. Both of my parents grew up with a single parent. It was only after I became an adult that I learned they had tough childhoods.

When my father was ten, his mother passed away. At a school sport festival, he and his older sister were too sad to see other students having a happy and luxurious lunch with their parents. They knew that their father had to work and could not come to watch their performance even if he wanted. They hid themselves in a classroom where nobody noticed them. My father said he still remembers the taste of simple rice balls that his sister made for them.

My mother lost her father when she was a baby, so she has no memory of him. Her mother worked at a construction site, where mostly men worked back then. My grandma was thoughtful, sweet, and small. I could not believe that she worked at a construction site, but I do know that she was a strong woman who did anything she could to support her daughters.

One day, my father said, "Do not be obsessed with things. When you die, you cannot take anything. But your faith will be passed on to your children, and to their children. In this way, you leave proof that you lived your life." My father is not a person who talks a lot, but he always gives me important and powerful advice when I ask him.

His message made me proud. I felt as if my father and my mother are and will be eternally inside of my heart.

Since both of my parents had difficult childhoods, they tried to give me and my sister everything. They wanted to ensure that we always had what we needed, so that we did not have to worry about anything and could simply enjoy our childhood. When I think of it now, while parenting young children of my own, my parents probably wanted to influence me by providing me many books so I would discover the joy of learning through reading. I do not remember what kinds of toys I had, but I clearly remember my books. Thanks to my parents' continuous efforts, I am now a parent who has the same wish for my children.

When I started attending elementary school, I was always excited about going to the school library during recess, to find and borrow new books weekly. I remember the very first book that influenced who I am today was a series of encyclopaedias on the bookshelf in my house. One of them was about language, mainly focusing on English. The first section was about how to greet and introduce yourself to other people in English. It was written using the English alphabet with a Japanese translation. I read the phrases and pretended to greet people from overseas. I doodled on paper pretending that I was writing in cursive script. I often imagined people speaking in different languages throughout the world. Since then, my interest in the language has grown. I wished to learn English, and to be able to communicate with people from different cultures. Even though I did not have much opportunity to meet foreigners while I lived in Japan, I was always excited about meeting new people and learning from them.

Being passionate about English, I enrolled in a local university and received a master's degree in English. My dream was to become an English teacher, focusing on conversation for children – I wanted to teach them to feel the same excitement about English that I felt when I was a child. I chose to work for a private company that operated English conversation schools for children. I spent hours and hours preparing lessons, wishing that every child who came to my class would enjoy learning English and would want to practise it with me. After about three years, I was promoted to be manager of a local branch office. About a year later, I got an offer to work in a head office in Nagoya, which is three hours away by car. Without hesitation, I decided to take the opportunity – I wanted to influence more teachers and encourage more children to be happy to learn English. I really missed classroom teaching, but I reminded myself that my work would lead to more children's smiles in the end. I kept reading books, both to build knowledge and for leisure. I was proud of myself for continuing to work at becoming the person I wanted to be. I was not scared of anything and was confident in doing what I believed. Nothing stopped me from moving forward. I was an independent and confident working woman.

In spring 2005, I reunited with my future husband, Jason (Jay). He worked for the same company, at around the same time, but left soon after I started working for the head office. We met through a mutual friend's party and clicked with each other. We married in fall 2006. In 2008, our beautiful son, Noah, was born, and in 2010, we had a beautiful daughter, Mia. Both children were born in Japan and enjoy having dual Japanese–Canadian citizenship for now. As an international couple, Jay and I have discussed a lot about our children's futures. In my mind, my parents were who I had in mind as ideal examples. I never doubted my parents' love for me. They allowed me to enjoy my childhood as a child for a long time. I was a lucky girl; however, I learned that due to our different cultures, Jay and I had many different expectations.

For instance, at one point Jay told me to go out for coffee by myself, to have a break from Noah and Mia while he took care of them.

"What? Why should I have a break from my own children? I am their mother, and I should be with them all the time even if I am tired."

It was not a typical way of thinking for parents in Japan, so I felt guilty when Jay took Noah and Mia somewhere by himself, and I was given some time to relax. Sometimes we did not agree about parenting styles and had to talk a lot, to figure out what future we would like to provide for our children. After some discussion, we decided to move to Canada to begin another chapter of our lives. We thought our children would enjoy learning in the Canadian educational system.

> *My dream was to become an English teacher.*

In summer 2011, we moved to Canada. I had never lived abroad, so I had mixed feelings about living in a new country and using my imperfect English. I left my job that I was proud of and had nothing here but my beautiful family. I did not regret my decision to move to Canada, but different feelings started growing in myself. At the time, I was not sure what it was. I felt like a part of me was missing.

Every night, both Jay and I read stories to our children in both English and Japanese. They loved listening and got excited about picking which books they wanted us to read. They would run to their bedroom carrying many books in their small arms and usually fell asleep after we read for about an hour. Jay and I agreed that we should not buy too many toys for our children, but that we should provide them with any books they wished to read. We started building a home library for our children, which now has hundreds of books in both Japanese and English.

Raising young children made my life busy and filled me with happiness. However, I was left with such a halfway feeling. It was dependence. Excusing my language and knowledge about my new community, I started depending on Jay. I became reluctant to communicate in English due to the lack of knowledge in certain subjects and my unfamiliarity with social systems and norms. I hated saying, "I do not know" so many times.

I was an independent and confident woman before I moved to Canada. That woman did not exist anymore. I started to dislike myself.

Jay's family and friends welcomed us, and we often got together with them. I was able to communicate with them in English for basic conversations; however, I sometimes had trouble understanding when people spoke in slang or talked about specific content that I did not know.

For instance, a lady said once that it "was raining cats and dogs." I got confused and thought, "How come she is talking about cats and dogs? I thought she was talking about her weekend. Oh, now she does not talk about 'cats and dogs' at all. What were they about?"

Every time I had a moment when I did not clearly understand people, though nobody ever said anything, I felt that I had failed. I became disappointed with myself. I felt that my existence was useless, powerless, and meaningless. I became reluctant to talk to people I did not know because I was afraid of not being understood. I knew that everyone wanted to get to know me and was trying to be nice to me, but sometimes I wished that nobody invited me out, so I would not need to deal with those negative feelings about myself.

At a house party we were invited to, as usual, I enjoyed meeting people at first, but later I started feeling alone again, despite there being many people in the room. I did not want to be rude – I tried to smile at people, but I did not have the energy to initiate conversation with them. I made myself busy with taking care of my children, so I would not need to talk to people. I escaped from being social.

While I was doing that, I was arguing with myself, "Yuki, don't escape. You should talk to people. That's the only way to overcome this loneliness."

But another me said, "Yuki, you are doing enough and you don't need to push yourself."

I was getting tired of arguing with myself. I went to the bathroom and shut the door, and I burst into tears. Jay and some of our friends noticed something was wrong with me and asked if everything was okay. I did not know how to explain to them the mixed feelings inside of me. I did not want anybody to feel sorry for me because of what I was going through. I decided to move to this country for a better future, for all of us, but I found that I was not really ready myself to overcome all the negative feelings I had, to make the necessary changes. I wanted people to recognize me as the woman I used to be, but I felt as if that woman had become useless, powerless, and meaningless. I loved my family and was proud of what I was doing as a parent, but something completely changed in me as to how I valued myself as an adult woman.

In winter 2014, I heard about an ESL program called LINC, which stands for Language Instruction for Newcomers to Canada, a government-funded program. I wanted to make changes for myself and registered for the program. In class, I met many students from different countries. We learned how things worked in the Canadian community. I felt as if I had found the missing puzzle pieces to my brain, to help make conversations with local people understandable to me. I truly enjoyed the feeling that I was learning more about this country and my community.

We were also given opportunities to share our feelings about moving to Canada. I learned that many of my classmates had feelings similar to mine: isolation, frustration, uselessness, powerlessness, meaninglessness. All the feelings were negative. None of us spoke perfect English, but we understood what we wanted to express as if we had known each other for a long time. Without having perfect language skills, I realized that we could understand each other. The LINC program helped me to build a small community where I felt my existence was valued. It provided me with a sense of belonging.

Our teacher, Sara, was empathetic and understood that we were facing those negative feelings. One day she said to us, "You guys should be proud of yourselves for learning a second language. Not many Canadians speak a second language, so you do not need to feel negatively about yourselves because of your English competency."

It was a simple but powerful message. Something had changed inside of me. She made me realize that there are people in this community who value us. I started to regain my confidence and positivity. Learning vocabulary is not enough. Languages are alive, and we can use them practically only when we know how the words work in real life. For example, to use the word "e-transfer," we need to know how an e-transfer works. If we do not understand the concept, we need to learn it. In Japan, I wanted the children I was teaching to feel excited about the language they were learning, but once I moved to Canada I lost my own excitement about learning something new. Instead, I felt ashamed that I did not have the knowledge and ability to express my thoughts clearly.

In class, Sara introduced us to abridged versions of historical novels for people who speak English as a second language. She said, "Reading is powerful. Once it becomes a habit, you cannot stop."

I knew what she meant. I remember how it felt when I read books in Japanese. I tried to read books in English but gave up on it. It seemed like a long time until I could understand and enjoy reading books in English. I did not have time to do so because I was a busy mom with two little children. I made many excuses for why I could not read. Who was this person who was good at making excuses? Where was the woman I liked? I wanted to make changes – I needed to do so. I decided to trust Sara and give myself a second chance at reading books in English. I wondered when I could find the time. I was exhausted and could not keep my eyes open at day's end, after taking care of my children. Should I wait until they get a little older? But I needed to stop disliking myself. I needed to start doing something for myself. After thinking for a while, an idea popped into my head – a perfect place that I go to every day where I can be by myself. The bathroom! I started taking a book into the bathroom with me and read in the tub every day. It was a tiny bathtub, but it became the place each day where I could set aside some time for myself. It was only about ten to fifteen minutes, but I looked forward to it during the day. The excitement I used to have about books was coming back to me.

Sara, you were correct. Reading is powerful, and it inspired me again, like it did when I was a girl.

In spring 2015, Sara asked us what we wanted to do after completing the LINC program. However, instead of asking myself, "What do I want to do?" I was telling myself, "I can work as a waitress in a Japanese restaurant because I am Japanese."

But I was always left with a question: "Do I *want* to work at a restaurant? Do I have a passion for it?"

As a girl who was excited about books and learning English, I knew what I wanted and who I wanted to become. I became a language teacher to teach children the excitement they can feel in learning English. But that all happened in the past. I could not allow myself to dream of teaching a language when I am not a native speaker.

I heard me talking to myself: "Yuki, your English is NOT sufficient enough to teach people English." So I buried my passion somewhere deep inside of me.

When I was a student in the LINC program, I was asked to attend a seminar as a volunteer panelist with Jay. Abbotsford Community Services (now Archway) wanted to hold a seminar with the theme of international marriage. Some international married couples, including Jay and myself, attended the event as panelists. We were supposed to answer questions that the audience asked.

One of the last questions was, "What do you wish to do in the future in your new community?"

I had to think of an answer quickly, although I did not know what I wanted to say. I kept asking myself, "What can I do?" instead of "What do I want to do?" Without knowing where my answer would go, I started talking about my experience as a language instructor in Japan and how much I loved the job and sharing my experiences and memories with children. While I was talking, I suddenly became emotional. I did not know why, but tears filled my eyes.

After the seminar, I tried to understand what had happened to me. My brain has been trying to find something new that I might be able to do in Canada, but my heart has always known that being a language instructor is the most exciting job for me. I loved getting to know my students and wanted to be there for them. I remembered the excitement I felt being in a classroom. After being put through situations where I felt I was useless, powerless, and meaningless because of my own feelings and the limits of my ability, I had forgotten about what I loved and what had always pushed me forward. I had been ignoring my inner voice, telling myself that I need to become a different person. I realized that I had given up my own dream because I was not a native English speaker. Should a non-native speaker not teach the language? Were there any advantages for me in teaching the language? There was no correct answer, and I did not need to be told by anybody else. I needed to admit to myself that teaching English was what I wanted to do. Nothing had changed about me. I was the same person who loved the language and loved supporting people. After that seminar, I decided to be honest with myself. I started by telling Sara and my classmates that I wished to become a language instructor even if it took many years. Sara and my classmates acknowledged my efforts in the program and encouraged me to move forward.

In September 2015, I was hired as a teaching assistant in the LINC program. It was an exciting time – I was starting a new career in education here in Canada. Mala was the first instructor with whom I worked. She was a fantastic instructor. She was caring, thoughtful, and respectful. All the students Mala taught loved her very much. She taught me how an instructor could build strong trust with their students, and how doing so would affect students' motivation to learn.

In April 2017, I received a message from my colleague: "HI YUKI. MALA HAD A HEART ATTACK AND PASSED AWAY AT HER HOME."

When I saw the message, my mind went blank. I was confused and struggled to understand what I had just read. I had to read it multiple times to process it. After a few minutes, I burst into tears. Jay looked at me in surprise.

"Mala passed away!"

He hugged me and I cried in his arms. I could not see Mala or talk to her anymore. We had worked as usual only a few days earlier. She looked fine, although she was concerned about her health a bit. She said she had a doctor's appointment.

I was in shock having to accept the reality that our lives could end so suddenly and unexpectedly.

After Mala's death, I continued working as a teaching assistant. All the instructors there were inspiring and supportive of their students. I wanted to become like them one day – one day in the future. I was not yet strong enough to be honest with what my heart was telling me. I was conflicted over whether I should spend more years improving my English before moving forward and taking a certificate course to become a language instructor. But how many more years would I need to spend improving my language skills before I felt confident? Would it ever happen? I asked myself these same questions over and over, and I was getting tired. I felt stuck in the same place for a long time.

One day, I was thinking of a time when I was working with Mala and heard an inner voice saying, "Do you want to end your life without doing what you WANT?" Suddenly, I got scared. To be honest, I knew what I *wanted*, and I did not want to end my life without trying.

In February 2019, I told Jay that I wanted to take the Teaching English as a Second Language (TESL) certificate course, a required qualification for a language instructor. He was a little surprised because I had never clearly or seriously expressed my interest to become a language instructor in Canada.

He said, "Babe, you should do whatever you want. It could be challenging, but you could do it. I will support you one hundred percent."

I started looking online to learn about the course, asking people for advice regarding my new learning journey.

In September 2019, I was at the University of the Fraser Valley campus in Abbotsford. I was working two part-time jobs, so I decided to take one class each semester to deepen my understanding of the course.

On my first day at the campus, I looked around the classroom and found that almost all the students were native English speakers. I did not feel like I belonged there, but I told myself, "Do not worry about what people might think of me. Focus on what I *want*. My family is supporting me!" I spent hours each week reading textbooks and doing assignments. Quite often, I had to read the same parts two or three times to make sure I understood correctly. My text became full of my notes. My study time started after I finished work and my kids had gone to bed, so I stayed up until midnight or later during weekdays. But I never got tired. I was excited about doing what I had wanted to do for so

I felt stuck in the same place for a long time.

long. The classmates in the course were supportive and my nervousness seemed to disappear. I started to look forward to seeing my classmates at campus.

Then COVID-19 hit in March 2020 and everything changed. Our course shifted to online learning completely. Online learning was another new experience for me. My nervousness came back as we had to have discussions with people I had never met in person, but I told myself, "Just do it!" My professors gave me positive feedback, and I completed my first year successfully.

In August 2020, at around 1:00 a.m. on the night when the Vancouver Canucks won against the Stanley Cup champion St. Louis Blues, I heard someone banging at our door.

I woke Jay up. "Jay, I think someone is banging at our door."

We went downstairs. I thought someone drunk was celebrating the Canucks' win and was causing trouble.

When we opened the door, our neighbour shouted, "FIRE! FIRE! Get out of your house right now!!"

"What? What did he just say? A fire?"

Jay and I looked to our next-door neighbour's townhouse. There were huge flames from his garage to his roof. We rushed to Noah and Mia's rooms and woke them up. They were half asleep but we sent them outside immediately.

Jay shouted, "Babe! Grab whatever we must have in one minute!"

I ran back to our room and grabbed the diaries that I had been recording about Noah and Mia's growth, and our passports. Then I stood there and thought of what more I should grab.

Then I heard Jay shouting, "Babe! Hurry! We must get out right now!"

I ran down to the door. The flames were bigger. About ten to fifteen minutes later, a couple of fire trucks arrived. The firefighters carefully started investigating the townhouses.

Noah and Mia were trembling. They kept asking, "Mom, are we going to be okay? Are we losing our house?"

"We will be okay. Nobody got hurt and we are safe. That matters most."

The fire had spread from roof to roof. We sat outside for hours just watching our house on fire as the firefighters got organized.

My daughter, panicked, again asked, "Mom! Are we going to be okay?"

I tried to appear calm, to take care of my children and their rising fear.

Firefighters started tackling the fires, but the blaze did not seem to go out. An official told us that we did not need to be there since they did not know how long it would take to extinguish the fire completely. She gave us each an emergency blanket and some essential care products. Jay, Noah, Mia, and I walked to a hotel in our pyjamas and sandals at around four in the morning, in a sprinkling of rain. I wished it would have rained harder, to extinguish the fire.

The next morning, we heard it was almost noon when the fire was completely put out. We met with an insurance adjuster. He told us that nothing was really burned in our house, but everything received either smoke or water damage. So, we were told to give up most of our things.

I wondered, "What happened to our books, our little library?"

In the early evening, I went back to our townhouse. I was not allowed to go inside and was told to give the restoration company a list of items that held important memories, things that were irreplaceable. I asked them to find my wedding picture frame, the traditional Japanese decorations celebrating Noah and Mia's lives, their drawings and paintings from when they were little, other diaries that I'd recorded back when they were still babies, and a picture frame that Noah and Mia had made from a bunch of tickets from where we had gone for Jay's birthday.

When I was explaining to a lady at the site where she could find them, my eyes filled with tears. I said, "They are nothing of monetary value but irreplaceable to us."

She said, "We understand. Tell me what you want me to get. I will do my best to find them."

After she brought out the things I asked her to find, I realized I needed my textbooks in which I had written a lot of my notes. I told her where she could find them on our bookshelf, but it was difficult for her to locate them because we had so many books.

I begged her, "I know where they are, and I can grab them quickly! Can I go?"

She said, "No. It's dangerous."

I continued asking. Finally, she came back with an extra helmet and said, "Okay. I'll give you one minute to get your books."

I ran to our bookshelf and found my textbooks. They were wet and damaged from the water, but I felt happy to have them back. I glanced at some of the other books sitting on our bookshelf. They looked perfectly fine, but we had to say goodbye to them, to the books Jay and I read to Noah and Mia when they were little. The books that Noah and Mia had read by themselves. We lost our little library full of memories.

After the fire, the days passed quickly. Under the COVID-19 pandemic, everything changed. I was still taking a few courses online to get my TESL certificate while we lived in a rental house. Our friends knew that Noah and Mia loved reading and gave them some books. We bought a few bookshelves to start rebuilding our library.

In June 2021, I completed the TESL course. During those two years I studied the hardest I had in my life. I am proud of myself. I graduated from the University of the Fraser Valley with a dean's medal. It was an honour to be recognized. Furthermore, I was happy because I had re-discovered my passion and have moved forward. I was determined to make my dream come true. I am an independent and confident working woman who will continue being honest with her heart and developing this new me that I admire.

Our new library is not as big as it was, but we will continue to fill it with books and resources on teaching, and with our family memories.

PART 3

Stories of Belonging and Exclusion

10

Finding My Place

Ana I. Vargas

LET ME TAKE YOU on my journey as a child of immigrant parents.

I was born in Tepatitlán de Morelos, Mexico, in the central Mexican state of Jalisco. It's called "Tepa," for short.

In 1967, my parents moved to Riverside, California, in the United States, a country very different from theirs – the language, the culture, the food. What was especially different was that they had left behind their own parents. I know how much it hurts to leave behind people you love, to never know if you'll ever see them again. My parents moved to the US to give me and my siblings a better life, which they did. I thank my father and mother for all their struggles and every sacrifice they made for me and my siblings.

I was four years old when my parents moved to Riverside. I remember when I started my kindergarten class. The teacher took my hand, took me to my desk, and gave me a colouring book and some crayons. Confused, I looked up at her face. What was said was not in Spanish. I didn't understand a word. I put my head down then, and tears ran down my cheeks. The teacher was nice, but as much as she tried to make me feel comfortable, I was still sad not knowing what was happening.

I was not the only one who was sad. My mother was sad, too. She comes from a big family and was very close to her six sisters and two brothers. She was very lonely in America, very isolated. She missed the noisy streets of Tepa. The property that we lived on was where my father worked. It was about twenty acres of land on Sunny Lane. From where we lived, you couldn't even see a car or people walking on the street. I remember it had a long driveway, and as you drove up it you'd see a big yellow house on the right side and our small trailer on the left. The sister of my dad's boss, an elderly woman, lived in the house by herself. We were isolated from everyone. My mother was busy taking care of us: myself; my brother Luis, who is a year and four months younger than me; and my sister Hilda, who was one year old at the time. My father was hardly home. He worked long hours on the property and would return when the sun had set.

I understand now why my mother decided to go back to Tepatitlán when she got pregnant again.

I was in first grade, so I must have been about six years old. This baby was her fourth child. She wanted the baby to be born in Mexico, which was the opposite of what other people wanted at that time. People would do anything to have a baby in the US, but no, not my mother. She wanted to have the baby in Mexico. My parents waited 'til we'd finished the school year to move us back to Tepatitlán. This must have been around June 1970.

During the time we lived in Riverside, my parents were building a house in Tepatitlán, in the suburbs near the downtown area. The house was still under construction when we arrived, so my mother rented a house across from our future home. The house that my mother rented was old, built out of adobe bricks – just one room, a small kitchen, and a small patio with dirt. It wasn't a nice place to live. It would be a month or two before we would move into our new home, not finished but with all the necessities in place. We moved in around July or August 1970.

It was the beginning of the school year, and my mother enrolled me in a private school run by nuns. It was a different experience for me. Not that the nuns were mean, just in that I couldn't have my hair loose and had to wear a uniform consisting of shiny black shoes and ribbons that matched my uniform (white, red, and blue) – no pants, no tennis shoes, no T-shirts. Everything had to be clean and in its place. In the US, I didn't have to wear a uniform and there were boys in my classroom, in the entire school. In Mexico, my school was an all-girls school. At that age I didn't understand what was happening, and I wasn't happy there.

One morning on my way to school, as I was walking down the side-walk, I stretched my arm out and touched the walls of the houses with my fingers as I passed, like any child might do. The houses were all built side by side at that time, with no space between them and no yards.

When I entered the classroom that morning, we all stood by our desks, waiting for the nun to enter the classroom so we could say good morning at the same time. I remember I could only see her face. The nun was wearing a traditional long black habit. We were not allowed to sit down until she walked through each aisle. As she did, she carried a long thin stick in her hand, moving it up and down and hitting it against her other hand.

Then she said, "Everyone, put out your hands, facing upward."

I asked one of the girls next to me, "Why are we doing this?"

She said, "If you don't have clean hands, you will be hit with it."

"Oh!" I said to myself.

I started spitting on my hands and rubbing them hard on my uniform. I must have done a great job cleaning my hands, because I didn't get hit. It was very scary moment for me, to see the nun with her stick striking a student on her hand. I remember when it was recess time, at my old school in Riverside, I played kickball, four square, and tetherball, with boys and girls. Naturally us girls would scream loudly if a boy chased us. In the private school in Mexico, it was different. There was the normal screaming and chatting of girls, but very low. The school building was old; it had big hallways and tile floors, and a garden patio with no dirt or grass. I loved sitting on that floor and playing jacks with my new friends. We would also play an elastic game where we had to see who could jump the highest. These were all new games for me, and I liked them.

I wasn't happy at that school, so one day I decided not to go to school. I was only seven years old, and I ditched school and walked straight to my grandmother's home. It was probably three blocks away from the school. I remember the look in my grandmother's eyes when she opened the door and saw me: warm and kind, not judging, with a knowing smile.

She asked, "Don't you have school?"

I recall telling her that there was no school that day, yet there I was, wearing my school uniform and carrying my backpack. She just smiled at me, let me in, and told me to sit down near her big patio area and wait. She came back with a ball of yarn and a crochet needle. She sat beside me and taught me how to make a basic crochet chain. I must have done that for less than an hour, but for me, it seemed like an entire day. My grandmother continued mopping her pink-and-white tile floor while I continued to crochet a chain that seemed about my size. I rolled it into a ball when I got tired. I recall at some point telling my grandmother that it was time for me to go home. She must have taken me home since we had no phone at our place.

After that incident, I guess my mother figured out that I didn't like the school, so she enrolled me in a government school that my aunt attended. I still had to wear a uniform, but it wasn't as strict as the other school, and boys attended this school.

I was adapting to my new environment – to my school, to family reunions, to playing on the street near the sidewalk outside my grandmother's house. It was very common for children to be on the street playing since we didn't have a park and only three or four cars would drive by. I learned to play new games that I had never played before, street games like Vivora de la Mar, Trompo, Loteria, Changay, and Canicas. My friends and I also got together at my grandma's house to watch a children's show called *Topo Guillo,* since my grandma was the only one with a TV in her home. Once a week in the afternoon, she had all the neighbourhood children in her living room. Those are my favourite childhood memories. We had lots of time to play since we didn't have a television.

My mother finally had my baby brother, Hugo, but my father wasn't present as he was still working in the United States. My mother seemed happy, but being a mother myself, I now know that she was sad because my father wasn't there with her. On the day that my brother Hugo was born, I recall walking down the sidewalk with my Aunt Fela, leaving my great aunt Trine's house. It was cold and very dark. My aunt held my hand and said that we had to leave my mother there, at my great aunt Trine's home. There was a midwife, and my grandmother by my mother. I didn't understand what was happening, but I felt comfort holding my aunt's hand. It was common to have a midwife deliver babies at that time. A doctor would come to your home with his black bag if anything happened. My parents had six children total. Two of my siblings and I were born at my grandma's home. The only two born in a hospital were my youngest siblings who were born in the US.

My brother Hugo was about seven months old when my mother received a phone call from my dad's friend. My dad had been in an accident and was in the hospital in Riverside. We learned that while he was fixing a tire from a cement truck, it had exploded in his face. My mother had to leave us with her aunt Trine, who had three children of her own. My mother told me later that seeing my youngest brother on the bed there as she left us was very emotional for her, but she'd had to make that difficult decision. She cried every day.

My mother's journey would be a long one. She went with her cousin Pablo to cross the border illegally. In those years, men would travel across the border, not women. She was the only woman in that group of about ten men. They paid a *coyote*, a person or group that walked people across the border and into the States where someone was waiting for them on the other side. Not knowing what had happened and not having a parent with me made me feel sad and lonely. My mother's aunt Trine treated us well. My memories of that time are mostly of taking care of my youngest brother, Hugo, going to school, and helping my aunt.

I felt bad one time when my aunt asked me to wash the dishes, and I refused.

I said, "No. I can't. I just did my nails."

That conversation stayed in my memory for years. I felt bad that I had told her no. Now I realize that I was only a seven-year-old child at the time.

> *In those years, men would travel across the border, not women.*

Eventually, my mother told me what had happened to my father, and why she left us there. She had been gone for five or six months. She was heartbroken, missing us, and crying daily. She and my father were saving money to pay a coyote so that we could all cross the border and be with them.

My mother worked for a lady called Loy. She took care of Loy's children, and Loy became her good friend. Loy saw the pain that my mother was going through and offered to cross us into the Unites States (via Tijuana and the San Diego border). My mother accepted.

My mother phoned Aunt Trine to let her know that Loy would cross us into the US. My aunt got on the bus with my brother Hugo, Hilda, Luis, and me, to take us to Tijuana, Mexico, to meet with my mother's friend.

I still recall meeting my mom's friend Loy. She had straight, long black hair. Her skin was tanned, and she was slim and petite. Her beauty stood out to me. Loy and Aunt Trine had never met before, and my mother had only given a description of each other over the phone. The meeting took place at a park in Tijuana. Aunt Trine found Loy first and handed us over. I don't remember what my aunt said to us. She hugged us, cried, and left us there. Another person that I knew was leaving us again.

Loy was very nice, but when she spoke Spanish, it was a broken-down Spanish. She was a *pocha*, a person that mixes the Spanish and English languages when they speak. Her Spanish was not the same as the Spanish I was used to hearing back home – different intonation, cut-off words. As it turned out, she was born in the States and her parents spoke Spanish.

We got inside her car, not saying a word. I sat in the front passenger side, and my two brothers and my sister sat in the backseat. Loy told us not to say a word and gave us snacks. When we got closer to the border, an officer asked her a couple of questions. Loy used the birth certificates for her own children to cross us into the United States as if we were hers. I remember that my baby brother started to cry. My sister, Hilda, said something in Spanish then. I remember looking into the backseat, seeing my sister and baby brother there. The officer put a paper on the driver's side by the windshield wiper and told her to park on the side. I don't know how she did it, but she didn't go inside the inspection area. Loy kept trying to get that paper off her window. She was moving the windshield wipers and was finally able to grab that paper and drive off in a different direction. I can still see her look of desperation and relief. She was never followed. This happened fifty-two years ago, so there were no security cameras or any of the technology that we have now. It was very easy for us to cross the border into the US.

Loy didn't charge my mother a single cent. She risked being put in jail and having a criminal record, all to help my mother. Thanks to her we were reunited with my parents and were together again as a family. Loy was our family's angel; she helped my mother and father so many times. I'm thankful that she was the right person, too – crossing the border illegally like that is how so many children get abducted.

For the second time in our lives, we were illegal citizens in the US, but we'd been reunited as a family. The trailer, with its one bedroom, one bathroom, kitchen, and living room, was now too small for our family, but Loy's parents had a house on Mull Avenue. We moved there. The house was very old, cement flooring, no air conditioner, no heater, and only two bedrooms. You could feel the wind coming through the edges of the windows. It had the ugliest bathroom – when you opened the door, it was pitch black, with no light switch, no windows, no drywall, and the walls were covered with black tar. I was always afraid I might step on a water bug, or even touch one when I had to pull the string hanging from the bulb in the centre of the room. It was like entering a haunted bathroom –

I expected scary music to start playing and then something to reach out to grab me. I hated taking a shower there because as soon as you pulled the shower curtain, it got dark and you couldn't see anything. There wasn't a faucet in the bathroom, so I had to go the kitchen to wash my hands.

I started school late, around November 1971. I attended third grade at La Granada Elementary School, which is where I met Christopher. He was standing by the door, and he looked at me and said, "Would you like to watch *Sesame Street* with me?"

And of course, I said, "Yes."

This is how I learned English, by watching television and interacting with others. Christopher and I had a lot in common – we spoke the same language, we were the oldest in our families and had siblings about the same age, and we didn't like pickles. As we got older, I found out he was illegal, like me. We did everything together and had a lot of fun! Having him in my life helped me a lot. He was like my brother, and our friendship continued until he passed away in 2016.

A neighbour must have complained to the city that there were children living in this old house, the Mull house. One day, the Child Protection Agency came to our house with a notice and told our parents that the house was not a safe place for children, that my parents could stay but not us.

We moved back to the trailer, which was kind of hidden down that long driveway. Eventually, we were able to move into the nice house there, where my dad's boss's sister lived until she passed away. I don't know what happened to her as she never interacted with us. It was a beautiful house, with four rooms, two bathrooms, a big kitchen, and a big living room with wooden floors.

I went back to Twinhill Elementary School, in Riverside, where I had attended kindergarten and first grade. My appearance was different from that of the other children, at least that's what I thought when I was young – not because of my skin tone but because of the way I dressed.

My mother used yarn to braid my hair instead of ribbons. She didn't use hair gel, instead, she would cut a tomato in half and slide it down my hair, brush it and make sure not a single hair stood out. I probably had tomato seeds on my head. I can still remember the smell of the tomato and how sometimes the juice would go down my forehead and face.

I wore dress-up clothes to school – shiny black shoes, crochet blouses, crochet dresses. I just wanted to wear what other kids were wearing, like T-shirts, jeans, or shorts – comfortable clothes. I felt different from the other kids. The teacher always complimented me on how nice I looked, but the children would all stare, which at that time made me uncomfortable. The children were not mean. It was me that felt out of place and different. Even though my skin colour blended in, my clothes were different, my hair was different, and my last name was "Vargas."

One day, I undid the yarn that was braided into my hair while I was out waiting for the bus. I felt happy but worried. I thought that my mom might get mad at me, but at least for that day I felt like I belonged.

When I was ten we moved again. My dad's boss had reported my mother to immigration authorities, but her plan backfired. My father was at the house at the moment when authorities arrived, but my mother wasn't there. Since my father didn't have documentation, the immigration officers took him instead. My dad's boss pleaded with the immigration officers not to take him. She wanted my mother to be deported to Mexico – she didn't like my mother, and my mother suspected that she had been interested in my dad. Fortunately, Loy had taken my mother to get groceries that day. On their way back home from shopping, my mother's friend recognized the green immigration van and never took the turn into the driveway. I now have three children, and I could only imagine in that moment what my mom was going through, not knowing where her husband would be at or what to do. My father was deported.

> *The house was not a safe place for children ... my parents could stay but not us.*

Loy took us to her home until our dad returned. My father was back in only a couple of days. My mother and father always saved money, just in case anything happened to us. My father was able to hire a coyote who walked him to the border where a car picked him up and took him to his friend's house. His friend paid the one hundred dollars for him. During the early '70s, you paid anywhere between fifty and one hundred dollars per person, and it took about three hours to cross the border between Tijuana and San Diego. My father never went back to work with his old boss. He was able to get some belongings, clothing, and documents from our old house, but no furniture.

After that, my father found a job in Pomona, changing oil for trucks at a company. We moved to a beautiful neighbourhood there around Christmas time. We didn't have a normal Christmas tree or gifts that year;

our Christmas tree was a branch that my father had cut from the backyard and decorated with cotton and lights. But what a memorable day! It was my favourite Christmas day ever! We didn't have any gifts, but my dad was with us. We lived there for about seven months. I barely remember my classroom at the time or the school there. What I do remember is I had a friend who had a wooden playhouse in her backyard. I loved playing there.

We moved again. My father didn't like the company he worked for and got another job working nights. We moved to a place called Mira Loma. I finished my sixth, seventh, and eighth grades at Jurupa Middle School. I was very independent – I rode a horse, rode my bike, had my skateboard, was on the honour roll, volunteered at the library, and was on the school basketball team, I had friends from different nationalities. I was shy, but at the same time, I did what I liked to do. I was a very happy girl!

My parents never told me that we were in the country illegally. Everything that had happened to me – crossing the border, my dad being deported – I never thought of it as wrong. I guess my mother thought I was too young to understand. When I returned from school one day, my mother was crying, and I could see that something was wrong. Someone had reported the entire family to the Department of Immigration. They didn't take my parents because my siblings and I were at school and they were going to come back in a couple of days to get us. When you're a child you try to understand what is happening. There were times when I wish my parents would have told me what was going on, but I think it was probably better not to know. I could see how worried they were, the sadness in their eyes. My parents got a lawyer in Los Angeles who told them not to worry, he would handle everything. And he did. My parents applied for Permanent Residency, as my youngest sister, Delia, was born in the US, which meant they qualified. We got our Permanent Resident card two years later.

At a young age I would help my father and mother translate. I can still see the desperation on their faces, not being able to say what they wanted or to understand what others were saying. This was especially true for my father. When he was laid off from work, I accompanied him to the Employment Development Department (EDD), where he needed to verify that he had been looking for work. I would fill out his form for the two weeks and explain why he couldn't find work, so he could get his unemployment check. My father would get very frustrated and would even say words that I did not want to translate. Now I understand the frustration he felt. He only completed first grade. My mother had to help him write his name.

I went many places with my parents – to auto parts stores, doctor appointments, school offices, the bank. I felt bad sometimes because I couldn't help them like I thought I should have been able to. Sometimes my translations were incorrect, or I would say what other people wanted me to tell my parents. I felt responsible and guilty for not helping them more, and yet I was only a child. There was even a time when I felt shame for not having English-speaking parents. I must have been ten years old. What a terrible thing to think. My parents were vulnerable and good people, and they were taken advantage of so many times.

My parents bought their first house in Rubidoux, California. It wasn't in a nice neighbourhood. I completed ninth grade there, and in the summer of 1978, my parents sent me to Tepa with my sister, Hilda. That's where I met Arturo, my first and only boyfriend and the man who would become the father of my children. Well! Remember that old house on Mull Avenue? On our return, we came upon that house. My parents sold the house at Rubidoux not long after. They didn't make a profit, but they made enough to buy the Mull House in 1978. Loy's parents sold it to my parents for ten thousand dollars. My parents sold the home they had in Tepa to be able to afford the Mull house and fix it up a bit. My mother was pregnant again, and my youngest brother, Edgar, was born in November 1978. I started tenth grade that year at Norte Vista High School, which is where I would graduate from.

Our new home was a two-bedroom house with one bathroom, but now with a family of eight. It was the ugliest house in the neighbourhood. But for me, it was the most beautiful house to live in. It was our home. Just seeing my father and mother happy made me feel secure and happy. My parents never moved from this house.

Arturo was my first boyfriend at the age of 15. In 1981, the year I graduated from high school, Arturo had a motorcycle accident in Mexico, so I went to Tepa to be by his side. I lived there for a year and half, until he got better, and then I moved back to my parent's home in Riverside. Arturo and I got married in Tepa in 1984, when I was twenty, and we lived there for about three years before moving back to the US.

We had three wonderful children: Arturo, Isaac, and Melina. They were all born in Riverside, California. They spoke English all the time, but at home it was Spanish – I didn't want them to forget their culture and language. But, Arturo never liked living in the US and, in 1999, we decided to return to Tepa. At that time Arturo was fifteen-years-old, Isaac was fourteen, and Melina was nine. I had loved living in Riverside where I had everything – my family, my job, and our lovely home – but I supported Arturo in this move. I thought I could adapt to living in the small town of Tepa again. Our move reminded me how much I cried every time I had packed a box; every time I left friends; every time I left a place I loved. I realized that I was doing the same thing to my children that my parents did to me and my siblings – taking them to a new country, away from what was familiar and comfortable.

We packed everything into two trucks – my father's work truck and our small one. The house in Tepa was very beautiful, and even though it was not completely finished, I loved it. I lived there for a further fourteen years.

Speaking English had its advantages as I was able to find work as an ESL teacher and an English coordinator in my hometown of Tepatitlán. Coming from the United States had its advantages and disadvantages. I was working at three schools and even worked Saturdays, trying to help out financially. I made many friends amongst my colleagues, but my outgoing nature created gossip in the community. I used to drive a colleague home or go for lunch with a fellow teacher. Others saw me and disapproved of my relationships with male colleagues and spread gossip. I was called nasty names. If I held hands with a close female friend, I was called a lesbian. No one supported me, or believed that my relationships were innocent, just friendly – not even Arturo. It was a difficult time. It took a lot out of me emotionally, and I finally decided to separate from the man I had known for thirty years.

You're probably wondering how it is I came to Canada. In 2014, I had a lot of expenses and debt, and all I did was work to pay off the interest. At the time, my brother-in-law asked if I could help them pack and take care of my nieces because they were moving to Canada. He offered to sponsor me, since he's Canadian. I thought I would be returning to Mexico in a year or so. Leaving my children was very difficult, even though they were all in their twenties, but the money I'd make in Canada would help me pay off my debt, and then I would go back home. At least that's what I thought.

I met Larry at a Starbucks in West Vancouver in January 2015. I'd seen him walking outside. There was something about him that caused butterflies to flutter in my stomach. He came in, and introduced himself.

His voice was deep and calming. I couldn't stop looking at his eyes: they said everything about him. There was a connection.

I said to myself, "No, Ana. This cannot happen. You are going through too much now! You can't fall in love with him."

It was like we had known each other for a long time. We've been together ever since. He's taught me to stand up for myself and to be me.

I have never considered myself an immigrant in Canada. My learning experience as an immigrant child has helped me understand what others go through when they move to a different country, speak a different language, have a different culture, dress differently than others. I always tell them to embrace where they come from – not to lose their culture but to embrace the country that they're in, that is giving them new opportunities and a better life.

I'm proud to be the daughter of Lidio and Carmen Vargas. Their journey made me the person I am now.

11

Amaluna

Angela Manetti

WHAT BROUGHT YOU to Canada? Why are you here?

These are the questions people generally ask. The answer is pretty romantic. "I moved for love and the desire to raise a family."

People respond, "Must be a great love to move to Abbotsford, Canada, from Florence!"

And as a veracious Italian woman, I always say, "Yes, it is! You should tell my husband! He always seems to need someone to remind him!"

I actually remind him often, especially when I feel lost and everything seems challenging and impossible. Let's start from the very beginning, when this true love started.

I met my husband, Filippo, in Florence some years ago. We were together for a while but had different ideas about the future and our paths diverged. Experiencing a crisis in his professional field, he foresaw a lack of job opportunities and cultural impoverishment in stunning and glorious Florence, Italy.

I couldn't see this because I was so attached to my city and my life there. I was willing to discover another country, have adventures, improve my English, but I wasn't ready to leave everything familiar and move to another country. I couldn't leave my job after years spent building professional skills teaching Italian as a second language, not to mention my position as a dance teacher.

Dancing has been always part of my life. I was always happy seeing my mom and dad dancing in a ballroom. I relished trying to imitate them.

It was like being in my own magic world: free, elegant, beautiful, loved. I promised myself I would become a ballerina.

I didn't become the kind of ballerina I dreamt of, but I had the opportunity to study dance, perform, teach, and pass my passion on to my students. I wasn't ready to give up on my cherished childhood dream, but Filippo was ever so determined to start a new life. He moved to Canada without any fear of the unknown.

I stayed. It was painful, but I knew I could survive in my magic world. The silence between us triggered memories, regrets, questions about how we could have started a new life together in a new country. Several years of separation and silence brought new experiences, new learning, new struggles, and even a new house I had bought for myself.

It was during one of Filippo's trips to Florence, to visit his family and pack some of what he had left behind, that the unbreakable silence between us was defeated. We ended up meeting again. Both of us in our forties but like two teenagers on our first date, we found ourselves walking closely together along the river Arno.

Thousands of unspoken questions floated through our minds, but we were too shy and too afraid to ask them. The moon, the same wonderful moon that lights up the night and my room, now, as I write this, was our steadfast companion. Maybe it was the moon's influence, maybe the growing desire to raise a family – perhaps it was the yearning to become a mother that made me feel like something in our relationship was changing. Step by step we started putting our cards on the table, asking questions, providing answers, sharing experiences. We opened our hearts and expressed our feelings. Then we realized: we were ready for another chapter of our lives.

A New Chapter Begins

I started packing my existence into boxes and trunks, giving away plants, books, dance costumes – it was as if I was gifting friends with fragments of myself.

Soon enough, I found myself on a plane to Canada. I was overwhelmed with mixed emotions: I was sad over leaving my friends and family, excited to reach my love, and hopeful that I would become a mother. I kept repeating to myself that I would be just fine and would overcome any obstacles. After all, I wasn't alone. I was with my loved one, and I was moving because my desire to raise a family was stronger than ever. I quickly realized that even if you are doing it for the right reasons, even if you have carefully weighed the pros and cons of leaving, moving to another country is never easy.

I landed in Vancouver with my heart beating like a drum to the point that I was afraid everyone could hear! I looked frantically for Filippo's eyes in the crowd. I wanted desperately to be in his arms and to go to my new home and rest. Proud, joyful, fearful, and hopeful, I stepped onto foreign soil.

Full Moon

Once again, the Moon is my muse as she urges me to continue my writing. The night is so bright, a magical energy is all around me. I am trying to write, but I can't refrain from staring out the window and thinking of my daughter, my angel, my miracle, my Moon.

Her name, Amaluna, is a fusion of two words: "Ama" refers to mother and love, and "luna" refers to the moon. Her name evokes a mother-daughter relationship and love for this planet.

I became pregnant surprisingly quickly, just two months after starting my new chapter in Canada. I felt like I was floating on air. I felt alive in a way I had never experienced before. We were going to be parents!

After basking in these idyllic moments, a pragmatic matter brought us back down to earth – my status in this new country. I entered Canada as a tourist, and we were about to start the process of applying for Permanent Resident status. In the absence of this and health insurance – no private insurance company would cover a pregnancy – I had no choice but to return to Italy.

Divided Between Two Worlds

I was again divided between two worlds, and once more an ocean separated me and my Filippo. I gathered a few things and flew back to Florence. It was painful to leave my love, but the life inside of me gave me the strength to deal with this separation. I wasn't alone!

Back in Italy, I was soon immersed in my old life and able to resume working with my previous employer, though in another position. Relatives and friends welcomed me, opening their houses and giving me a place to stay. I was so happy and proud of my pregnancy. My heart was bursting with joy and gratitude, and everyone around me shared in those sentiments. I had the opportunity to meet extraordinary people and re-establish old relationships. It was one of the happiest times of my life.

My belief in creating a new and exciting life in Canada was in jeopardy. I was missing my husband dearly. He wasn't with me for doctors' appointments, for the preparation of the delivery, not even when I felt my baby move. I was tormented by thousands of thoughts.

"Do I really want to live in Canada and raise my child there? Should I stay here in Italy where my daughter would enjoy and benefit from the love of an extended family?" I could have my daughter, my love, and keep my work. I could still be a teacher and live in my cherished world of dance. I felt so unsettled.

The time of our child's birth was soon approaching, and instead of wallowing in these feelings, I allowed joy to guide my steps.

I am going to stop writing now. The Moon is shining through the big windows of my bedroom and I don't want to lose this magical moment. I need to pause my thoughts and enjoy the peace this bright night brings.

* * *

My husband joined me in Italy two weeks before the due date. Finally, after a long and troubled labour, my daughter graced us and the world with her beautiful presence. I can still feel the joy and the strong emotions of that moment.

We were living in a magical bubble surrounded by relatives and friends, celebrating the arrival of our angel. And the more time I spent in that bubble, the more my doubts grew about living in Canada.

Even if I were to move for the love of my husband, I didn't want to leave my country anymore. But he was so well adjusted in Canada and proud of what he had accomplished that he didn't want to take into consideration the possibility of returning to live in Italy. I felt like I was trapped. My brain and heart were overwhelmed with tumultuous emotion. I was torn, emotionally distraught, but finally, I chose to live out my motherhood adventure in Canada.

After a big celebration with all our relatives and close friends, among dance and joy and tears, my husband and I flew from Florence to Abbotsford, British Columbia, with our month-old baby daughter. At the Canadian border, my daughter was accepted as a Canadian citizen in process of receiving her passport, but I was still a visitor. This made it more complicated to navigate the health care system and to secure routine follow-up appointments with doctors, all of which became stressful and labour intensive for my husband, who had to fill out the endless documentation necessary to apply for Permanent Residency.

I was a new mom in a new country. Being a mother was and is beautiful and joyful, but it is also challenging. Contending with motherhood in a new country magnified my challenges. I was no longer on vacation, exploring the beauty of Canada, free to go about without worrying about my knowledge of English. I was now responsible for another life, and terrified at the idea of something serious happening and not being able to address it. What would happen to my daughter if my English wasn't good enough and I had to call 911 and explain a problem or relay information and instructions? At the beginning of my stay in Canada, I even avoided answering the phone. I left the answering machine on to perform this task for me, waiting for my husband to come back home from work and deal with any messages.

I felt like I was trapped.

During certain times, I even experienced strong negative feelings about Canada, such as being asked to cover myself while I was breastfeeding my daughter in a mall. I felt so humiliated. I asked myself, "Where was all the open-mindedness of this country?" The urgency to leave Canada rose again. I adamantly stated that I would never cover myself while nursing my baby, and I was reassured that it was my right to breastfeed in public. That was my little conquest in my motherhood journey.

Every day I fell more in love with our angel, and every day she surprised us with something new. I was so happy to be a mother, but I was also incredibly homesick. I wanted to have all my family and friends around to share this extraordinary experience. Social media and electronic devices became my bridge.

Attending programs at Archway Community Services in Abbotsford helped us to connect with other families, and helped me to connect with other moms who were coping with the same difficulties.

When I found an envelope in my mailbox one day with a card inside, I was thrilled to discover it was my Permanent Resident card. I'd waited two years to receive this and was as excited as a child opening gifts on Christmas Day! My heart started beating fast and loud, and warm tears streamed down my cheeks. I hugged my husband and closed my eyes to savour this special moment.

My status in Canada was official. I was finally able to leave the country and visit my family, which I did a few months later. Returning to Canada, I was re-energized after breathing my own country and enjoying the love of people and family I had left behind.

It took me a long time to adjust to my new life. Attending English classes for newcomers at Archway Community Services was a crucial and positive step in adapting to life in Canada. The first day of class I was as excited and nervous as a child coming back to school after a summer vacation. The faces of all the immigrants I had taught back in Italy flooded my mind. In that moment more than ever I understood what they were going through: homesickness, language barriers, and sometimes discrimination. Their resiliency increased my motivation to improve my English, which I did thanks to the help of an amazing teacher. She encouraged and helped me and my classmates to step out of our comfort zones, to learn more about Canada and reflect on our identities and our skills. Not everything was lost. We just needed to reinvent ourselves and count on the experiences we'd accumulated in our own personal journeys.

Regaining a little of my confidence and sense of belonging in this country, I started reflecting on the possibility of returning to the working world. I missed my job but was aware that it would be very challenging to work in the same profession as I had in Italy. Yet, I was determined to find meaningful employment in the field of education.

Working with children in a non-profit organization has always been my passion and my mission. With time, I was fortunate to be able to secure a job as childminding teacher at Archway Community Services. I shifted from being a client to becoming part of a working team.

I imagined myself as one of the trees I used to draw with my children back at school in Italy, when I taught them about seasons and nature: the roots big and solid underground; large branches extending toward the sky, expressing gratitude to the universe; green leaves and flowers showing the power of spring.

I was a mother, a wife, and now, again, a teacher. I was finally able to showcase my educational experiences and skills, all of which I had thought were lost and forgotten. I was excited to meet and learn along with my new little students, confident that this new journey would reinforce my own motherhood journey.

My tree was flourishing and fruitful, but seasons change and soon my tree lost its crown. Winter, with its snow and ice, shook the roots and my tree so hard it felt as if it might have come to the end of its cycle. In April 2018, I was diagnosed with ovarian cancer, a very advanced stage.

"My" beautiful Moon lights the night. Everything looks so enchanted! I wish I could find a safe shelter in this magical land, to be protected from this life. My life. Tonight, as I write this, I feel so unsettled – I've received news from the BC Cancer Agency that I have an additional genetic flaw that could lead to another type of cancer.

I try to live day by day, hour by hour sometimes. I live in the present and try my best, but nothing can change the fact that I am a cancer patient, and the path ahead is uncertain. Every time I go for blood work, every appointment, every piece of mail I receive from the agency evokes conflicting feelings: appreciation that I have good care, but also fear, hope, and dismay toward my upcoming results.

> *I was a mother, a wife, and now, again, a teacher.*

Choosing to Fight for Life

Very often people tell me that I am a strong woman fighter. I don't consider myself that way. I am neither strong nor brave. I am a mother, and despite my mistakes, my yelling, my Italian temper, I love my daughter above everything else. She loves me. She needs me, and I must fight. I have no choice. But sadly, I have learned that there is a limit to what love can overcome.

September 12, 2018

My first day of chemo I was in anguish. I tried to separate my mind from my body, to convince myself that it wasn't me walking into that room. When the nurse called my name and approached me, I shook my head as if a child trying to hide something. I felt like I was in big trouble, and I was about to run away in tears. She immediately understood and hugged me. She helped me sit down on the bed and tried to calm me down. Within seconds another nurse, an oncologist, and a counsellor joined her. They surrounded me to support me, to provide explanations, and to help me make my own decision. I didn't want to start the treatment. I didn't want to start living in the hell I already knew this would be, as cancer had been part of my family history since I was a teenager. I looked at my husband, but he couldn't give me the answer I was looking for.

My assigned nurse, who had been looking after cancer patients for thirty years, sat near me and held my hand. And like a mom, with a calm and reassuring voice, she told me what I needed to hear. "You don't have to do it for anyone – not for your husband, not for your friends, not for your daughter, but only for yourself."

I knew then that I had decided to start the treatment mostly for my daughter, but the nurse's words released me from the pressure of obligation. She was my special angel. I owe a lot to her.

Changing Identity Again

I stepped into chemo hell: five hours for nine cycles. It is impossible to describe to loved ones how chemo treatment affects your brain and body. The physical and emotional fatigue are inexplicable. I can't even explain it to myself.

As the Moon changes, showing us its different phases, I was changing my identity once more. This time I wasn't the author. My illness was. Cancer changed my identity completely – physically, psychologically, and relationally.

I became a fighter, but I was still very vulnerable. I am still raw and vulnerable today. During treatment I was extremely moody, and it was quite hard to control my anger with my daughter and my husband. My brain was often foggy, and sometimes even classical music, which I have loved since childhood, was difficult to handle. Now I am not as volatile, but my balance is so fragile and hiding my emotions is not always an easy task. Cancer stole part of my vitality and energy. I am not the same person I was before, and I don't think it's just a fleeting feeling. It's a reality that I can't put in words. You have to live that experience to understand.

As I changed, so too my relationships changed. I consolidated and reinforced some friendships, and I met new people who became important and supportive friends. I stopped spending my energy and time on relationships that were not deep or those that were unilateral. My relationship with my daughter changed as well. It's for sure more mature now, and not just because she is growing up; because despite being a seven-year-old child, she has had to learn how to deal with potential loss, and with a very sick mother who is changing physically and emotionally, and behaving differently. She still struggles with accepting these changes, and it is heartbreaking to recognize this.

I push my daughter to be independent now more than before. I am encouraging her to be more responsible and focused, which sometimes leads us to arguing. Despite this, our bond has grown stronger daily. I am so proud of her and blessed to be her mom.

It has been very hard for my husband to deal with my illness and my emotions, especially my anger. He hasn't been able to express his feelings, and silence has become his self-protection. His practical ways of supporting me during this time were important, but I desperately needed him to show me unconditional affection and love.

During the days of unbearable physical pain and lack of energy due to the treatments, and when my husband was working out of town, I doubted our love. I wondered, "Was it the same love that brought us together? Do we still love each other, or are we still together because we are trapped in this personal hurricane called Cancer?"

We still love each other, but we are learning to live even without each other, focusing on giving our daughter opportunities and helping her to grow independent and strong. Our love has become more practical than romantic, but often my mind flies to the night we spent walking along the river Arno with the Moon as our companion. I miss that romance tremendously.

My body changed during treatment, and it continues to change now. With no hair, no eyebrows, no eyelashes, I looked like an alien. When I had enough energy, I tried doing makeup, wearing wigs and scarves to feel better, but at the end of the day removing the "props" – as a dancer would after a show. I found the reflection in the mirror to be unbearably awful, nothing even close to that of a ballerina. I often cried alone in disgust and despair.

Whenever I open the beautiful wood coffer that a friend gave me, and look inside at the treasure there – my long, shining hair braided carefully, lying on an old handkerchief I painted for my mother back when I was in elementary school – millions of memories flood my mind. My head spins and I pray to God to wake me up and stop this nightmare.

Bureaucratic Hurdles

At the beginning of my healing process, I felt the Canadian health system had totally failed me. I was completely abandoned. From the time I discovered a lump in my left groin to my first surgery, I waited for an interminably long nine months. Between tests, I waited for two or three months. When I was first diagnosed with cancer, I had to wait for at least a month before even meeting my oncologist!

I had to do a PET (positron emission tomography) scan, which is a very accurate scan that shows even the smallest cancer cells in a patient, but once again the wait list in BC was about three months. I couldn't wait so long anymore. I needed a complete picture of my cancer stage and needed to undergo surgery as soon as possible. The BC Cancer Agency arranged for me to go to a laboratory in Bellingham, in the US, for the PET scan. Thankfully, there is an agreement between BC Ministry of Health and Washington State Department of Health to accommodate cancer patients who need to take such tests as soon as possible.

At the border I was treated in a demeaning way. I gave the customs officer my passport and a detailed letter from the BC Cancer Agency, explaining the reason for my trip to Bellingham, but she didn't even look at it. She started questioning me, and my answers didn't seem to satisfy her. She finally took a look at my letter and verified my statements. She was upset by the fact that I was going there and stealing a medical spot from an American citizen!

I felt intense rage at her and wanted to cry and yell. "I didn't want to be here! It isn't my fault the health systems in these countries are lacking."

I was in utter disbelief, but I kept calm so as to not worsen the situation. Finally I was permitted to leave.

That lack of compassion reminded me of the astonishment and anger I had experienced after my family doctor first told me that I had cancer. My husband, my daughter, and I were sitting in his room. He opened the computer and he gave me the lapidary diagnosis in three words, "You have cancer."

These words were like stones being violently hurled at me. I was frozen and unable to express any reaction at that moment. I couldn't. My daughter was there! My husband tried to ask some questions, but my doctor dismissed him by saying, "I can't give you answers. This isn't my field."

We were out of his room in five minutes, without a word of comfort, without any explanation or guidance on how to proceed. I only knew I was going to see an oncologist as soon as possible.

Why did the doctor dismiss us this way? Why didn't he spend more time with us and offer a few words of reassurance? They couldn't change the results, but at least they would have helped me not to feel completely lost and abandoned. Is this cold and clinical encounter the normal procedure for letting patients know they have cancer?

The family doctor is your starting point in the health care system. He should be able to not only prescribe medicine but also support you with kindness and compassion, and help you navigate the health system. No patient deserves to be rushed or not taken seriously. No patient deserves to wait for weeks before finally seeing a family doctor or having to resort to a walk-in clinic. No patient deserves to wait for months to see a specialist or have urgent tests done.

My family in Italy tried to convince me to return for better care, as well as their love and support. I was like a little boat in the middle of an ocean during a storm. I was angry not only because of the devastating news I'd received but also because I couldn't understand why it was happening in Canada, in such a great country that I'd learned to appreciate over the years.

I was in such despair. I knew that in Italy I could receive all the support and help I needed from my family, but what about my daughter who was about to start kindergarten in Canada? How would my choices impact her? I could not make this heart-wrenching decision with only myself in mind.

I decided to stay despite the fear of not understanding completely what was happening to me, what was going to happen, and my medical terminology. Despite my intense fear of not having help and support, I wanted to give my daughter some stability in the hurricane we were experiencing. I know today that I made the right choice.

During this dreadful time, I faced language obstacles. Every time I went to an appointment with the oncologist, I struggled with understanding the medical terminology and the volumes of information I had to absorb. I had the impression I was receiving new information and a new diagnosis with every single appointment! My anxiety escalated, sometimes to the point that it was difficult to breathe. I had to adopt a denial technique in order to not completely lose control. The doctors tried to explain it in a way I could understand and asked if I needed an interpreter. Though my husband and I were quite confident in our knowledge of English, finally we had to ask a friend to come and help us to better understand.

I have made peace with the Canadian health care system; I waited too long, since my family doctor didn't take the situation seriously, but when I finally was in the process, I received very good care. I have been treated with such professionalism and kindness from doctors, nurses, secretaries, counsellors, and volunteers at the hospital and in the chemo room – more than I ever could have imagined. I was not ever treated as an ID CANCER NUMBER, only as a person, and every act of kindness I have experienced has made a huge difference in the healing process. I have learned that it is not only the clinical medical treatment you receive that helps you in the healing process but also compassion and kindness.

June 24, 2020, 12:00 a.m.

I am writing from the kitchen, staring at a big bowl full of water and filled with flower petals and aromatic herbs. I look at the sky, searching for the Moon, but it's not in its shining phase yet. The sweet aroma brings a lot of memories. My mom, who was stolen from me by cancer when I was still a teenager, used to prepare this same fragrant water on this night. The same night she departed.

In Florence, on June 24, we celebrate St. John the Baptist, the patron of the city. According to tradition, the soul of St. John comes to bless the aromatic water. People prepare for this by putting water outside to be blessed. What a magical moment it was for me as a child to follow that tradition with my mom! I see many faces in those petals – faces of relatives and friends taken by cancer. I also saw my face as I won a crucial battle with the illness, but the war is not over.

I also see the face of my precious angel. It is my daughter, Amaluna, who gives me the strength to fight. I pray to the universe that I didn't pass on my genetic predisposition for cancer to my daughter. This is something a mother couldn't live with.

On this special night, I need to try to let the pain and the sadness go and just live the magic.

Reflections on a Full Moon: July 4, 2020 Sorrento Full Moon

Living with cancer and the COVID-19 pandemic, I know now that uncertainty is my new normal. More than ever, I have to live day by day and set very short-term goals. We should all live following this philosophy. Unfortunately, we often only learn through adversity.

As an immigrant, it doesn't matter why at a certain point in life you choose to move to another country. Regardless, the immigrant journey is always a hard step to take. There are always sacrifices to make, challenges to encounter, and something and someone you will miss. You will always be divided between two worlds, recalling old memories and reproducing and maintaining scents, tastes, and traditions in the new country.

I greatly miss my extended family, my ballet teaching, dance, and performance in Italy, but I have learned to love Canada for so many reasons. I learned the importance of reaching out to my community and asking for help, and creating new connections with people beyond one's nationality. This was the key for me to get me to come out of my shell and start rebuilding myself. It takes time and a lot of work, energy, and courage. There are no short cuts to any place worth going. Diversity and multiculturalism are the beauty and the power of Canada.

I like to think about Canada as a giant pomegranate, which shows its pointy crown with diversity and multiculturalism as invaluable gems. A thick leathery skin encloses and protects countless shining seeds as rubies with different shades. All unique, with sweet and tart flavours, separate, with a hard core, but all part of the same fruit. I am glad to be one of those seeds that thrives with others, that maintains uniqueness but shares a common place.

12

Canada Reimagined

Camille McMillan Rambharat

I WAS SIXTEEN WHEN I first visited Canada. Years later I landed here as a
newcomer and am now married, a mother of three, and still in love with
the country. But maturity and decades of experience have made me
observant. As a human rights activist defending against social injustice,
I never realized that a day would come when I would have to fight for my
own human rights and dignity.

You see, I often wondered how President Barack Obama led the United
States for eight years – unprecedented and unlikely in so many ways – and
how Michaëlle Jean was Canada's Governor General for five years, and
still both countries exhibit many facets of prejudice, discrimination, and
unfairness.

I ask this not for myself but for my family, and for BIPOC who call
Canada home.

My ancestry is African. My husband and I are Caribbean-born and
Canada is our home. Unlike me, my husband can trace his roots – he
knows the meaning of his surname and the village and time period during
which his great-grand-parents arrived in Trinidad and Tobago, from India,
175 years ago. In contrast, I inherited the slave name of the family that
owned my ancestors, who were shipped off to the Caribbean, making
different stops along the way; Tobago was where they were dropped off
to slave on plantations.

Along with my family, we moved to Canada, not the US, because I
felt Canada would be non-discriminating for our three Black children,
especially our sons.

Before we moved here, my grandmother lived in Canada for over forty years until her death. Three of her grown children lived here also, and in her travels back and forth, her son, my uncle Clyde, accompanied her. I always looked forward to their visits. For that reason, growing up, I was always connected to Canada, mainly Toronto. Canada itself has had a permanent presence in Trinidad and Tobago since 1910, sharing in the country's oil, natural gas, asphalt, cocoa, and sugar fortunes.

As the years passed, I became more and more intrigued by this picture-perfect country that gave family members and friends a different kind of glow. Canadians showed a different happiness and calm compared to relatives from the US who always seemed to be on the hustle and exhausted during their visits. The Canadian work-life balance I'd heard people speak about was what I wanted to be a part of.

When I was sixteen, my aunt Joan gifted me a ticket to fly to Toronto with my cousin Denise, known as Den-Den, to spend a summer with Grandma. This was my first visit to Canada, and it was a summer to remember – it was a love at first sight. I was home! The wide clean streets. Smiling faces that greeted us as we walked downtown, where uncle Clyde took us before we went to stay with our grandmother at her one-bedroom apartment. On the way, he took us into a brightly lit shoe store with shining mirrors, which I can only describe as like being in that scene in *Pretty Woman*. Do you remember when Julia Roberts goes back to that very expensive store from where she was rejected earlier? That was me! Except I was there with my very tall and handsome uncle Clyde who only knew the finest in life and wanted us to experience that during our trip.

Denise and I were giddy without our parents. Uncle Clyde told us to choose whichever pair of shoes we liked. I found the most beautiful candy pink semi-high heel pair. I remember him asking if I was sure I wanted them, and grinning from ear to ear, I said, "Yes!"

We approached the cashier, and as my uncle Clyde was pulling his wallet from his back pocket, he said, "Miss Camille, I'll drop you off at Yonge Street so you can make back this money, eh?"

Of course, we had no idea what he meant. Want to guess what unplanned stop we made after leaving the store, on our way to grandma's apartment? Yep, Yonge Street, with all those beautiful working ladies. That's the closest I've come to my *Pretty Woman* scene. To this day, Uncle Clyde reminds me that he's still paying off his credit card from that purchase.

Uncle Clyde never once spoke poorly of those working ladies. I loved that Canadians were open-minded and non-judgemental. This meant a lot to me as I had always been judged just for the colour of my skin. I felt safe here.

It would be years before I would have to confront certain realities of Canada, which would distress me and awaken in me my instinct for justice, fairness, and dignity.

If there's a perfect picture of what "home away from home" looks like, it would be of the beautiful city of Toronto. Being in Canada made this tourist, and future citizen, forget about the blazing heat. By the second week of our stay, I called Mac – what we called my dad – and pleaded with him to allow me to stay.

Giggling nervously, I said, "Mac, I want to stay with grandma, please, please?"

Without missing a beat, he said, "Listen, listen girl. Bring yah little black tail home, eh."

His voice was stern but I heard a slight chuckle somewhere within. I laughed at his non-threatening command.

"Come nah? PLEASE?" Which was met with a swift stupes, a sucking of the teeth. Two weeks later I returned to Trinidad and Tobago, but Canada never left me.

Dad was my strength through womanhood, marriage, pregnancy, miscarriages, childbirth, life's ups and downs. He scolded as required, even when I used his teachings for raising my own children, his grandchildren.

He would chuckle and say, "You're too old school, so leave my grandchildren."

That's how grandparents get back at their children. Ironically, it was my dad's death in Trinidad and Tobago and events which followed that brought me face to face with a different Canada.

Canada saw me again, vacationing with my children, in the summer of 2008. One morning I received an email from our host notifying me that we could not stay at her home. I was floored and turned to Uncle Clyde, letting him know what had happened.

Without missing a beat, he said, "Well, stay at my place."

Later, I reached out to my childhood friend, Natasha, and she invited us over to spend time with her and her boys. As our children played video games in the basement, Natasha and I sat on her back deck and chatted about everything under the sun. I was telling her about our landing documents and my husband's dislike of Toronto winters. She had an intense look on her face. She dragged on her cigarette and nodded.

She blew the cigarette smoke into the air and finally said, "Why don't you guys move to Vancouver? Their winters are really mild."

Clarence, my husband, called me the next day from Trinidad. I said, "Guess what? Natasha said we should move to Vancouver!"

"What are you talking about? I thought we were just vacationing?" he said in a flat tone.

Back home in Trinidad, Clarence went online and researched Vancouver. When he joined us for vacation a week later, he was already convinced that we should move there.

The Summer Olympics were happening and Canada was doing well. It was a good time to be in the country. With the five of us together, one still requiring a car seat, we went sightseeing through Toronto. We'd packed knapsacks with frozen bottles, hot dogs, napkins, bus passes, lost toys, and a pink polka-dot baby stroller for our two-year-old. It was adventurous!

I still remember the looks on our children's faces – they beamed with excitement, giddiness, as they, too, fell in love with Canada. The warm sunshine on our faces mixed with the occasional comforting, reassuring breeze from Lake Ontario. Our amazing week-long stay at a beautiful two-bedroom lodge in Niagara Falls removed any doubt – we would one day call Canada home.

We returned to Trinidad at the beginning of September and the boys went back to school. But we had returned with Canadian eyes. Nothing felt the same. Even the kids felt it.

We made a decision. Three months later, we had sold everything we owned in Trinidad, made some arrangements in Canada, and packed up to move to Canada.

Soon we were on our way. We landed in Vancouver just days before Christmas. As the aircraft taxied to the gate, the captain reported that there was a little snow, but that it would be gone by tomorrow as it hardly snows in Vancouver, and when it does, it melts quickly.

Natasha's brother, Leon, and his family collected us at the airport. As introductions and hugs were taking place, Leon said jokingly, "You guys brought the snow with you? But don't worry, it will be gone tomorrow when the rain washes it away. It rarely snows in BC."

That was about to change.

Within a couple of days, we went to look at our rental, and we purchased a car and some furniture. It continued to snow until February 2009. It took forever for the chunks of ice to finally melt.

Moving to Canada in December was intentional, as we figured the cold introduction would be perfect for our children and ourselves, to get us used to the "mild" winter we were told to expect. Nothing prepared us for sidewalks we would not see for weeks, and vehicles spinning as their tires locked. Our layered clothing, toques, and tall cups of hot chocolate warmed us. Welcome to Canada!

The forecast was for an unprecedented snowfall. Everywhere we went, friendly Canadians spoke about the weather, asking where we were from and insisting, "It never snows like this in BC."

My response became, "Are you guys paid to say this to newcomers?"

We would all chuckle, and then they'd say, "You guys did this to us."

We moved into our rented home in December 2008 and immediately started meeting with the banks to sign up for a credit card with a two thousand-dollar limit, as every purchase we needed required it. This was denied because we didn't have a credit history in Canada and we were unemployed. Even though the bank we went to was the same bank I had done business with back home, we did not have a credit history in Canada – which made no sense because my deposit was much more than the minimum I was asking for. Unfortunately, this delayed our purchasing a much-needed cellphone, to reach our families back home and to have a number to put on our résumés.

We were desperate and needed to keep in touch with Leon and his wife. With our newly purchased desktop computer, my husband turned to Craigslist, as we often did for the next year. My husband tracked down a used SIM card on Craigslist. We needed to meet the seller close to the Surrey Central SkyTrain Station. When we got there, it turned out to be a store in a strip mall just opposite the Station, one that seemed to carry lots of used electronic stuff. Maybe I've watched way too many *Law & Order* shows, but I was so scared to go in and felt that this would not end well. I started to wonder who would be my one phone call. I always joke with my husband about what seems to be a custom in his culture, for wives to walk a few steps behind their husband, but this time I was quite happy to stay behind him as I figured "last man in, first man out." After identifying himself to my husband, a fellow led us to a dark room at the rear of the store. If fear and anxiety didn't kill me, it would be the cops that I imagined raiding the building at any moment. What an adventure it would be, but really there was nothing shady about the purchase.

We were excited to have a card to call home, and to make enquires about info sessions, child subsidies, schools, etc. We put money on the phone right away and found out the hard way that money on a phone expires after a certain time.

The snow continued its "out of timing" display. With no vehicle and the need to walk or use transit, we felt like penguins in the Arctic, a scene most glaring when it was all five of us slipping and sliding with inappropriate shoes and gear. The sidewalks were impassable, the snow almost knee-high at times.

The internet and our faith became our tools for exploring BC: banking, children's schools, and newcomer support. Our job search had begun in Trinidad before even purchasing our tickets. My husband and I took turns looking at job opportunities. He felt it would be much easier for me to get a job as there were hundreds of openings for clerks, administrative positions, receptionists, and greeters, and we were fine doing whatever we needed to, to provide for our family. Unknown to us, it was not a question of how educated or uneducated we were or pretended to be. It was about Canadian certification and Canadian experience, two expressions we would hear for many months to come.

My first job interview followed a call from a hiring agency for a receptionist position. I was excited and we were hopeful.

"You got this honey," my husband said. He kissed me and watched as I headed out with my certificates and Google map in hand.

I waddled through the snow, one minute on the sidewalk and then in the middle of the road the next, using the path vehicles left behind as they too struggled to get through. When I got on the bus, I told the friendly looking white-haired driver my destination and asked, "Am I on the right bus?"

In a kind voice he said, "Don't worry. I'll let you know when it's your stop."

And sure enough, he remembered me and my stop by looking up at me as we approached. I stepped carefully off the bus, checking my coat pocket for the Google map I'd printed, and it was not there. I checked the other pocket and still no luck. As I waited for the lights to allow me to cross, I found it in my bag. I began walking, which took forever. Again, walking and slipping in and out of the mountain of snow, literally following in the footsteps of others.

I did not get the receptionist job.

I have heard and read many newcomers express frustrations about the "lack of Canadian experience." Soon enough I understood that it is not really about work experience but Canadian culture: way of life, values and principles, laws and regulations, workplace culture, dos and don'ts. I also understood soon enough the need to experience Canadian culture first-hand as much as possible – in malls, stores, churches, and on buses and trains. I started to pick up free newspapers, especially those in my community, to follow national news as well as provincial and city news. I knew this was about knowing that the Canucks were playing and maybe not doing too well; that the BC Lions had a new player; that the SkyTrain extension was being discussed again; or that something new was coming to the Bell Centre.

It struck me that there was a form of certification for every imaginable thing in this country. This is what drew us to our city's website, Parks and Recreation, and our world of volunteering. Job searching was a learning curve. We had over forty-five years of work experience, both in the Caribbean and in other countries. None of that mattered. We faced rejection.

"We would have hired you, but you don't have the Canadian experience." Or my favourite, "We're so sorry, but you're not the fit."

Why would companies put newcomers through two or three interviews to tell us we lack Canadian experience? Surely, my resume would have clearly shown this.

I attended numerous immigrant services, to be cloned into "the fit." From resume writing, to networking (my favourite), mock interviews, even how to dress for success.

One afternoon, as Clarence and I watched our little girl play, I turned to him and said, "This makes no sense." We were juggling to get our two boys into elementary and high school, job searching, rewriting resumes.

Then came further barriers. My first experience of biased or un-biased racism came relatively early on, when we made signing the children up for school our priority. In fact, we came to Canada to ensure that registration took place before the new calendar year. An ill-advised and ill-informed administrator had other ideas. A school administrator noted that I checked English as our primary language. Her facial expression changed as though she'd caught me lying.

She asked, "What other language do you speak?"

Without missing a beat, I responded, "English."

She questioned me again, "So you speak no other language than English?"

"Only English," I responded. Our eyes met like a matador and a bull, checking to see who would look away first.

As she walked away, I felt I had won. I looked at my family seated behind me and shrugged my shoulders in disbelief. It was cold and I was exhausted as we had gotten very little rest since landing in Canada. Christmas was approaching, which meant we still had to shop for a tree and gifts for our children.

When the administrator returned, she handed me a document for our son to attend an ESL class.

I reminded her, "We only speak English."

"I am just following the rules," she said.

Perplexed, we gathered our children and waddled home through the non-stop snowfall. We felt belittled and embarrassed as our children looked on.

We were all exhausted. We arrived home and took hot showers and had an early dinner next to the fireplace. I was furious about being judged and treated like we were not being truthful about only speaking English. I had to not allow myself to feel upset by her ignorance and enjoy the time and our new home with my family instead. I didn't like the administrator's unwelcoming and dismissive attitude, or her unwillingness to do a quick Google search about languages spoken in Trinidad and Tobago.

The next day, Clarence decided that he would take our son for his English assessment appointment. He wanted me to take a day off. As a Canadian citizen, I have had to comfort our children, themselves Canadians, because they sometimes experience racism and discrimination. Our daughter has faced it in school, from teachers unsettled by her brilliance and unwilling to concede to anyone relying on anything but merit.

Her elderly white male teacher told her, "You're not as smart as you think you are."

A male classmate constantly teased her about her mother being an N-word. Later, he took his sharpened pencil and stabbed it into her palm. This was in third grade. Her teacher rationalized the classmate's behaviour away; however, I made a report to the RCMP in case it continued or got worse.

Our sons have been followed around in stores by security. On one occasion, as I walked through Shoppers with our second-born, the security guard looked at us and began walking in our direction as we made our way to one of the aisles. He followed us down every aisle. I looked at him at one point and asked if he was following us, and I guess "the angry Black woman" made him uncomfortable and he left us alone.

When my second-born son started work, he was also called the N-word and was told that he had monkey feet. I've asked our children to tell their friends that regardless of their ethnicity, the N-word is unacceptable. Our children had to educate some of their friends because the school and parents have failed to do that.

> *Our sons have been followed around in stores by security.*

When we were looking to purchase a townhouse, the white female realtor told me I couldn't view a particular unit, which was on the higher end.

She said, "You can't afford it."

She seemed offended at my insistence to see the place. At this point my daughter-in-law, who is Canadian born, white, and of Dutch and German heritage, walked in and was taken aback when she heard the comment. That's when the realtor allowed me to view the unit. I refused to purchase the unit and bought our current home, which cost way more.

My son's ESL class never happened. An agency employee dismissed the English question, saying she'd faced the same profiling as an immigrant from Fiji. She pronounced our son and our family as proficient in English to an expert level.

Our son got into the school. As our children entered new schools, from daycare to Grade 9, we got busy attending informational sessions, secretly praying that we would be accepted into a suitable program. Being assigned to Pat, my case manager, was such a blessing. Pat went above and beyond to get me into the right program, the amazing World of Work program at Douglas College. This provided me with the Canadian work experience employers were asking about. It gave me a sense of belonging and purpose, which I felt every morning when I headed to work after dropping our youngest off at daycare and before seeing the boys head out to school. Into the New Year, people were so warm and welcoming as we started moving around in our first vehicle. It was a joy to meet colleagues from around the world, to share our stories, customs, food, and loads of laughter. The World of Work program also provided us with Canadian references, which were essential as references from our home country weren't accepted.

Parallel to attending this program, our family joined YMCA Vancouver's Newcomers program. As part of this program, I volunteered my time as an event planner and photographer, which provided references, great support, and the forever golden ticket of Canadian experience. Attending YMCA events – a trip to Capilano Suspension Bridge, Thanksgiving, a weekend at Camp Elphinstone to meet other families – was great.

A day or two before we left Camp Elphinstone, some of the adults and their children were hanging out. I was asked if I used sunblock as my skin was so dark – and as I was processing that remark, a youthful white lady asked if she could touch my skin as if I was a pet. As though she was at the petting zoo and I was some exotic animal. Who does that REALLY? Did she know how insulting and dehumanizing that was? To think she was doing the exact thing her ancestors did to mine, only this time this pet was unchained and uncaged. Appearing shocked, this explorer complimented me on how soft my skin was. I thought of educating her about why her lack of respect and boundaries were offensive, but again, with me being the "minority" in the group, I did not want to be the angry Black woman.

The flow of generational trauma from the capture and slavery of my ancestors was triggered by her unwelcomed discovery of my Black body. My ancestors were thought of and treated as less than human by their oppressors. Denying my dignity, I smiled to ensure her and others that I did not feel uncomfortable. The memory remains with me.

On the Obama and Jean question I asked at the beginning, I believe that racism, discrimination, and unfairness take many forms. Our oppressors and bullies hide behind another word that gives them some sort of comfort: systemic.

I did not want to be the angry Black woman.

After 107 job applications, four interviews, and one informational interview, the World of Work program coordinator sent me a posting for a job developer, and I knew right away I had to land this job.

Spending over ten hours on my resume and cover letter was overkill and at times frustrating. On mornings, after I watched our boys and my husband leave, I dropped our daughter off at daycare then returned home and sat next to the telephone practicing my "Tell me about yourself" script, which I said about a million times, keeping in mind to speak slowly.

Speaking slowly was golden advice. My husband's case manager suggested watching *The National* with Peter Mansbridge, to learn to speak at Peter's speed. Do not be rushed, speak clearly, and keep focused on the listener. We never missed *The National*.

With the lead on the job developer position, I picked up the cordless phone, inhaled, and dialled the number from the posting. I silently prayed that no one would answer

I heard a quick, "Hello"—a female voice who then said, "Good morning. How can I help you?"

With my best Canadian training, I said, "Hi, how are you today? I saw your job posting and would like to get the manager's name and email address please."

"Her name is Darlene. Let me put you through."

"Oh. Okay. Thank you," I said, thinking to myself, really? I get to speak to a manager over the phone about a job posting I need to email to her?

"Hello! This is Darlene, how can I help you?"

"Hello, Darlene. I am calling about the job posting I saw, and I wanted you to know I am the perfect person for the position."

And with a friendly chuckle she said, "Oh really. Tell me why you'd be the perfect person for the job."

And so, I marketed my brand (me) to Darlene. She seemed impressed and provided me with her full name and direct email address. I had woken up that morning feeling lucky. I calmly released only positive thoughts and energy into the universe as I typed in my password, held my breath, and sent Darlene my cover letter and resume. I needed this job as our projected six months of budget was approaching its end and I had to help my husband with our bills. The phone rang within five minutes.

It was Darlene. "Thank you for your email, but there were no attachments."

"Oh, sorry!"

"Don't worry about it. These things happen."

Sigh! "Focus, Camille," I said to myself.

And with complete focus and precision, I tapped on the "Attach" and "Send" icons, and then smiled because I somehow knew I would be hired.

I did indeed get the job. I got to work with amazing at-risk youth, helping them with life skills, job searching, and connecting them to employers.

Finally, being the right fit for something signalled I had been accepted. Accepted. A Black immigrant female finally felt accepted. Growing up in the Caribbean, the darker your skin colour, the more one has to "fit in," even among people of my own race. I was even teased by my own brothers about being too Black as they laughed and mocked my melanin-pigmented skin. This teasing was not my brothers' fault but the effects of colonization, which teaches people to hate themselves and others. As I grew older, not being the fit became part of life and I, too, no longer saw my Blackness. How could I? How could I pay attention to the thing that people noticed first and judged?

With the values and morals of my upbringing, I focused on working harder, always proving myself by how I dressed, how I kept my hair, how I spoke and walked. I worked with amazing coworkers – it was the greatest first job I could have hoped for. As time passed, I got other offers and was being hired elsewhere. Then came my dream job with one of Canada's top employers working with newcomers to the country. There I worked as a career coach and mentorship specialist. As always, friendships were developed within and outside the office.

As a member of the newly created Diversity and Inclusion Committee, my excitement to join was short lived as it became clear my inclusion was just a box being checked. This was confirmed when someone on the committee announced she didn't know it was me someone was speaking about after our staff Christmas party, even though at the time I was the only Black person working for the company. I later resigned and returned to Trinidad and Tobago to support Clarence in his 2015 campaign for Parliament. He got in as a senator and is now Minister of Agriculture, Lands and Fisheries.

Three years later I returned to British Columbia and found work quickly. I was rehired by an employer, and just as in Jordan Peele's *Get Out*, I would soon find out the "sunken place" existed. In the sunken place, I was left alone to deal with the effects of an abusive manager on my mental health, my career, and my family life. If the roles were reversed, if I was the abuser and my white manager the victim, I would have been fired immediately.

The manager questioned my doctor's medical note about my need to recover from a concussion and lower back injury, which I suffered while in Trinidad for my father's final farewell. I suffered micro-aggressions, unethical requests, and gaslighting, but I brushed them off. I did not want this abusive white woman to feel uncomfortable. Yet she used her supposed discomfort and tears to change the script and hide the truth just as colonizers have done throughout history.

On my first day of medical leave, while driving, I accepted a call from this person. Her call quickly turned abusive, which traumatized both me and my daughter who was with me.

"When are you returning to work?" she demanded. "I need to know NOW!"

I responded, "I cannot tell you now, but my doctor's note says I'm off for one month."

Accusingly, she yelled, "You are holding the company at ransom!"

My daughter held her hand over her mouth as if she wanted to scream. She grabbed my hand as we tried to make our way home. Wanting to get off the phone, I said, "I promise to call and let you know Monday morning."

Her numerous messages to both my personal and company phone followed non-stop. I refused to respond to her as she had already crossed the line.

On Sunday evening, in one of her messages, she said, "I am coming to your home to collect the office laptop and phone on Thursday."

I didn't want that woman at my home, so I delivered the items to the receptionist on Monday morning. As I left the office and was heading down the two flights of stairs to my car, something caught my eye. I turned my head. My abuser, drunk with white privilege, was running toward me.

I hurried to drive away, but she jumped in front of my vehicle, causing me to slam on the brakes. She was screaming, hands flailing like an inflatable sky-dancing tube man.

She slammed her fist onto the hood of my vehicle and demanded, "Get out of that car now!"

She shadowed my every move as I tried to reverse and go around her. She ran alongside my car and jumped in front of it several times.

Shocked, I signalled through the windshield, "Please move."

I parked and activated the handbrake, and she started banging on my window. This felt like a public lynching, a white woman yet again putting an N-word in her place. Not wanting to get into trouble, I felt the presence of my ancestors keeping me safe and calm.

Onlookers went by. People from nearby offices must have seen what was happening. No one came to my rescue, though. Had it been the other way around, everyone would have come to *her* rescue and the RCMP would have arrived in a second. That's my reality.

Feeling like a runaway slave who was being hunted down, I fled the scene, almost crashing into an oncoming vehicle. I called HR, told them what happened, and said, "I am coming to the office."

Management began by asking, "What did you do?"

I felt dehumanized by their immediate protection of her and blaming of me, the victim.

I was traumatized. Tears flowed. Then a text came from my predator, while I was talking to HR: "Shame on you!"

I cried louder. My knees buckled as I showed this message to those in the room.

There was no empathy. I still refused to become the angry Black woman.

I spiralled into depression. Anxiety, isolation, and suicidal thoughts consumed me. After months of struggling to find my way out of this sunken place, I realized I *had* to become the angry Black woman to regain my humanity. I had to remove the shame the predator had placed on me like a bounty placed on a runaway slave.

The workplace bully never apologized, and neither did the organization. In fact, threats to silence me, as well as intimidation, accusations, victim blaming, and monitoring me instead of the perpetrator, continued. She stalks me online; I have screenshots of her viewing my LinkedIn page. This angry Black woman refused to be dehumanized and left for dead. The unprovoked workplace violence inflicted upon me and my family has been traumatic

I've asked myself, "What was I to be 'shamed' about?" Did my abuser want to shame me for escaping her public lynching? Did the Minnesota police officers send George Floyd a text saying "shame on you" after they murdered him?"

I'm beyond exhausted by the code-switch and seeing, daily, the public lynching of my Black brothers and sisters along with the generational trauma we carry in our DNA. My ancestors ran away risking death so I could be free. I honour generations of them by demanding respect and dignity even when I'm called an angry Black woman. I will continue to honour them until we are accepted and treated equally.

I am a very proud Canadian of African descent, an immigrant from the Caribbean and a female who won't fit in; my children won't fit in; my husband won't fit in – all because that's not what being Canadian is about. If your idea of us being "the fit" means we have to dumb down our education, work history, culture, and most importantly the history of our ancestors to make you comfortable, then that's more of a *you* problem than a *me* problem.

Across Canada, in workplaces particularly, BIPOC should be given what we give so generously: dignity and respect. We want to lean into those spaces and behind titles where our abusers hide. I want the world to take its knee off our necks so we can breathe. This isn't a request but a demand!

O Canada! I stand on guard for thee.

13

Travels to My Here and Now

Taslim Damji

THAT I AM SITTING DOWN to share a little of my story as an immigrant feels, somehow, painful, telling, and correct. Painful because it underscores my identity as "other" to many white settlers and immigrants in Canada as well as to those in other nations who, in my experience, often essentialize the characteristics of a "Canadian." It is painful because it speaks to the fact that my identity continues to be placed on me like a suffocating blanket by others. It is telling, because it reveals an attitude: that despite my almost lifelong relationship with Turtle Island – this land that we call Canada – I am still not considered, by many, as belonging to or being of this place. It reminds me that the relationship between the immigrant identity and belonging, however long mine has been, remains unresolved. It is correct, because I am an immigrant, and I am grateful for the quality of my life here, and simultaneously I am conflicted about my presence on these lands – unless your ancestors are indigenous to this land, you too are descended from immigrants to these dishonestly and violently procured spaces.

My name is Taslim Damji. Taslim is a Muslim name that means peace and submission to the will of God. It is also a greeting. Damji is a Hindu name meaning lucky; and unless your name comes from the Indigenous cultures of this land, your name is foreign, too. I didn't always love my name, but I do now. Without me knowing, it feels like it has somehow shaped me.

It is not lost on me that as I begin this journey, recanting vignettes from my past, I am in the air, over the ocean, between lands – both for which I carry citizenship but neither to which I belong, and neither of which claims me fully as their own. I am far away from the lands of my ancestors ... to whom I would likely present as a curiosity. I am traversing that space that feels best to me, a sort of interspace where my identity is anonymous, unquestioned, and free ... away from the geographical land masses that for so long represented an absence of belonging.

My story, like all our stories, began centuries before I was born. It is intertwined with conquest, imperialism, and subjugation; the proselytizing nature of religion and its own strain of imperialism; colonialism and oppression; political alliances; and attempts at assimilation. It represents an endless intergenerational quest for freedom, safety, acceptance, economic prosperity, and social mobility – an unspoken obligation to both our ancestors and also our descendants to survive, thrive, and actualize. And as I write, it occurs to me that these motivations may represent some of the defining features of human migration through the centuries – and that my experience is shared. Through central and south Asia, east Africa, England, Central Europe, and Canada – or rather, Turtle Island – my family seems only ever to have journeyed. I am from a long line of migrants, and in some ways, I am lost in translation, while in others I am defined by it. I don't have a single identity. I have layers and pasts that intersect – aspects of which reveal themselves, or recede, depending on where I am or who I am with, a sort of perpetual, instinctual, survival-driven switching of codes.

My identity continues to be placed on me like a suffocating blanket.

Last year, I turned half a century; it was as if a great weight had lifted. Why, I am not sure, but it felt as if the preoccupations of a lifetime had left me. As I reflect, I notice how these existential pre-occupations – isolation, rejection, self-consciousness, fear, a sense of being lost, having a seat at a mythical table of belongingness, doubting my own human value – which have framed my being across contexts, have moved away like clouds. Recognition landed: of the impossibility of belonging to a single place, to a single tribe, or a single history. That the tired and narrow parameters of identification, given the complexities of human histories, were neither relevant nor useful to me – nor, perhaps, to others like me. My family has been in Canada for over fifty years. We were educated *here*, worked *here*, loved *here*, laughed *here*, grieved *here*, have friends and family *here*, moved through the rituals of life *here,* and paid our taxes *here.* But because none of us were born in Canada, we all remain first-generation Canadians – immigrants.

I am curious about this. For how long will I be branded in this way, as an "immigrant" – a mark of otherness? Is there any point at which I will no longer be seen as a newcomer or an immigrant, with all that implies about my legitimacy and belonging? My own children are technically first generation, but the Canadian-ness of my children is generally not questioned. They present as white, and their accent is Canadian. At fifty, I recognized that I could never belong to the groups of "Canadians" around me, but I do not crave that anymore. I have questioned: If I am of different places, would it be possible, or even desirable, to belong to just one? I think the meaning of belonging has shifted for me. My understanding of my relationship to the land I live on extends to all the places I am connected to. I feel a sense of belonging to myself, to my family, friends, and colleagues, to whomever I happen to be with or pass in the street. Even those I have never met feel, in some small yet significant way, connected to me. Belonging now feels like part of this relationship. I feel now that "relationship" determines the quality and nature of my belonging. Relationship feels credible, tangible, cultivatable, measurable. Who do I call? When do I call them? Where are they? Who do I trust? Who will I turn to when I am in need? What would I be willing to ask for? How present am I for them? What do we bring to each other?

I am glad of this shift, which took a long time in coming.

Go West

> *My story, like all our stories, began centuries before I was born.*

Canada was never implicated or complicit in my "displacement." Unlike migration that happens due to war, religion, famine, unstable politics, or soft currencies, my family's move to Canada was guided by the advice of the present-day Aga Khan. Our migration to Canada in the early 1970s coincided with the purging of Indians from Uganda, during the time of Idi Amin. Indians, among them Ismailis who had made their homes in the nations of East Africa since the late 1800s, were forced to leave. When I listen to the oral histories of family and those in my community, I understand how anger, resentment, hate, and the desire for autonomy seemed to propel their expulsion from Uganda – a reaction to a history of colonial injustice and abuse in which Indians also had their unwitting part to play. Fuelled by a desire to be like their white colonizers – actualized, respected, and caught in the learned behaviours of colonialism – many of my people treated the people indigenous to those lands without feeling and respect. My oppressed ancestors participated in the oppression of others with little understanding or recognition of the impacts of their attitudes and actions, or that the oppressed in those lands might someday rally to emancipate themselves.

My knowledge of my community's history and practices is limited, and I share the narrative passed down through the generations of my own family and Vancouver's Ismaili community – an interpretation of our diasporic history. At this time, Canada's prime minister, Pierre Trudeau, approached by the Aga Khan, offered Ismailis from Uganda refuge in Canada. For this, the Liberal Party of Canada seems, from what I have observed, to have earned an almost unshakeable allegiance from that community. This allegiance might seem to represent a demonstration of loyalty to perceived friends, a recognition that in some way our people were worthy of saving, worthy of being brought into the fold. I feel that we did not disappoint. The focus on community service – first within the community, and then, with a nudge from the Aga Khan, within the broader community – seems to have aligned well with Canadian values around volunteerism and community service. There was an active investment in education, belonging, and community actualization. Many years on, I am able to see how these commitments and values reflect some of the Indigenous teachings around self-actualization and building sustainable community.

At this time, my own family started their very different journey to Canada – from London, UK, the seat of the Empire. Canada was regarded as a multicultural, safe, progressive space, evolving in the direction of a pluralistic society. Its doors were open to the subjects of the former colonies of a collapsing empire. These countries were now part of the Commonwealth of Nations, and their people, as British subjects, could move with relative freedom among other member nations.

But before we continue, I'd like to share how my family arrived at this point in our migration story.

My mum's family can accurately trace itself back to Gujarat, in western India. The *sub*-continent. They were farmers and had suffered through crop failures from several years of drought. They travelled to Africa in the late 1800s. They had no schooling. Their knowledge had been passed down through the generations: working the land, building homes, cooking, raising children, healing, religion, traditions, and community. Because the crops had failed, my family couldn't afford the taxes they were required to pay by the British Empire, so they left their villages, first making their way to the coast on wagons, and then travelling from there on dhows from colonized India to the eastern shores of colonized Africa. My dad's family's migration to Mombasa started with my young orphaned great-great-great-grandfather who had convinced an uncle to take him aboard a boat to Africa, where he'd heard there was good money to be made. Four generations of my family were born in Tanzania, Zanzibar, and Kenya. Although my grandmothers were born in the Omani territory of Zanzibar and the German territory of Tanganyika, after the war these territories were ceded to Britain. My maternal grandmother would have lived under three different empires without ever having moved.

My mum, Khatun, and dad, Bashir, were both born in Mombasa in 1936 and 1942 respectively, which at that time was a British Protectorate with different rights and "privileges." Mombasa had been carved out as a separate piece of Kenya, so in some strange, fortuitous way, they were born as British subjects. In 1954, my mum, aged eighteen, left for the University of Glasgow. In 1953, my dad, age eleven, flew to London with his father Badrudin, who had planned to supply British sports equipment to businesses in East Africa. They travelled on small twin-engine, two-propeller planes that carried twenty-seven passengers. It was a three-day journey. My dad recalls the four stops needed to refuel on the Nairobi to London route: Juba, Wadi Halfa – where they stayed on the Nile – Malta, and Nice. My mum remembers other routes from East Africa to the UK – Addis Ababa, Entebbe, Casablanca ... names of places I have never been, flights toward a welcoming, post-war, socially oriented "first world" future into which I would be born.

In 1968, UK laws changed to stem the flow of migration, and being a British subject was no longer sufficient to guarantee inclusion. Identities shifted and my parents were required to register themselves as citizens of the United Kingdom.

Because of the unstable nature of my parents' relationship, mum went back to Africa to be with her mum. I was born in Dar es Salaam, the city of peace, in Tanzania, the home of my maternal grandparents and aunties.

My mum brought me back to England when I was a month old. I have never known anything other than a transatlantic family – the separation of family by land and water, an identity with no fixed address. That is my normal. I was registered at the British High Commission as a British subject in 1971. I was born British. I was born with choice and relative freedom to live in any nation of the Commonwealth. I was born with, among other privileges, the gift of citizenship, language, access to education, and social and economic mobility – a member of the "free" world. Britain and Canada needed workers and educated professionals. My family could and continues to have been able to deliver on that for decades. We are practical in that way. Migration has motivated and encouraged our capacity to explore and adapt, to support each other, to reach out.

A Cumbersome Move in Three Parts

The story of my migration to Canada feels like a cumbersome one. It wasn't one in which my body was transplanted onto a new terrain and from there my life started anew – clean, light, without a past attached to it. It happened over a series of moves as I travelled in my small brown body through places of disorientation, curiosity, remembrance, grief, and nostalgia. Through severed connections and cultural confusion, I strove to belong. For decades, I couldn't find that mythical place of safe landing within the constructs of race, culture, and nationhood.

Innocence

I have a memory: a sunny day in East Putney – I'm balancing on a garden wall, walking along it and holding my mum's hand on the way to nursery school. We climb the stairs to an old brick house, and I am excited to go in. I'm wearing a white crocheted hat with navy blue trim, made by my gran to protect my ears – I had chronic ear pain. A woman opens the door – white, middle-aged, dark-haired. She greets us warmly. Suddenly, I am overcome with shyness and hide under my mum's calf-length forest green dress. I remember the toys strewn over a claret-coloured carpet, the colours of the toys and my wonderment at the sight of a real little brass trumpet. Next thing I know, I'm off to play, running in the garden, excited, curious, happy. I have a black-and-white picture of this time: Doug, Samantha, Fiona, Willie, and me in my little white hat all looking at the camera. I'm in the middle. I'm happy and I belong. I have no awareness that I might be different. All is well.

I have another memory of this time. I am sitting in the kitchen on a blue linoleum floor in the morning light. My parents are sleeping, I have opened the fridge and pulled out the cottage cheese. I am eating it. There's no worry, or fear; there are no boundaries or rules that I have learned of yet. I remember our home is in a 1930s mansion block, Millbrooke Court. I remember the garden in the back and a stone pond with goldfish. I remember Mr. and Mrs. Patience, the elderly caretakers. I remember white-haired Mr. Patience setting me on his knee as a grandparent might, reading to me, talking to me, and offering me chocolates from the box that always sat next to his armchair. And then it ended.

I didn't understand then that Canada was a refuge for mum from her marriage. In Canada, she had family – her mum, her siblings, and all her relations had arrived in 1973. In my earliest memories of Canada, I am three years old. Mum is teaching at the University of British Columbia, on what we now know are the lands of the xʷməθkʷəy̓əm (Musqueam). We are living in a townhouse in Richmond, on Lulu Island, near some railway tracks. The year is 1974, and I remember sleeping in a big bed with my mother in the basement of the house that my family had rented. I remember the darkness of the unfinished basement, the smell of the laundry room and Sunlight detergent. The smell of laundry detergent is so different in Canada than it is in England. Sunlight. Persil. They evoke different feelings for me: Sunlight – I'm a visitor, an outsider, a voyeur. Persil – familiarity, my heart is full and whole. The scent cloys, and yet it is comforting to me. I remember the green-patterned heavy bedspread we slept under. I remember standing under the doorway while all of Richmond shook during an earthquake. I didn't even know the earth could do that. We all lived together: my mum, recently graduated with her Ph.D.; my auntie Shirin, a fashion designer; my uncle Abdul, a railway customs inspector; my uncle Safder, a linguist and communist; my uncle Nizar, a chemist; my uncle Sadru, an accountant, and his wife, Auntie Gully, and their two children, cousins Aslam and Aly; and my grandmother Zera who everyone called Bai. Except for mum, they had all arrived a year earlier, put their pennies together, and started a restaurant at 970 Granville Street. Next door was Tom Lee, who back then had a long narrow store specializing in pianos, and Kripps Pharmacy. They're all gone now. I walked down that way the other day and there was just rubble and construction, but I still remember these little snapshots as if it were yesterday. The heart's snapshots are multi-dimensional: space, emotions, smells, voices, sensations, objects, time – all there, captured. They named the restaurant Papaya Gardens. The menu: sandwiches with chunks of avocado, thick old-fashioned cream cheese, little pink shrimp, slices of roast beef, handfuls of alfalfa sprouts; served with a side of carrot sticks on a white rectangular, polystyrene plate. There was always fresh soup in the sunken stainless-steel soup warmers – vegetable, chicken noodle, minestrone, or beef barley; Shirin auntie, in her floral-patterned duster jacket, made them every day. I remember a choice of flavoured drinks that came in three giant plastic dispensers – mango, papaya, passion fruit, or piña colada; and there was ice cream, too – strawberry, chocolate, and vanilla – served by the scoop with a little fan-shaped wafer for decoration. Safder uncle built the orange Formica counters and other furniture – dark stained tree stumps for stools and tables, and a rotary-style phone hanging in the doorway. The walls were plastered with giant posters of beaches with palm trees at sunset. My uncle Abdul kept the accounts in the back office. They all pitched in and worked at that restaurant until one by one, they found their legs and broke away and into their new professional lives – independent professionally, but holding on to the connection of family and community as naturally as a child might hold their mother's hand.

I remember the leather jackets and Cowichan sweaters that people wore on Granville Street; the theatres and the movie theatres; The Bay where my mum took me to get my ears pierced with a piercing gun – my cousin Aslam was so nervous about the shot, I still remember him flinching and tearing up. We were three years old. I remember details long forgotten, unlikely details. Cowichan sweaters were new and unfamiliar to me ... intriguing. The lonely-looking, sometimes drunk people on Granville.

My mum sometimes tells me how in 1974, she was teaching at the University of British Columbia (UBC), and at the time it was strange to her that she never saw any "Indians," as Indigenous people were called then. She'd asked why and had immediately felt her question was unwelcome, met with disapproval. She was confused by the responses she received. She could not make sense of their absence; why we had no articulated relationship with anyone Indigenous.

During the days, while my mum worked, I went to preschool. I had a blue plastic tricycle with a yellow and red trim. It had a seat that lifted up and down, covering a little storage space that I imagined was for sandwiches. I rode my plastic tricycle to and from preschool. I remember a paddling pool and eating beets for lunch. I was aware the teachers were different; they were big and tough, and they expected you to take care of yourself. They didn't like the criers. I see now that I had become a crier. The children interacted differently, too. I played on my own, and I remember the feeling of confusion and isolation I experienced when I slipped next to the paddling pool. I remember the dark colour of my blood on the concrete, the grazes and gashes on my knees. I remember feeling there was no one to turn to and recognizing that I did not matter here – not to the teachers, not to the other children.

As I think about that year, it is as if I were watching a movie, observing from a distance. Three years old, sitting under a Chinese paper umbrella under my mum's desk in her office at UBC; the faculty Christmas party – carols, the pa rum pum pum pum chorus of "The Little Drummer Boy," Santa, and little elves; my family; the warmth of so many members of my maternal extended family in one home. And then I remember my dad arriving with hugs for my mum and a giant-sized stuffed donkey for me. He'd named the donkey Burrito. I remember standing between them as they embraced in the basement of our townhouse in Richmond, holding onto their legs, smiling. My heart felt happy; I felt the wholeness of our little trio, absolute safety and belonging with no feelings of separateness. I want to say that where we were didn't matter, but I'm not sure that's true.

We went back to South West London. In my memory, I recall a sort of happy expectancy and joy, that all had returned to what it should be. It was a new home we went to this time. A little Victorian garden flat on the other side of Putney – 34 Clarendon Drive, with a beautiful weeping willow in the garden. At last, we had our own tree! My Dadima – my paternal granny whose name was Bachi Bai, another new school – light blue blazers and berets, and school dinners. These were the anchors I recall. I had already started to be identified as being different from the other children. The belongingness that comes from being in one place of established relationships of having set ways of doing things – of safety and routine; of being from the dominant race, socio-economic group, and culture – was lacking. There were fissures, and even then, I could feel myself falling. My belongingness was beyond my control. I was not white, English; I did not attend the Church of England, and I was not perceived as middle class. My parents struggled. They struggled with their identities and with their careers; with separation, instability, cancer, racism, roles, shared vision, and values. I went to different schools, depending on where things were with them. That was the turmoil my brother was born into. But there was joy, too – Battersea Park, Wimbledon Common, the Museum Gardens, Putney Common, Kew. There were holidays in the countryside and at the seaside, meals at restaurants, nights out at theatres, and family. But my parents were swimming against the current. Two bright and brave humans, barely able to acknowledge the extent of what they were battling against and knowing they couldn't afford not to succeed. The battle was divisive.

Lost

One morning I woke up in a Victorian conversion in South West London, and that night I went to sleep in a wooden house in a rainforest in North Vancouver that I now know are the lands of the Sḵwx̱wú7mesh (Squamish) people. One day I am in a private school for girls on Queens Gate. I wear a uniform, royal blue, with a cloak and a bowler hat; our lunches are served on blue-and-white china in a refectory; our class goes riding once a week, and I curtsy to my teachers. I study Sanskrit and philosophy. The next week I am in a public elementary school, disoriented. Mr. Mitchell was my homeroom teacher and saviour. Every morning, he handed out photostats of the words to a song, took out his guitar, and we all sang along. He was my first and best introduction to North American culture. Singing was good for my soul. His grounded presence – gentle, sensitive, slightly distant, and not entangled.

When I was eleven years old, I was moved 7,568 km from home. With each move, my identity fractured further. I made my way through the last bit of elementary school, through high school, and university all waiting to go home.

I knew where home was and I finally made it back to South West London when I was twenty-one. I'd had no plan to return to Canada, and no sense that I'd come back again at thirty-three with my partner and that we would raise our children here.

I am thankful now, but it wasn't always that way. I know that I am fortunate to make my life on the lands of the Coast Salish people, on the lands of the Sḵwx̱wú7mesh, Stó:lō, Səl̓ílwətaʔ (Tsleil-Waututh), and xʷməθkʷəy̓əm nations, but this was very far from my mind for many years. I didn't really know what this meant, although there was a boy at school who I think came from the reserve – I didn't even know what that was. I remember my mum had a pair of earrings that she had bought from a little shop at the bottom of Capilano Road. Now I know that the little shop had been on the edge of Capilano Indian Reserve No. 5, χʷəməltʃ'stn (Homulchesan). Dangly earrings. I think they were made from porcupine quills and red beads. They were called Indians, the people that lived there, and I didn't know any better. I had thought I was Indian. I couldn't understand why I was called East Indian. I didn't understand that even the name India was part of a Raj and Post Raj colonizer's construct. Now we call the people on whose land we live Indigenous, and the descendants of guilty ancestors are making first steps to distinguish between the nations. I am still described as East Indian, and it still feels like a snub, a refusal to acknowledge my identity except in colonial terms. Why would the people of a country with a current population of almost 1.5 billion, plus all the diaspora, be referred to as East Indian when they are Indian? Would this be unconscious or conscious incompetence? Sometimes, when I am feeling brave, I *gently* let people know.

It was 1982 and my mother was alone again. This time, she arrived with two children – my brother, Sulman, was five. Canada was still a refuge from her marriage, because here, she still had family. I went to Cleveland Elementary when we arrived back here in 1982. It was hard. I was eleven and had already been to five different schools. This would be my sixth attempt at belonging. It was not successful. By now, I existed on the fringe, an observer wanting to join in, trying clumsily to insert myself but not succeeding. I was younger than everyone else, I had an accent, my values and mannerisms were from a different land with a different history. I was out of place to all these children who had known each other through the years. They told me I was not welcome – through their choice of words, their lack of words, or their backs. I had landed in a vacuum of the unfamiliar.

I tried to learn fast, but I made too many mistakes and didn't know how to fix them. My parents' values didn't match what I saw at school. I made some shallow connections, but it was hard to find anyone to play with, to talk to. Lunch hour and recess were dreaded, lonely. It continued like that until the end of my second year at university. I no longer acknowledged to myself that I wanted to belong – it was not even a possibility. I was "less than." I felt shame and humiliation. I defined myself by counterculture. It was a time of tears and grief – I couldn't make sense of things. I didn't want to go to school. I barely finished high school and dropped out of university in my first year. Every interaction accentuated that I was not welcome, that I didn't belong. Eventually, my dad came to help me finish.

He created an emergency shelter for just long enough that I could finish university. I am lucky that I kept going with my education. I'm grateful for all my supports – money, food, housing, family, friends, all that was invisible to me for so many years – but I will never like the smell of a wet, West Coast rainforest or bark mulch, because it reminds me of that rootless and solitary time. Those years when every time I saw a doctor, they offered to medicate me.

Now I understand a little more about trauma and anxiety. I understand those feelings of not having control, of being forced, of choiceless-ness, of fear and paralysis. I understand how trauma and anxiety can interrupt learning, impact behaviours, hinder relationships and interactions, distort our vision of what is and isn't possible ... because we are consumed. I don't know how I escaped, but I did. I recognize how our lived experiences can show up in our hearts, minds, and bodies. I have a tremor, and I have always wondered when it started. I recently met a friend from forty years ago in Soho. I actively seek out old friends these days. I feel like I'm strong enough to define my own belonging – the shame is gone. She told me I never shook as a child. So, I now know that whatever triggered it happened after this second move.

Coming to terms

I'd been living abroad, with no plan to ever come back to Canada. I'd travelled alone, started a family, and was living on the outskirts of Warsaw with my partner, Arkadiusz, and his mum Janina – my unofficial teściowa (mother-in-law). We lived in a big old falling-down house with a kitchen garden, a German shepherd named Rex, and a tall metal fence around the property. I realize now that every decision I made after university allowed me a more dignified space to not belong. I went to places where I had no connections and spoke none of the language. I was exempt from most rules because I was an outsider. It felt good. Lonely, but somehow more comfortable. Being an outsider removed the problem of not belonging because there was no hope or expectation to belong; no awkwardness or humiliation. And expats were often so much friendlier, so much more open to seeing you as one of them.

Then, my mum was diagnosed with cancer. I thought I would lose her. Our children were five years old and fourteen months. Now Max is twenty-four and Seraphina is twenty. They are Canadian ... and Polish, and Indian, and British. I think Canada is their home, as it is mine, now – I can't really speak for them. I know that they also feel deep connections to Poland, to their Babcia (grandma) – and that every year they return. They were raised belonging to more than one place. Togetherness is time together, eating, talking, making our way toward our goals, travelling, walking ...

In the beginning, re-entry felt exciting. We moved into a light, bright, modern apartment in Yaletown overlooking the park. The neighbourhood was being newly developed as a residential area – it was the opposite of where I had been living. The sun shone, my mum recovered, my brother lived down the road. It was a time of reconnection with family and a small number of friends. I had come back with a stronger sense of self, and with an understanding that, in a general sort of way, our human experiences may sometimes be shared in ways we least expect. I found work easily, and once more it was time to rebuild. This continued building since that return in 2003 has slowly healed me over the years. Yes, I still look different, I still sound different, and I interact and think differently than many Canadians. I have been openly and covertly judged for my ancestry, skin colour, accent, attitudes, and behaviours. My differences continue to be highlighted by peers, by the learners I work with, and by members of the public that I may not even know. This experience is unwelcome. As an educator, my non-white status is constantly the subject of inquiry and scrutiny. And the question "Where are you from?" is one I am asked every day. Recently, I was asked it again by a group of students at the end of a class I was teaching. I felt my heart sink a little. I thought for a moment, and then I asked them, in the spirit of curiosity, what sort of answer they thought I might give. There was a moment of quiet consideration. One started to speak about my features, another about my accent, another complimented Indian people. Someone praised my English – which is my first and only language of proficiency – while the others listened and observed. It was a powerful moment. I didn't end up answering their question – not because I don't have an answer but because there had been a pause in which there was a moment to consider why they were asking, a moment in which I could witness them trying to make sense of my identity and uncover their own motivations behind such a question.

Yet my life here is fairly content. I enjoy as much a sense of belonging and acceptance as might be realistic to wish for. Throughout the years, my circle has become wider – friends, neighbours, colleagues ... Time, stability, and shared experience has helped me build relationships and belonging. At the same time, my sense that I am occupying someone else's lands is increasing and I am left questioning how happy a person can be in that knowledge. I am conflicted in both heart and spirit.

Here and Now

I believe it's the wealth of my relationships that have held me through my journey. And of my many teachers, mentors, and guides, there are two that I have to thank for teaching me about relationship and for giving me the language to articulate myself: Aaron Nelson-Moody, from the Sḵwx̱wú7mesh Nation, and Justin Wilson, of the Híłzaqv (Heiltsuk), who I thank for introducing me to what it means to explore and be in relationship to myself and to others; to the land; to our past, present, and future; to the importance of knowing that we are loved and needed. For helping me recognize that my individual story of migration, that so much of the geography of my heart is anchored in relationship.

I have come to understand that my family are like great rooted oaks that support me wherever I am in my transatlantic journey. Feelings of connectedness and belongingness come most readily when I recognize the kindness and good will of others; when we can exchange smiles or stop to talk; when I can share or be useful. I feel most at peace when I am in the garden, near the water, at the beach, or in the forests, because nature makes me feel welcome and not judged. Walking, breathing, and reflecting are like friends that help me process and accept what is and reveal to me what would best come next.

The opportunities I have received as an immigrant to Canada have often felt like double-edged swords. People see me as racialized, and it has been often pointed out to me that opportunity is being offered on account of my immigrant identity – my identity as "other." Who wants that? I want to know that I am enough. At the same time, after all these years, I have settled into my life in Canada and recognize the contemporary nature and value of my intersectional identity.

> *My family are like great rooted oaks that support me wherever I am.*

I believe that many of us in Canada share these overarching commonalities: that we each have different histories, dreams, and experiences of the world that shape us; that we want to feel safe, be heard, be valued, and to belong – on our own terms; and that we all live in relationship to each other.

And now, it emerges for me – that we have come full circle. My family was colonized, and we went on to enjoy the relative privileges of racial hierarchy in the British colonized parts of Africa. Now, we live as colonizers in Canada. I have made my life and raised my children enjoying the comforts and privileges of Yaletown, a pleasant and fairly affluent neighbourhood of Downtown Vancouver. My building was built on the lands of the Coast Salish people – land sold by the BC government and developed by Hong Kong Developer Li Ka shing. I know that the life my family and I enjoy comes at the historical and continued cost of the Indigenous people on whose lands I make my life, the Sḵwx̱wú7mesh, Səl̓ílwətaʔ, and xʷməθkʷəy̓əm nations. It is also clear that gratitude is insufficient. This truth, and my relationship to it, implicates me and asks what I will do now. I am needed to meet a new perspective of history and experience, to be led by those voices, and to demonstrate my willingness to adjust in ways that reflect a relationship that is shaped with and honours an Indigenous vision for our shared future.

PART 4

Stories of Displacement

14

Child Soldier

Albino Nyuol

IN 1983, THE SECOND SUDANESE Civil War broke out in Sudan. The army
of the Republic of South Sudan was called the Sudan People's Liberation
Army (SPLA). The SPLA was founded as a guerilla movement against the
government of Sudan in 1983 and was a key participant of the Second
Sudanese Civil War. More than 2 million people were killed and thousands
of others were displaced by this war. Many children, aged five to thirteen,
were forced to flee their villages because the Islamic government of Sudan
began systematically torturing and killing South Sudanese families, burning
their villages, and enslaving young boys and girls. This led to an exodus
of more than twenty-five thousand boys to Ethiopia and from Ethiopia
to Sudan on foot. This story describes my journey, from Bahr el Ghazal in
South Sudan to Ethiopia, from Ethiopia back to South Sudan, from South
Sudan to Kenya, and then finally to Canada.

A Tortuous Walk

I was thirteen years old on February 4, 1987, when civil war in Sudan
drove me from my home village, Mabil Thon, in Akoc Payam, Twic
County. Mabil Thon, where I lived, was a village of nearly three hundred
families. Most of the buildings were traditional huts made out of grass
thatch and mud. The community was a peaceful one, relying on farming
and cattle-keeping and fishing. When the war forced me to leave Mabil
Thon, I began a long journey, eventually walking one thousand miles to

a military training centre near Dimma, Ethiopia. On the way there, I survived starvation, wild animal attacks, and diseases. My food was whatever I could find: wild fruits, leaves, even the dry hides of dead animals. In South Sudan, people are accustomed to walking, but long-distance walking nonstop for three months, travelling night and day, was horrific for young children like me. Dying in the desert is a painful and horrific way to go. The landscape that the boys and I walked through was barren with only shrubs and a few acacia trees. A local community, Bor, one of the Dinka tribes in Jonglei State, promised me and a group of boys, upon leaving Ajak-Ageer village, that barrels of water would be ready for us under an agreed-upon acacia tree. But when we got there, there was nothing. Stuck with some other boys in the middle of two deserts, the Tingling and Ajak-Ageer, we waited for three days without any visible water. Thoughts of death filled everyone's hearts – we knew these deserts had killed many South Sudanese civilians trying to cross to SPLA training centres in Ethiopia. Human bones and skulls were scattered everywhere from those who had died of thirst. The only thought that came to everyone's mind was that death was waiting around the corner. Each of us was praying in his or her own dialect, asking God for a miracle, especially to bring rain down. Luckily, God answered our prayers and rain started to fall from what had been a cloudless sky. We got up immediately and started to collect rainwater with our containers. We were so happy and energized, and we started to walk toward Pibor Post, which was just captured from the government forces. Some of us were singing traditional songs while walking and the rest of us were singing an SPLA song. I sang a traditional song in the Dinka dialect: "Akuei Duk koc Akuei yo Deng ci Jal."

We walked night and day. Some of the boys were so very weakened by hunger and lack of sleep that they could go no farther and sat down by the roadside to be prey for lions and other animals. I was lucky to survive this horrific journey because I was being pushed by my half-brother, Santino Nyuol, to keep going. He was older than me and very tall, someone who always had a smile on his face.

"Albino," said Santino, "I want you to be walking with me always. If you walk behind the people, lion might grab you and take you away."

"Okay, you are right, my brother," I said, "I will be walking in line with you always." Walking with Santino gave me hope, and this is how I survived the tortuous journey.

Sudan People's Liberation Army – Dimma Training Center

After three months, one thousand miles from the village we fled, we crossed the border into Ethiopia. The training centre was situated in a mountainous area, and when we arrived it was little more than a clearing with some trees around it and a big river nearby. At Dimma we were divided into battalions, companies, platoons, and squads – we were trained by the SPLA to help them fight the Sudanese army. At that training centre, numerous battalions of red army soldiers were also being trained. Recruitment was compulsory. Every individual had to be trained to be a reservist for the reinforcement force. Because there were no buildings and there was no running water at the training centre, we had to build quarters by chopping trees and cutting grass for thatched roofs with machetes. All the recruits were segregated – we were not allowed to mingle with, or even visit, the adults in the residential area. Even boys who had relatives in the residential areas had to seek permission for an hour or two because authorities were afraid that recruits might try to escape and hide in the residential areas. This social isolation hurt most of us because children learn from adults. We were cut-off from the outside world with no phones, televisions, or computers. We depended on each other for survival: the older children cooked for the little children and made sure that they had rooms to sleep in and blankets to cover themselves with during the night.

We all learned unpleasant facts through trials and hardship. Unpleasant facts that turned out to be war propaganda from our leaders. When the army leaders spoke, they made lies sound truthful. For example, in order to convince us to remain in the army and do their bidding, our leader in the SPLA used to tell us in a raised voice, "You are the fruit of the nation and the leaders of the future."

A Cruel Overseer

One of the mistakes the SPLA made during our military training was putting a prisoner of war (POW) in charge of the training centre at Dimma. Thousands of recruits had died at the hands of this POW, Abule, a Sudanese Arab captured in the war zone in Sudan, who seemed tall and scary to me. He intentionally starved most of our recruits to death during our military training. He began by reducing our ration whereby we could count the pieces of maize on our plates. According to Abule, he was training us this way in order to teach us to cope with hunger. But there was something else behind it. Most of our recruits literally died because of this harsh training, lack of food, and severe punishments, which included Abule interrupting our breakfast early and making us run up and roll down rocky hillsides in hot weather, injuring ourselves. He even forced us into a cold fast-flowing river. He was not really bothered by the dead people in the training centre, instead he presented these deaths as normal casualties of the training. Many people were buried in mass graves. Obviously, Abule was enacting revenge for his being captured by the SPLA. During our training, maize and sorghum were not allowed to be ground into flour. Abule prohibited it because ground maize could reduce incidents of diarrhea or sickness among the recruits.

> *He intentionally starved most of our recruits to death.*

Our military training was prolonged for six months instead of only three or four. His intention to prolong this training was to make sure that many recruits would die. Some of us who survived this brutal training were very skinny by the end. There were no visible muscles, not even buttocks when we were finally discharged from our military training. The battalions, which graduated with us and were sent to Bahr el Ghazal immediately, were really thin and weak. They were not able to stand up during the military parade or even carry their own guns. Finally, after graduating from military training, about 4,500 boys were eventually sent back on forced march to Sudan, as reinforcements to fight alongside the SPLA.

Another Dangerous Trek

I walked back to South Sudan through muddy forests over a period of two months. It was a rainy season and very difficult to walk while carrying my own ammunition and the ammunition of others who were not strong enough to carry their own. I was also carrying food on my head. My boots plus other supplies, like loading-bearing equipment, an assault pack, and an extra uniform, were left in the mud. There was no choice but to sleep on the wet grass or the ground. My comrade soldiers and I hiked through muddy bush loaded with supplies including Kalashnikovs and rocket-propelled grenades, which I carried on my shoulders. Each of us was exhausted all the time. My comrades and I were heading to the border of Sudan, Ethiopia, and Kenya, where former president Omar al-Bashir was about to put his soldiers at the border to attack the SPLA. However, reaching the border was not easy. There was another dangerous desert, the Maruagapi. Crossing the Maruagapi was another terrible and horrific situation we faced as child soldiers in 1989. Our three battalions stationed at the border were ready to cross, but there was no water available nearby. There was only one water tanker, which was not enough to carry pure water for the entire army. Therefore, the commanding officers decided to add a barrel of diesel to it, to make it undrinkable, which would make it last longer – all in an attempt to save the lives of the child soldiers.

Conflict in Taposa

The desert brought us hot sands and land that was not only flat but had no trees at all. We were lucky to cross the Maruagapi desert without losing any soldiers on the way to our final destination.

Once there, we found no available buildings. We had to build our own thatched houses, and there was no food to eat.

We survived off the leaves of local trees in the nearby forest. These trees, aniet and apoor in Dinka dialect, helped us to survive. We feasted on these leaves for a full year, until there were no more leaves left in the forest.

We were not allowed to take anything like goats and sheep from the local community in Taposa. If we were caught doing so, we could be killed by firing squad.

The community at Taposa was not happy to be so near the army because they feared we would take their resources by force. Therefore one day, the Taposa community leaders asked our commanding officers to agree to a peace between us. The commanding officer sent a squad with one of their sons to attend the meeting. Unfortunately, the squad was ambushed and the local Taposa community killed all the soldiers. The killing of our soldiers made us angry, and we launched an assault on their community. They all had guns, but we managed to take their goats and sheep as a revenge. It was also our only chance to acquire food from the local community. Though I felt conflicted because it was civilians we were fighting with, I had no choice. I had to do it to survive. This was how we survived in the army.

A Fortunate Assignment

On May 28, 1992, the Sudanese military unexpectedly captured nearby Kapoeta military base, and tens of thousands of refugees were forced to move again. Nearly all unaccompanied minors at Narus base surged into Kenya. Three of our battalions went back to Kapoeta to offer reinforcement to the SPLA. I was lucky to remain at Narus with only sixteen officers in the entire town, to work in the military intelligence office because I was trained as intelligence personnel. All other intelligence personnel at Narus base had been sent to the frontline to fight the enemy. Some officers were left guarding the prisons where POWs were held, while others stayed to guard the ammunition storage areas.

Within a week, injured soldiers were sent back to Kenya for treatment, but most in the battalions were killed in battle. I felt guilty at the time because my fellow soldiers had been killed. Those of us left were scared that local Taposa were going to kill us, too, but they were too busy collecting maize, sorghum, oil, lentil, and many more items left behind by the refugees.

Bleak Refugee Camps

A month later, I got sick with typhoid and was advised by my military intelligence officer to go to a Kenya refugee camp for treatment. He arranged for my transport before I even knew about it, but in the military, you have to obey the orders of your senior officers. I joined refugees in this bleak Kenya refugee camp, which was prone to sandstorms and flash floods and year-round temperatures near one hundred degrees Fahrenheit. Life in the semi-arid desert environment of Kakuma is challenging. It also had poor infrastructure and low access to essential services. For example, there were no latrines or showers in the camp. Refugees only received dry food rations from the United Nations High Commissioner for Refugees (UNHCR), but materials to enable cooking, including firewood, were not provided. The Kakuma refugee camp was full of dust storms, poisonous spiders, snakes, and scorpions. Outbreaks of malaria, pneumonia, and cholera did not spare refugees. In 1995, I left the Kakuma refugee camp for the Dadaab refugee camp in northeastern Kenya, approximately sixty miles from the Somalia–Kenya border for search of resettlement. Dadaab is a semi-arid town in Garissa County, Kenya. It is the site of a UNHCR base across three camps: Ifo, Dagahaley, and Hagadera. Refugees received food rations containing maize, legumes, and oil, but we were not eligible for the initial rations until one year after arrival because Dadaab refugee camp was mainly for Somalis. We were denied food ration cards by the UNHCR. As such, I had no access to food in Ifo refugee camp for a year. There was no work at the camp. All South Sudanese in Ifo were paid by local Somali refugees to dig a latrine. To me it seemed almost like slavery, but we were hungry so we accepted the work.

Sometimes I went into the bush with other boys searching for firewood that we later sold to the local Somalis. In the bush, we were at risk of being attacked by bandits – usually poor Somali Kenyans who hid in the bush waiting for refugees out searching for firewood. Sometimes they even attacked United Nation's convoys bringing food into the camp. They wore scarves tied over their faces and they were often quite violent; sometimes they beat refugees or raped women and girls at gunpoint.

Quail Hunting

I sometimes went with some other boys into the bush to hunt for guinea-fowl and other wild animals. It was not easy to catch a guineafowl with a net or to kill wild animals. Our lives were more miserable in the Ifo refugee camp than in the Kakuma refugee camp because we were at least getting food rations in Kakuma. It was a dry season in the Dadaab camps and there was no water for wild animals and birds. I made a trapping net with some other boys in order to catch African quail. We tied bird netting to a bendable strong post, then we planted the trap in the ground so the quail

In the bush, we were at risk of being attacked by bandits.

would walk through the net and get tangled in it. Then I poured water on the ground to attract the quails – when a flock of quails sees water on the ground, they immediately fly down to try and drink the water. I depended on these quails for food for three months before I was finally issued a food ration card on August 31, 1996. I was happy to receive my food ration card, but I still planned to try and trap more quails in the morning, to make into soup. But our plan was different from God's plan. Ironically, on the same day we received our rations, it rained heavily during the night. In the morning, there were no quails to be trapped as they had gotten their fill of water in the night. So, I was only left with my food ration. This was how I survived in the Ifo refugee camp.

Getting an Education

In 1992, while I was in the Kakuma refugee camp, and after some time in military uniform without schooling, I started Grade 4. Being a student in a refugee camp was not easy for many reasons. Necessary resources such as a library, computers, study lamps, etc., were not available. I went up to Grade 7 in the Kakuma refugee camp before I went to the Dadaab refugee camp in northeastern Kenya. For the eight years I was in Kenyan camps, I was a student, and I eventually became a teacher in the Dadaab refugee camp in 1999 as there was no higher education to attend. During this period, I had many challenging experiences as a student and as a teacher. I was paid 2,500 Kenyan shillings a month, which came out to around fifty dollars USD. It was the first paying job I'd ever had and I was happy. I taught primary school until 2002, when my life changed.

A New Life

In 2002, as part of a program established by the Canadian government and the UNHCR, I was offered resettlement with some other South Sudanese. Life was extremely challenging in the camp, so I was overjoyed when I was selected for resettlement to Canada. This is how I left the Ifo refugee camp in Dadaab, Kenya, after several years of suffering. Thousands more South Sudanese were granted refuge elsewhere and are now scattered around the globe. My half-brother Santino is safe now, back in our village, Mabil Thon.

From 2002 until 2011, I started upgrading my education in Abbotsford, British Columbia and received my Dogwood Diploma, a Grade 12 equivalency. During that time, I was thinking of doing business administration, but I started part-time work at Abbotsford Community Services, which is now Archway Community Services, as a Settlement Worker. I liked that work and I like helping people. So I decided to study for a Social Services Diploma at the University of the Fraser Valley – I completed it in 2012.

While I was studying, my mother and many of my siblings and relatives were telling me to get married. "Come home!" they all insisted. So I went back home.

The family invited many young girls to come and see me, and everyone had an opinion about which one I should marry. There was one attractive and special woman who came to my village to see me. Many other girls came too, but I wanted to decide for myself who I should marry, so, I talked to the one special woman, Arual Manyol, and I chose her. On May 3, 2011, in Twic North County in South Sudan, she and I were married.

I returned to Canada later, alone, and did not waste any time continuing with my education. After graduating with a diploma in social services, I was accepted into the Bachelor of Social Work program, and I graduated from that program in 2016.

The year 2016 was very good for me because Arual was finally able to come to Canada on January 20, and my son Nyuol was born later that year, on December 2. In 2018, we were blessed again, this time with a little girl: Abuk Nyuol.

I learned a lot while going through such difficulties. One day, things can simply change. I did not have a good life when I was a child soldier and living in refugee camps, but today I have learned more and I have more opportunities. My experiences have taught me to look on the bright side and always have hope.

I am a survivor. Many people have helped me get to where I am. Now I am a settlement worker helping newcomers to Canada understand their rights and responsibilities, and to find the programs and services they need to survive in this country.

15

An Uncertain Journey

Jummeiz Kambidi

ONE SUMMER DAY, I was taking a break from a long day of teaching and sitting on a cool concrete bench in the schoolyard, under a tree. Another teacher came and sat beside me. In confidence, he said, "I would like to tell you something, but promise not to tell anyone. After all these years of work, I have found you to be a good and friendly person. I did not need to work as a teacher, but I did it because I was on a mission to watch you." He continued, "I am working for the Sudanese government's intelligence service."

He was sent to spy on me at Comboni College, in Khartoum, and to report on all my activities, connections, meetings, people who visited me at school, and places where I went after school, in order to find out if I was a threat or potentially harmful to the regime in any way.

He said, "After you finished work, there would be another agent who would follow you until you got home."

And this used to take place every single day.

After school, I used to attend church leadership meetings. I wasn't aware that I was being followed around by a security person wherever I went. This continued for over three years without my knowing. This fellow and I had always treated each other with respect, never had any heated arguments about the regime's policies. From my life experience, sometimes when you treat people with respect, even if they are your enemies, they will pay you back with respect.

Frightened, overwhelmed with fear, I thought about my life and my family. I had been unaware of what was surrounding me. After dinner that evening, I told my wife, Amal, about the astonishing conversation at school.

Amal was surprised and scared.

I suggested, "We need to think about leaving."

Amal agreed. "Where to?"

"Egypt." I added, "Since I have applied for a master's degree in England, I could follow up with my application from Egypt."

"How could we do that?"

"We would say we were going on vacation."

We looked into different options and tried to come up with a concrete decision for leaving the country.

My fear increased when one evening a stranger tried to open the door to our house, pretending that he was wandering and looking for somebody else's house. Clearly, we were in danger. I barely slept that night – it was the longest night of my entire life. I was not sure if I would make it to the next morning; I was expecting security forces to break in and arrest me. We knew we had no choice but to leave.

We could not tell anyone. I immediately started preparing our passports and exit visa. I didn't go to the passport office myself, though, as I was afraid of drawing the attention of the intelligence agents. Instead, I hired someone to renew our expired passports and prepare our exit visas. I gave this man some extra money, like a commission, just to stay away from suspicion, and trusted that he would prepare everything necessary for us to travel. I had a different person book my travel by train, which was safer and avoided the more accurate scrutiny of an airport. All this without informing my colleagues. I had asked the school principal for a letter to show I was going to Egypt for vacation, in case I faced questions at any checkpoint at the border.

I was forced to leave my country of origin against my will because of risk factors that threatened my safety. This threat, I realized, began during my time as a university student, when I acted as a socio-economic and political activist. I used to provide social and political orientation and political awareness about university life and activities for newly admitted students from Nuba Mountains, from where I descend. Doing this became an obstacle to my employment and career choices post-graduation. I was always spotted as a bad apple, for my ideas were contrary to the regime of that time.

Employment Dilemma

Looking back, I see how it is that I became known as a bad apple. After graduation, I started a lengthy job search. Based on my background in political science, I wanted to work for the Ministry of Foreign Affairs. When jobs were posted for the hiring of thirty diplomats in the ministry, I applied. I knew in advance what would happen, but I applied anyway, for reasons of ethnic belonging, religious faith, and some political views. In the back of my mind I knew I was fighting a losing battle, but I decided to launch it to the end, no matter the outcome. The first phase of the process was a written exam, with two questions; one of them I considered a trap, to distinguish those who did not share the regime's political point of view regarding foreign policy. My essay was solid and did not include any flattering expressions, which they expected to see, matching their ideology. My essay showed my competency in my chosen field, and what a knowledgeable and qualified diplomat I would have been. Surprisingly, I found that I passed the written exam, which I believed was a way to get me face-to-face with the oral interview panel members in the second phase.

The time finally came for me to face the panel in an oral interview. The chair of the interview panel was a high-profile member of the Islamic regime and the Sudanese ambassador to Iran. During the interview, I was sarcastically asked to recite some Qur'anic verses, even though they knew I was a Christian. This panel's sarcasm and disrespect didn't have any impact on how I conducted myself and reacted to such questions. I had a message to convey – a fair, just, and equal opportunity for everyone, irrespective of ethnic or religious background. I continued to answer all the questions steadily, confidently, and competently, and demonstrated my capacity in every aspect of the interview. I did not get the job.

I tried to find a job with non-governmental organizations, but I could not because the regime was monopolizing and dominating all opportunities for its partisans. I didn't dwell in despair, but I remained always hopeful. It was only with such hope and determination that I was able to overcome these obstacles.

In the end I worked as a teacher for Comboni College Khartoum, a private school. I built a house, got married, and settled, but the regime wouldn't leave me alone. During work hours, this man kept his eyes on me, was around me all the time, and talked to me about different issues – sometimes about the regime's policies, just to hear what I would say.

This alarming background narrative, being denied my rights as a citizen, set the foundation for my decision to leave Sudan.

The Day of Departure

In June 2000, Amal, now five months pregnant, and I boarded a train and left Khartoum. It was one of the most difficult and emotional moments – saying goodbye to our relatives, not knowing what the future held. My father, who used to stay with me, moved into my older brother's house, the house in which my mother had passed away five years before. It was hard for me, letting him return to that house. I knew it would trigger strong emotions all over again. Sadly he passed away a year later. My siblings shed tears for me, and I was in deep pain for having to leave them.

> *I had a message to convey – a fair, just, and equal opportunity for everyone, irrespective of ethnic or religious background.*

Other dreams vanished. My wife's mother, who wished to see the first grandchild from her eldest daughter, now found her dream evaporated. We were stepping out of our comfort zone, leaving relatives, friends, and acquaintances, and moving into an uncertain future.

On the day of our departure, my older brother escorted us to the train station. Adding to our stress and anxiety, the train did not leave on time. Finally, the station personnel rang the bell and the train blew the departure whistle, and my stress abated. My brother said goodbye to us and we hugged each other, in tears, not sure if we would meet again. As the train moved slowly away, I kept waving to my brother.

Our destination was the terminal station at Wadi Halfa, a small city on the Nile in the far north of the Sudanese-Egyptian border; neither Amal nor I had ever been there before. We knew some people from our community who lived there, such as Amal's cousin. From there, we would take the ferry to Egypt.

The train arrived at the station in Atbara, the biggest city in Northern Sudan, where we met a man we knew bidding farewell to his nephew, going to Wadi Halfa on the same train. He handed us his suitcase to keep in our compartment and told us to keep our eyes on his nephew because he did not book his seat in advance and had no place to sit. Not everybody could afford to book a train. Some people just showed up and sat on the roof. My anxiety went down – the boy would be our guide, and we might stay in their house.

From Abu Hamed, the last train station along the Nile, the train slipped through the Nubian Desert the whole night. We could see only extended desert and stretches of sand dunes. We were still far from our destination. It took us another ten hours through the desert to finally arrive in Wadi Halfa around three o'clock in the afternoon. Arriving at such an early time in only one and a half days, we were told, was a kind of miracle. I considered it a sign of good luck – the train used to break down on the way, resulting in delays. Still, when the train was crossing that desert, many questions and thoughts lingered in my mind: What if something happens? What if we run out of fuel? What if the train stops in the middle of this desert?

In Wadi Halfa

Upon arrival at the train station, I met a friend who had been with me at the same elementary school. He was working for ferry security and right away took our passports, had them checked, and booked us on the ferry to Egypt. The boy who was with us on the train invited us to his family's house, which was a great relief. We spent two days there, never leaving the house, waiting for the day of departure. In that remote city, my worries and stress remained so long as I was on Sudanese soil. I waited anxiously for the sailing that would take us across the border.

On the day of our departure, Amal's cousin who worked on the ferry carried our luggage ahead of us. My friend accompanied us to the ferry, had our passports checked, went with us, and stayed until it was ready to sail around noon. I breathed a sigh of relief as we moved away from the dock. It took us one and a half days to arrive in Aswan.

In Egypt

In Aswan, we prepared to take a train to Cairo. We booked our tickets and spent about four hours waiting, so Amal could rest before we resumed the journey that evening. I phoned my cousin in Cairo, who had been there for three or four months. I informed him to expect us the following day. The trip took the whole night. The spaces across the small compartment were not wide enough for Amal to stretch her legs, and the long journey caused her some discomfort. We arrived in Cairo and found two of my cousins waiting for us at the station.

The next day my cousin and I woke early and went to the United Nations High Commissioner for Refugees (UNHCR) office and registered for protection. We had to go early in the morning in order to get a spot in the queue – there was always a long line outside the UNHCR premises, and I had to wait for three or four hours for the office to open.

When the doors opened, I registered and was given a paper with a date to return after one year to receive an application form. I was unlucky because one month before my arrival, the UNHCR changed its policy regarding the duration of registration, receiving application forms, and interviews. It was hard to believe. One year, just to receive an application form. Before that, it used to be only a few months and all processes would be finished. Frustrated and disappointed, I had to swallow that bitter pill and accept the wait.

Tragedy Hits

One week after our arrival in Cairo, Amal was not feeling well. She was in pain and discomfort. Her water broke and she was admitted to the Evangelical Medical Centre. The doctors tried their best to save the pregnancy but couldn't, and she miscarried. We lost our five-month-old baby boy. Our excitement at becoming first-time parents quickly vanished. We felt only disappointment, sadness, and the pain of loss.

We never expected such tragedy would take place, or that it would hit us hard in a country where we had just arrived. It was the first impression and experience to mark our lives on this adventure; it wasn't the pleasant beginning we hoped for. Being far away from home, the lack of family for emotional support and comfort made for some really difficult moments. For Amal and me, it was painful to lose the first baby after so much joy and hopeful anticipation. Suddenly we felt emptiness.

I felt guilty and blamed myself, thinking, "If I hadn't decided to leave Sudan in the first place, this would not have happened."

I tried to encourage Amal as we both grieved. I phoned our families and the church and conveyed this sad news. They all remembered us in their prayers, which sustained us. My two cousins with their families, who all lived together in one place, were so generous and supportive to host us in

Cairo during this sad time. Also, a friend, a French researcher in linguistics who we had hosted in Sudan during his research into my tribe's language, Koalib, lent us financial assistance when I informed him of the tragedy.

Dual Challenges

We tried to move on and start a new life. All refugees shared the same difficulties of finding housing and a job.

Renting an apartment was too expensive for one family. Sudanese refugees and other nationalities were not isolated by the Egyptian government in separate refugee camps; we lived among the Egyptians, to avoid crimes that might be committed if we were left isolated. The landlords took advantage of refugees by raising rents, making it extremely difficult for both refugees and Egyptians to live. If there was a vacant apartment, the landlord would prefer to rent it to a refugee for a higher price than to an Egyptian for a lower one. This act of renting to refugees at higher prices caused resentment among Egyptians toward refugees. We were targeted. They hated refugees, attacked them at night, made fun of them in the streets.

Sometimes I sold nothing and didn't even have enough for bus fare to get home.

One of my cousins and his family rented an apartment with us and we shared the cost. It wasn't always easy for two families to share housing, but we had learned to live together. We made it work.

The other challenge was finding a job. I needed to pay my portion of the rent and food. Everybody was selling perfumes. My cousin and I used to buy perfumes from a retailer and resell them as street hawkers. Wearing a backpack with a strap over my shoulder, I moved during the day from one place to another, from one coffee shop to another. In the evenings, I stood by sidewalks until one o'clock in the morning. Sometimes I sold nothing and didn't even have enough for bus fare to get home. It became harder and more discouraging with every single day. When it became impossible for me to secure our monthly rent, my co-tenant moved out to find another place that he could afford. I was left with Amal to face our uncertain fate.

For some reason, we did not panic; we remained calm and felt confident that there would be some unseen breakthrough. We had faith that God would not abandon us. At a time when we did not know where help might come from, we kept hope alive.

A Miracle Occurs

As the end of the month drew near, worries about money increased. It was hard enough for me and my cousin to pay our portions of the rent back when we still lived together. It would be impossible to pay it by myself. Many questions tormented our minds through sleepless nights, stress, and what might happen if we failed to pay the rent in full.

After my cousin moved out with his family, some people in my refugee community viewed us with sympathy, others with cynicism, seeming to enjoy our misery and the possibility of us becoming homeless. I did not hint at or tell Amal directly to find a job as a housekeeper, as many women did. It was an easy job for women to find. Nobody had the courage to tell me to ask Amal to find such a job. She had just miscarried and was still recovering. I felt I could not push her into that as it would be putting her health at risk. Such domestic work required much physical strain, which would have been hard for someone in her state.

Then one day Amal received a phone call from a friend stating that there was an American professor visiting the American University in Cairo. The professor, Sherri McFarland, was researching courtship among the Nuba women of Sudan, and she was searching for an interpreter to assist her with questionnaires among the Nuba women in Cairo. Amal was recommended. Professor McFarland met with Amal and they put together a plan to interview various women.

I carried on selling perfumes. Every day when I came back, Professor McFarland and Amal would still be working together in our home. The professor, who was very open, often asked me, "How was it today? Was it good? How much did you make today?"

As my answer was the same every single day, she became alerted to our financial struggle.

When it was time to pay our rent, Professor McFarland informed Amal that she would pay her for her interpretation services and introducing the professor to the Nuba community. Amal's payment secured our monthly rent. The professor continued to pay Amal every month for facilitating these interviews and questionnaires. For me, this was extraordinary, a miracle. Those who were waiting to see our miserable downfall saw only stability and normalcy. That was the beginning for us, a sign of good things to come.

Later, I met a man I knew back in Sudan who used to be a teacher. Now he was teaching at a Catholic School for Sudanese refugee children in Cairo. He introduced me to another school, African Hope Learning Centre for Sudanese refugee children, funded by an American missionary couple. I met the school principal, who asked me to provide her with a written statement of faith, since it was a faith-based school. She offered me a volunteering opportunity with a monthly honorarium of 150 Egyptian pounds. She did not inform me about this when I first accepted the volunteer position, rather she surprised me with an envelope at the end of the month. I continued teaching there until the school year ended. The following year I was employed as a full-time teacher with a regular monthly salary, and I worked there until we left Egypt.

Amal finished interpreting for Professor McFarland after six months, and then she too found work with another school since she had also been a teacher in Sudan. Both of us working as teachers gave us some peace of mind and relief from financial pressures. Being involved in teaching and having a busy work schedule, we also at least had something to do, which reduced our stress over the immigration process. It did not really go out of our minds, however, as Egypt wasn't our final destination.

After waiting for one full year, it was time to go back to the UNHCR office and receive the application form. I was informed I had to fill out the form carefully, including every detail, establish my case, and return it after another year. I received the form. I had enough time to review it over and over, and to became familiar with the questions and what was required.

Two years had already passed since my arrival in Egypt. I was still waiting for my interview day.

Interview Day

The interview was on September 24, 2001. My claim number was 2378/2001, and the interviewer's name was only the initials SHS. The interviewers were infamous for their initials, and for being mean and resistant to recognizing refugees' claims. One of the most unpopular and terrifying initials among refugees was LS. I was so relieved that she wasn't the one to interview me; many of the refugees who had been interviewed by her had been denied protection.

On the interview day, we were requested to be at the UNHCR premises at 7:00 a.m. Amal and I arrived on time and waited for our names to be called. At 2:30 p.m. my name was finally called. I was interviewed for only half an hour and told to come back the following day to finish the interview. Then it would be Amal's turn. It was perilous and unfortunate to be interviewed in two stages.

I went home and tried to recall every single question I was asked and every answer I had given so that I wouldn't contradict myself the next day, which could jeopardize my claim. We returned to the UNHCR office the next day. This time we did not wait long. I was summoned right away and continued the interview from where I had stopped the day before. Amal followed and spent only thirty minutes with the interviewer because all her answers to the questions aligned with mine. We were informed that the outcome of the interview would be published on the wooden outdoor notice board on the wall of the UNHCR in two weeks. We waited.

Interview Result

I returned to the UNHCR office two weeks later and checked for the interview result, but I could not see my name on the board. I went back the following week. Still no result. I kept checking every week until finally I gave up. Even so, I remained confident that the outcome of my claim would be positive. After almost four months of delay, the result was eventually published. A member of my Sudanese community saw my name on the board, which meant my claim was recognized and found to be eligible for protection and refugee status. I sighed with relief, assured that we would be leaving Egypt sooner or later without knowing our next destination.

Resettlement Process

We returned to the UNHCR office several months later for resettlement to our asylum country, either the US, Canada, or Australia. We now had a three-month-old baby boy, Ezra, to include in our file. To my surprise, the resettlement officer was LS – those terrifying initials. But I had nothing to fear or worry about, since my claim had already been recognized. She turned out to be a nice person, not the fearful and scary character I had conceived of according to what was circulated among the refugee community.

She asked me, "Do you speak English?"

Jokingly, I answered, "Yes. I can speak English, German, Spanish, and Russian."

With astonishment, she dropped her pen and stared at me without saying a word.

I apologized and said, "No, I was just trying to break the ice."

Then, she continued explaining about the resettlement process and added our son to the file. She asked, "Would you prefer to go to the US, Canada, or Australia?"

Surprised by the choices, Amal and I looked at each other.

Together we said, "Canada."

She praised our choice. "Canada is a suitable choice for you."

I had visited the Canadian Embassy in Cairo several times before my interview with the UNHCR, for direct application. During my visits, something on a poster caught my eyes and heart: *People come from all over the world and make Canada their new home.* These words gave me the notion of an inclusive and multicultural Canada, which embraces diversity. It made me fall in love with the country.

To the Canadian Embassy in Cairo

When we had completed the resettlement process, our claim file was transferred from the UNHCR to the Canadian Embassy in Cairo. Some months later, one early morning, we received a phone call from the embassy informing us to report to the office for an interview in preparation for travel. We went there and met with an officer for this interview, and then we signed some documents.

He asked, "Do you know anybody in any part of Canada?"

I replied, "I have a cousin in Vancouver, but I don't mind going anywhere in Canada." I said this to avoid any delay related to the area of preference.

An Unforgettable Date

Shortly after the embassy interview, we received a call from the International Organization for Migration (IOM), the leading inter-governmental organization in the field of migration. We were informed we would be leaving for Canada in a week – May 21, 2003, to be precise. We had one week to get our documents and complete the exit process with the

Egyptian Ministries of Foreign Affairs and Interior, IOM, and attend three-day orientation and information sessions about life, culture, climate, employment, housing, and education in Canada.

It was impossible for me to accommodate all these events at the same time, so Amal attended the orientation and information sessions in my stead. It was one of the busiest and most restless weeks of my life.

In Canada

I left Cairo on the evening of May 21, 2003, excited about my new home but also sad about leaving friends and community members behind. Many did not know their fates. I wasn't sure if I would be able to help them get out of Egypt.

My feet touched Canadian soil on May 21, 2003, in Calgary, Alberta, where Amal, Ezra, and I waited for seven long hours to fly on a WestJet flight to Vancouver. We arrived in the evening and were picked up from Vancouver International Airport by the host agency, Immigrant Service Society of British Columbia (ISSofBC) and taken to the Welcome House on Drake Street, where we stayed for two weeks while we underwent medical check-ups, orientation, and applied for all necessary identification documents.

I did not have to worry that much when it was time to move out of the Welcome House and into permanent housing. My cousin and other friends, who had been with us in Egypt, had come ahead of us to Vancouver and assisted us in adjusting to our new life. They introduced us to shopping centres; provided us with rides to places of employment; and took us to driver's licence service locations, car dealerships, and helped us with other basic settlement information.

First Neighbourhood

We rented an apartment on Walker Avenue in Burnaby. We lived there for eight years. Our children went to preschool and then Morley Elementary School. It was a convenient neighbourhood with easy access to public transit, a small mall, a library, a community centre, a school, and a park, all within walking distance. We built our social network, explored the neighbourhood, utilized local resources, and started integrating into mainstream society. In this neighbourhood, we experienced moments of joy, sorrow, and some unpleasant incidents. An expensive floor rug was stolen by a neighbour from the yard where we had left it out to dry after cleaning it. My vehicle was broken into twice.

Then another tragedy struck.

In August, 2004, Amal lost her third pregnancy, a five-month-old baby boy. We went through the same emotional scenario that had happened to us three years prior. Some negligence on the side of our family doctor at that time played a role in the loss. Amal used to remind the doctor every visit to refer her to a gynecologist, but he kept postponing it to the next visit, until it was too late. Every one of our plans came to halt while we coped with the grief. If the doctor had listened to Amal, we would have not been in this situation.

A Plan in Place

We tried not to allow this misfortune to hold us captive. We looked ahead and moved forward. Amal and I made plans again. I wanted her to go to school.

I told her, "You go to school first."

And she said, "No, you go first."

"No, you go first, and after you finish and find a job, then I'll go back to school. I'll work in the afternoons after you get home."

So We Finally Agreed

After our Resettlement Assistance Program ended, I found work with A&R Metal Industries Ltd., a warehouse in Richmond. I worked there in the afternoons. I also worked a few hours each morning as a Newcomer Information and Support Worker, for DIVERSEcity Community Resources Society.

Amal graduated from the Community Development diploma program at Capilano University. After graduation, she got casual employment with ISSofBC, and then a full-time job with Multilingual Orientation Service Association for Immigrant Communities (MOSAIC) as a case manager for vulnerable and multi-barriered immigrant clients. In her position there, she helped newcomers navigate community resources and access settlement services. Now she is coordinator for MOSAIC's Moving Ahead Program.

In 2006, As Amal was about to finish upgrading her English, she gave birth to a precious baby girl, Mballany. God restored our smiles. Mballany is a joy to us both. For Ezra, who wanted to have a sibling, having a sister eased his loneliness. Whenever he saw other children playing with their siblings, he would say, "I wish my older brother was alive so that I could play with him."

Back to School

When it was my turn to go back to school, there were some voices in my circles that were against the idea. Many of them expressed their resentment and considered my plan insane. I was told to forget about education, maybe because in their social perimeter they had not seen a new immigrant go to school. I paid no attention to those negative voices.

But when the global financial crisis that began in 2007 dragged many of the world's economies into recession, Canada was not spared. Companies went out of business. Many people lost their jobs, including at my workplace. My warehouse supervisor suggested, "Jummeiz, you need to change your shift or get laid off. Maybe you should go back to school."

I chose the latter. I enrolled in a one-year Social Services Community Support Worker diploma program at Sprott Shaw Community College in Vancouver, to provide myself with an opportunity to serve new immigrants and advocate for service gaps. I was so lucky to be one of the first to take advantage of the Employment Insurance program and had my tuition fees and child care subsidy paid in full. I was so grateful to the Canadian government for this opportunity.

Career Evolution

Since 2010, my career has evolved in the immigrant settlement industry. I worked for MOSAIC in 2010, as a Project Evaluation Interviewer – an independent contractor role in which I collected relevant information from refugees and immigrants with multiple barriers such as large families, a lack of formal education, a lack of communication skills, health or trauma issues, and single parenthood, all of which would be used for the project evaluation.

With Options Community Services' First Steps Program, I assisted immigrant fathers of children from birth to six years old develop their parenting skills. I now work for Options Community Services as an Outreach Case Worker. I provide case management and wraparound service, and help immigrants with their settlement goals, objectives, action plans, and outcome measurement.

My advice to newcomers to Canada comes from my experience. If you dwell on your past, it will limit your thinking and slow your ability to pursue your goals and ambitions, and also anchor you to the past. Get *any* job and provide for yourself and your family. At the same time upgrade your English language skills and evaluate your credentials. Get enrolled in any program that will enable you to practice your profession. In order to succeed, interact with your informed social network, which will provide you with knowledge and information you will need to motivate you to achieve your goals and dreams.

I don't think I have reached my full potential. I still hold plenty of ambition. I feel that I have a lot left to accomplish. So many dreams – buy a house, start a business. I will keep dreaming and soaring on my wings, as high as I can.

16

Hiraeth

Malena Mokhovikova

Hiraeth (n) A deep, wistful, nostalgic sense of longing for home that is no longer or perhaps never was.

I KNOW THIS STORY by heart. I have recalled it countless times, at fundraising events, during newspaper interviews, and on awkward Tinder dates. Knowing when to pause, give space for *I'm so sorrys*, or when to reveal gruesome details.

I was born and grew up in cold and beautiful St. Petersburg, Russia. Seven years ago, I came to Canada as a refugee because of racial attacks, ongoing discrimination, and the fear of prosecution. My mama, Natalia Mokhovikova, is a Russian Jew, and my papa, Mokhsen Mokhovikov, is an Afghan. Growing up, I didn't realize how dangerous having a biracial family was in Russia. The country holds a very narrow-minded idea of what its citizens should be. We did not fit into that box. As a result, we were forced to endure endless racial attacks over the years from white supremacist groups, the police, and the mafia.

My parents did their best to shelter my younger sister and me, by sending us to Beit Sefer Menachem, a Jewish private school. Before the fall of the Soviet Union, everyone who looked the part quietly rewrote their passports to say "white." Now that socialism was no longer law, Mama pulled out the "receipts" of our Jewish ancestry. I was still a victim of physical and emotional abuse in the preschools I attended; one teacher ordered other children to hold me down and beat me up. When we switched schools, another assaulted me and told me it was a "massage." I felt nothing but shame coming home with new bruises every day. I was sure I deserved it.

The abuse did not exist solely outside of our house. Papa was born and grew up in Kabul. He served in the military, protecting his country in his youth. As a result of the traumatic events he endured, he suffered from what was called a "soldier's heart," or "war neurosis," and is now known as PTSD. At home, he got periods of angry or aggressive behaviour and let it out on Mama. Papa would get into arguments with her, which would often result in Mama tucking us in with bruises on her face and neck. It happened so often I thought she had some kind of skin condition where her face swelled up and changed colour on its own. My brother, Mamun, who was thirteen years older than me, saw what Papa did and started inflicting the same cruelty on Milana, my younger sister, and me. My first seven years were filled with physical, emotional, and sexual abuse and shame. I never complained about anything that happened to me or my family. I thought this was what everyone went through but did not talk about.

Despite their disagreements, our parents did their best to make Milana and me feel loved. Mama filled our childhood with magic. She wrote us letters pretending to be Santa and put them in a red letterbox on our kitchen windowsill; she crafted fairy tales about little gnomes that lit our street lanterns and sewed me a new dress *every night* because I didn't want to go back to my abusive preschool. After tailoring for hours, she would appear in my room at dawn with a sweet, exhausted smile on her freckled face. Like a fairy godmother from *Cinderella,* she made me feel like a princess, and I was running late to the ball.

"C'mon now," Mama would say. "Let's go show your friends the new dress."

This motivated me to go to school every day. You'd think that by the second week I'd have seen through her trick, but my need for validation won out. This went on for years.

Papa valued his masculinity, a part of which meant showing as little emotion as possible. Still, Milana and I were a force to be reckoned with; Ronald McDonald was our saviour and cheeseburgers were our mana. On our way home from school, we'd chant in unison, "McDonald's! McDonald's! McDonald's!"

We persisted even when the car was already in the parking lot by our apartment, its engine turned off. Milana and I kept screaming, "McDonald's! McDonald's!" until Papa sighed and begrudgingly drove us to the fast-food restaurant. I didn't realize it at the time, but those moments assured me that no matter how stoic Papa tried to appear, he had a soft spot for us.

In August of 2012, Mamun went missing. Time is divided into two parts: before this and after this. Days later, he turned up beaten up, with his hair, eyebrows, and eyelashes shaved and a green cross painted on his back. It was the signature of a white supremacist group, Skinheads who targeted people of colour and members of the LGBTQIA2+ community. A week later, my brother disappeared again. We searched everywhere – prisons, parks, and morgues – to no avail. The police wouldn't help us, so Mama hired a private investigator who found him in a psych ward.

Skinheads had bribed doctors to drug my brother, hold him there against his will, and test medication on him. I remember seeing him, a skeleton wrapped in skin. His mouth hung open and he stared back at me with hollow eyes as I fought the urge to cry. Fear smelled of vomit and antiseptic. We got him out in critical condition and moved him to a proper hospital. Months prior, Mama had booked a trip around Canada and back for herself, my sister, and me, for Rosh Hashanah, the Jewish New Year. She was conflicted about leaving when my brother had just gotten out of the hospital, but in the end she decided it would be a needed break for us. We left, while Papa stayed home and looked after my brother, who developed schizophrenia from the abuse he'd experienced at the psych ward.

Our cruise ship made a loop between New York and Quebec. It had a 24/7 buffet, and the cabin attendant twisted our towels into animals. Years later, when I saw the inflatable boats arriving on the news, I thought of the five-star liner and the irony of it being my transport to the promised land.

Upon landing in Quebec, Mama called home, and Papa said that someone was shooting at the windows where Milana and I slept. If we were there, we would've been dead. She realized that if we stayed in Russia, her daughters would either end up like her son, broken and traumatized, or we wouldn't survive at all. She sat us down and told us to pack only the most precious of our belongings. We were not going home. I gazed at her blankly, not realizing the full gravity of that moment. Numb and devoid of emotion, I did everything Mama asked so she would stop shaking. We put on as many layers as we could to make sure our bags looked light and natural, we walked off with other tourists, and then we ran. We took a Greyhound bus as far as we could, so the police would not find us and put us back on the ship (later, we found out about a Missing Persons report searching for a mother and her two children). The bus was headed to Vancouver. I didn't even know how to pronounce the city's name; Canada never appeared on Russian news. Three days and nights later, we found ourselves tired and starving in a foreign environment, with no idea where we'd sleep and no money. Vancouver overwhelmed me; the sounds felt too sharp, the colours too saturated. I was lost in a whirlpool of baffling neon signs, melodic conversations, and chattering autumn leaves of gold and scarlet. Thanks to selfless strangers who we met through the Kinbrace community, which welcomes refugee claimants with housing, education, and support, we found a temporary roof over our head, a food bank card, and a label that would follow us for the next eight years: refugees.

I was no one when I came to Canada, a lost tourist, an ill-fated statistic, a name on a foreign passport. Imagine the paradigm shift Milana and I experienced on our first day in Britannia Elementary, a small school in the heart of East Van. I saw more tattooed people than I did back home, and that was before lunchtime. Thankfully, at the tender age of twelve, I hadn't learned bigotry yet. I didn't care that my best friend had two moms or that my teacher was Chinese. If anything, I felt safer here, and despite being a foreigner, I no longer stood out. My new classmates helped me gain perspective on different cultures and backgrounds I wouldn't have gotten if I went to a wealthy West Van school. I was the translator for my family, despite only knowing greetings and numbers. For the first two years, I thought that "exactly" meant "exotic," thus marvelling at how condescending half of the people I talked to were.

I jumped at the first opportunity I had to make something of myself in this country by joining Britannia Secondary's basketball team in grade 8. I had never dribbled a basketball and could not speak English well enough to understand the difference between offence and defence, but it was a much-needed distraction from the countless courtroom meetings and lawyer appointments for our refugee status. Things started to progress: my coach gifted me my first basketball shoes, and my teammates started pronouncing my name right. We started winning games, and as the years went by, I was able to make a name for myself. As my basketball career improved, my mental health worsened. After going into hiding, Papa and Mamun were able to flee Russia. With their arrival, a new set of challenges emerged: I had to juggle school, sports, and two abusive men during the most vulnerable time in my life. Growing up, I was the most excited child in the room, so when I started becoming more closed off, others sensed something was wrong. Mental health was a foreign concept in Russia; we didn't see Putin talk about anxiety on TV or take days off in the name of "self-care." You were either "normal" or "crazy," so when my school counsellor suggested I try therapy, I didn't understand at first. When the clinician gave me a name to describe what was happening in my head, the weight I didn't know I was carrying lifted off my shoulders. I was diagnosed with clinical depression and post-traumatic stress disorder. Shifting the blame onto the ever-growing monster in my head, it took months of work to convince me that everything that had happened to me wasn't my fault. It was even more difficult to talk to my family about it. They didn't realize I was unwell mentally and that some of their behaviour was contributing to it.

After graduating high school, I was offered a basketball scholarship to play and study at Douglas College. I decided to go into psychology, to learn more about mental processes, so one day I could pay it forward. I was the first in my family to graduate high school in Canada and the first to get into post-secondary. I had no one to ask for help and was the one making a path through the dark for Milana to follow. I had to leave at five in the morning and transit to Surrey, so I could pay my family's bills and my living expenses. Then I went to college and to basketball practice, and would come home at ten at night and do it all over again the next day. My life seemed perfect: I was successful at basketball and did well at school, against all odds. I was the refugee poster child, appearing in several newspaper articles and telling my story at fundraising dinners.

Behind closed doors, however, my life was falling apart. We lived in low-income housing in an unsafe neighbourhood. We struggled to pay our bills, and my mental health got worse and worse. I had panic attacks at practices and started self-harming. Despite playing the sport I loved, I always felt drained, and my college coach put a lot of pressure on me every time I stepped on the court. *Fun* was not used to describe playing basketball anymore. I struggled with unhealthy team dynamics among other players, and the constant emotional abuse from my coach reminded me too much of my male family members. Being on the court was no longer a coping mechanism. Depression stole what should've been my safe haven. My clinician suggested that I leave the team, but I felt like if I did, I'd fail my family and the shiny image I'd built for myself. I was the one my parents turned to for help, and my younger sister for guidance. I didn't want to give up and seem weak in their eyes. I felt that I didn't deserve to be alive if I was not the most hardworking or successful person I knew because of how much my parents sacrificed to bring us here. I sucked it up and completed my first year, thinking the next one would be easier. I was wrong.

The second year of college and basketball brought even more struggles as my parents went through a divorce and Milana started having suicidal thoughts. I felt everything slipping through my fingers into a small box of antidepressants I kept in my cupboard. As things escalated, I was more and more inclined to pull the plug. I felt worthless and completely alone. My friends and family did not know how miserable I was as I didn't want to be even more of a burden to them. Then, one day in November 2019, I broke down while looking at childhood photos. I was drowning in memories I didn't know I had. Sitting in Papa's lap next to Milana, with a smile so pure that I didn't recognize myself. Chasing butterflies at babushka's garden in a small town in southern Russia. Pointing up at the mammoth display in the Zoological Museum in St. Petersburg. Milana and I, riding our bikes in matching rainbow outfits that Mama had sewn for us, training wheels still attached.

I saw how carefree and happy I looked, and I remembered finding joy in the smallest things, like chasing lizards and staring at rocks for hours. I had an epiphany: I was not tied down to my lifestyle. I had more power over my choices than I was giving myself credit for. That night I realized that basketball used me more than I used the sport. It was time to quit. That time off completely changed my priorities and helped me value myself more. I realized my friends and family will still love me at my worst; I didn't have to act invincible all the time. I got back into drawing, which had been my coping mechanism growing up, and I started meditating. Now and then, I still have nightmares about losing games and team drama, but they no longer solidify when I wake up.

Being an immigrant came with issues no one warned me about. There are obvious challenges, like the language barrier and cultural norms. There are also subtle ones, with just as profound of an effect. No one teaches mothers the words to the national anthem, and no one tells fathers to bring flowers to their daughters' graduation. I've never watched Mr. Dressup, used duotangs, or played street hockey with my neighbours. None of my friends had Pushkin's poems memorized, lived off old Soviet cartoons, or dressed up to take out the trash. The tiny differences build up until I am not sure whether I will ever feel at home here. No matter how good my English gets or how much I pluck my unibrow, I will always memorize phone numbers in Russian and prefer Ded Moroz to Santa Claus. Despite this, ever since we came to Vancouver, we avoided other Russians at all costs. I am still uncertain why, but even hearing my mother tongue on the bus makes my skin crawl. It's easier to despise Russia for what it did to us and say that it's a "rotten nation anyway" than face the fact that my homeland does not want me. I am not sure if my mental well-being can handle this level of self-awareness yet.

Milana was my rock throughout this journey. People spend their whole lives in search of their soulmates, while mine has been beside me all along. When I look back on all my milestones, my sister was always there. She was the first to hear the good news and the last to leave when I broke the bad. Fleeing home left Milana with wounds that she dealt with by working out. At the time of my writing this, our friendship is very unstable. At first, I was shattered at the thought of her not opening up to me anymore. After countless arguments and fights, I've realized that she has been dealing with the same dilemma as I: feeling ashamed of her weaknesses and fearing being a burden to her loved ones. I let her go. I accepted that she is no longer my baby sister but an adult with her own path and values. But I have made it clear that I'm always here if needed.

No one teaches mothers the words to the national anthem ... no one tells fathers to bring flowers to their daughters' graduation.

I didn't believe in angels until I grew up and got to know my mother. Mama is the strongest and most compassionate person I know; how can one lose so much and still love so deeply? In Russia, she followed what was in fashion, never smiled with her teeth, and devoted her entire self to Papa's ego. Here, she wears funky socks, stopped dyeing her hair, and doesn't let others define her happiness. Despite her change on the outside, her bright presence has remained the same. She loves Vancouver and cut all ties she had with her past life. It warms my heart to see her finally expressing herself and blooming as an individual. She's even allowed herself to wear dresses and go outside without makeup. But constructing a new identity in an alien environment came with its own set of challenges.

Back home, Mama was known for her three-dimensional leather illustrations or hyper-realistic flowers made out of polymer clay. Now, that artistic inspiration is harder for her to hold onto. With each new passion, I see that spark of purpose in her, but it evaporates just as quickly. Countless firecrackers of hope. Creativity can't be forced, but it's clear how ashamed and discouraged she is for not going through with another project. As a result, our house is cluttered with various arts and crafts supplies, our basement resembling Santa's workshop in the off-season.

It was just as difficult for Papa. He finished university and started a jewellery business in the Soviet Union, all while fighting racial injustice and the financial crises of the time. While he had finally established himself in St. Petersburg, he had to reinvent his identity to fit in here. He is still struggling and feels alienated from his culture. He rents a separate apartment and receives monthly income from Disability Benefits, but whenever we pass a jewellery store, I see the same regret and resentment in him.

> Western culture has monopolized the world and Russia is no exception.

"*Ah,* ninety dollars for a necklace?" Papa would click his tongue. "Real turquoise, from Turkey no doubt. You know, in Petersburg I made these from scratch and sold for more."

My parents' relationship was the textbook definition of domestic abuse, but it still hurts to see Papa like this. Sometimes, I see the shadow of his old self, sly and righteous. Whenever we meet up, I ask him to retell stories from his youth, where he is the main character. In Afghanistan, Papa had one of the top ranks in the military. When he moved to the USSR, he defended his brothers from gangs and racist policemen. Then, he and Mama built their own small business from scratch. They made jewellery, sold it at Rainbow Stone, their store across from our house, or at exhibitions across the country. Papa was my hero. I wish I had memorized his smile and laugh back home. I wonder if he felt as lost when he came to St. Petersburg as he did in Vancouver. Here, Papa worked so hard on his victim persona to get his Disabilities Benefits that he started to believe it himself. Mama said I got my passion for social justice from Papa. He's a shell of the man he once was – bitter, bigoted, and pessimistic. *How many meaningful conversations did we miss out on due to his pride? Will we ever be able to connect?*

Western culture has monopolized the world and Russia is no exception. I grew up worshipping English, envying cartoon characters with accents, and rapping along to songs I didn't understand the meaning of. When we arrived in Vancouver, I fell in love with its culture. It was everything I'd dreamed of, but now in colour. Turned out, the cartoons I watched didn't represent all the nationalities, races, and sexualities I would find here. It was enlightening to be surrounded by so many different types of Canadians, but I realized that multiculturalism also has its cons. In my Jewish school in Russia, I was known as Malena. In my high school in East Van, I became Malena, the Russian-Jewish-Afghan girl. My nationality became my main defining quality. I became "the other" in a society made up of others. Suddenly, I was *the character with an accent* I always dreamed of becoming. It came at a cost. As soon as I opened my mouth, people focused on how I sounded instead of what I had to say.

My fear solidified in ninth grade when I searched for my best friend at her birthday party. I found her at a park nearby, smoking weed out of an apple (out of *what*) with a group of older teens. I asked my friend to come back to the party, and a guy from the smoking circle looked up at me with a lazy smile.

"Is it true –" he inhaled the grey stench "– that during winter, you ride bears naked while drinking Vodka?"

I stared at him, befuddled. *Is this what they see when they hear my accent?* All I said was, "We prefer beer."

I wanted to weep. I wanted to yell. I wanted to scream at the top of my lungs: *We are more.* We are more than snow, Putin, and matryoshkas. More than tough-looking KGB agents and USSR villains in action movies. More than *Mother Russias* and *nazdorovyas*.

It's difficult to share my experiences of Russia because even that is subjective and specific to my own narrative. How can the largest country in the world with one of the oldest histories be defined by such shallow stereotypes? I grew so sick of it, disgusted with my identity and what it entailed. Whenever I see vulgar Slavic girls or guys in Adidas tracksuits, I want to hiss, *you are the reason they see us this way.* Sometimes I envy them, wondering who I would've been had I grown up in a world where my first name isn't an anomaly and my last name isn't a tongue twister. *If I made it that far,* I remind myself.

As a love child of two nations, for years I repressed both. Upon their arrival, refugees are expected to cut all ties with home, washing away anything that's left of their ethnic background. Kissing the feet of our Western saviours, we turned our backs on our culture and blended into the promised land. This narrative serves white supremacy and the cultural genocide this country is famous for. I became another thread in this evolving pattern, doing my best to seem grateful and naïve. I was the ideal refugee: a poor victim from an unstable country in need of saving by a civilized nation. *Look, what the refugee girl can do! Her English is great! She's so lucky to be here!* I avoided making Slavic or Middle Eastern friends until a few months ago, thinking it would somehow affect my integration with Canadian society. I had no idea how comforting it is to trade childhood stories and ethnic anecdotes with someone who experienced the same thing. I only recently started listening to music I grew up with. Pronouncing Russian lyrics correctly or knowing the rhythm of Afghan songs by heart made me emotional to an extent I'm embarrassed to admit. Memories of St. Petersburg are so fragile, so sacred, so tender. They are dried flowers I'm afraid will crumble under the slightest pressure. I have tucked these memories away, into the deepest corners of my mind, buried under piles of defensive opinions and a distaste for my people. At night, as I lay in bed with my eyes open, I cradle them and cry.

My childhood was stolen by men that will never know my name. They shot at me, beat my siblings, and tortured my parents. They are still there, roaming the streets I was banished from and listening to songs I have forgotten the words to. These men lick condensed milk off their calloused fingertips and lash each other's backs with birch twigs in *banyas*. They will grow old and die without altering their names to fit foreigners' mouths, without hiding their ethnicity to get hired. It took me years to accept that villains don't always get caught, and happy-ever-afters don't come in shiny leather covers from the Canadian Embassy. Childhood traumas keep replaying in my head. I chew on them over and over again, wincing at the rotten taste. Will this piece change my past? People's perception of me? My parents' marriage? I don't need it to. Maybe the reason my family went through this nightmare was so that one day, in perfect English, I could give a middle finger to our abusers. *We made it.* Our scars became our armour, our voice a sword. The fact that I'm writing this means my parents succeeded, that they didn't give their stability up for nothing. *Mama, we made it.*

My St. Petersburg has changed and so have I. Every birthday, as I blow out the candles, I make one wish: to go home. Not forever, just to say goodbye. I was torn from my motherland right as my roots were seeping into its soil. I had friends there, a future, and an established identity. My fate wasn't the brightest, but it was mine. In Vancouver, I had to grow and adapt again, under different conditions. Looking back on it, of course, Canada is a better place for me and my family. This doesn't rule out the fact that for years, I was lost and confused about how I was supposed to feel and what I identified as. I need that closure, to see that my St. Petersburg died along with my childhood. Some part of me knows that city is far from how I remember it. My friends grew up and our apartment is long gone. The other part of me is drunk with nostalgia. What I wouldn't give to see the Neva bridge rise one more time. To watch the Scarlet Sails under fireworks in June. To sled down the abandoned snow-covered nuclear bunkers. To wander the haunted halls of Kunstkamera at midnight during the summer solstice.

Our family is yet to recover from everything that happened to us. Each of us is trying to find our place in this country. We received so much support over the years; most didn't come from the government itself, but rather smaller non-profit organizations. Still, there are wounds that Canadian citizenship cannot heal. Here, micro-aggressions and injustices feel greater. I always remind myself that it must be tougher on my parents. They brought us to the promised land, and it turned out to be as flawed as Russia. Whenever faced with prejudice, we are haunted by the overwhelming sense of déjà vu. *What are we to do, flee again?* Experiences like those in Russia feel sharper and the familiarity bruises more. Whether it be men treating me like an exotic animal or police ignoring the racially motivated threats we've received in the mail. *Is anywhere safe? How much further must we run to find peace?*

It's difficult to write an ending for a story that is still very much a work-in-progress. This journey has taught me the importance of living in the moment and appreciating the little things, as trite as it sounds. At the same time, if I forget to ground myself and life carries me away, that's okay, too. The best illustration of this dilemma is my recent conversation with Mama. We finished watching *Rush Hour 2* and were sitting in our dark basement talking about our childhoods and relationships. The first time I watched that movie was on a VHS tape at babushka's house in Novoberezansky, a small village south of Moscow.

I said, "I envy how naïve my younger self was. She had no idea what went on around her. Wish I appreciated everything we've had in Petersburg while I could, you know?"

Mama nodded. "Yes, but –"

"But I know it wouldn't be the same," I interrupted, knowing what she was about to say, "If I reminded myself it would be over soon."

"It happened the way it was meant to," said Mama, teary-eyed. "You lived in the moment as your happy little self. Joyful and full of life, you were being a kid."

Hiraeth means "long gone" in Welsh. It took me almost a decade to realize why I yearn for a home that no longer exists. I miss throwing coins at the Hare Arseniy statue by Zayachy Island, chasing seagulls by the Baltic Sea, and knocking icicles off frozen pipes at Menachem, and not because it all happened in the Great Russian Federation. With an aching heart, I hold these places and memories close to my chest like they're mine to keep, because they commemorate the last time I felt safe and loved. My siblings and I have seen too much, were forced to grow up too quickly. I miss something so horrible to me because, amid the horrors and tears, we were *thriving*. As the world was ending, my parents cocooned my siblings and me into their loving embrace to spare us the dread. As bigotry progressed, as gunshots amplified, as racist chants grew louder, they shut the windows and smiled wider. If it wasn't for Mama and Papa sheltering us, hate would've choked me the way it did the white supremacists that tried to kill us. Instead, I grew up missing the nation that wished me dead. All because as humanity collapsed, my parents read us bedtime stories.

> It's difficult to write an ending for a story that is still very much a work-in-progress.

Now, my definition of home is alive and ever-changing. It's more than a place or a stamp in a passport. My family's experiences have taught me humanity, compassion, and the purest love there is. Subconsciously, I'm still on a mindless search for a shrine built on *I hope* and *what ifs*; a home that does not exist. This giant void is the invisible aftermath of fleeing your home that refugees have to make peace with, a wistful vacuum that devours from the inside out. My way of coping is sharing my thoughts out loud and writing, since I only recently learned how to put this storm of involuntary homesickness into words. Looking back on my younger self, I remind myself not to be envious or bitter. If I could give any advice to little Malena and others struggling with identity and belonging, it would be to not rush into figuring things out right away. To stay hopeful and patient instead. I'm glad I kept going because whatever this is, it's not the end. I'm thankful that despite all the hate, despite all the fear, despite all the suffering, she didn't give up. I'm only here, in a place where I can be honest with myself, because of me not giving up. Now, it's neither nostalgia nor regret. Only gratitude.

17

A Journey to Safety

Rasha Haj Ibrahim

IT WAS A BEAUTIFUL DAY, a calm day despite the fear I felt. It was Friday, which was usually known as the day of protesting. Anyone might be arrested by the police on this day, on the pretext that they had participated in a protest. I was standing in the kitchen preparing breakfast with the window open. A cool breeze mixed with the smell of jasmine. Jasmine trees were everywhere in the neighbourhood, as if they were a part of the houses. They stood like sentinels and moved with the breath of the wind, spreading their beautiful smell throughout the neighbourhood. The smell of jasmine remains in the memory of anyone who has lived in Damascus. It is known as the country of jasmine and roses.

I was living in a new building that contained many windows overlooking old houses. Pigeons and birds lived on many roofs and were treated as pets by the residents of the houses. They hovered around, sometimes sitting, and sometimes flying.

In the morning, the birds chirp and sing their beautiful melody. It breaks the calmness and shakes the sleepers. It's a wonderful melody, like the tune of famous international musicians – only the musicians are beautiful little birds. That chirping is like a daily alarm that wakes me early and starts my every day with joy.

All the houses stand in a row and are separated by a high wall. The streets are narrow alleys, and they look like a maze for visitors who do not know the area well. Despite being very old houses, they still attract people. When you walk down these streets, all you see are high walls. The neighbourhood's hidden beauty can be seen only when you enter a house to find a fountain in the middle of a courtyard and lots of plants like roses, basil, and jasmine. This is why poets describe the houses here as perfume bottles. Anyone who visits Damascus and does not visit these houses has not seen the real beauty of Damascus.

I love the view from here because I adore old houses. I watch these houses and imagine the generations that have lived in them. I wonder about the people who built the houses, and who was the first to live there. Every day when I watch the movement of the people between these narrow streets, mixed with the smell of jasmine, it gives me the same pleasure.

While I was preparing breakfast, there was suddenly a huge explosion. The sound was so loud that it felt like the building was vibrating. The sound shook my body with its severity. I stood silent, watching out the window and not understanding what had happened. All those joyous pigeons started to take flight out of fear. They spread out across the sky. They felt the same horror, but I could not run away like they did.

A beautiful day had turned bloody.

I stood silent in amazement. I remained in that state until a second explosion occurred. I started hysterically as I realized what had happened. My child followed me to the kitchen, staring at me to understand, but it did not look like he was afraid like me. It was like he felt safe when he saw me. I checked all the windows to see the reaction of people in the street and to know whether what I had heard was real. I realized what had happened when I saw a cloud of smoke rising over the area, followed a few minutes later by the sounds of ambulances.

Oh, my goodness! It was close to my house, down a road that I always take when I go shopping or visit with my friends. The road is close to my husband's work, and before the war began, I was living there. It is a busy road during the week, but today was the weekend and there were fewer people out.

There was no way to know what happened except by turning on the television. The event was breaking news, confirming an explosion but without any further information. Several hours later, they confirmed there had been many deaths and injuries. A beautiful day had turned bloody.

That explosion is imprinted on my mind because it was the first time something like that had happened in Damascus since the war started in

2011. Elsewhere, war had already begun with the protests and revolt of the "Arab Spring," but now it had arrived in Syria – in the form of bombs. The explosion remained in the memory of everyone who heard that voice and felt that fear, but unfortunately it would not be the last event of its kind. It was the beginning of infinity – our real fear started that day. We started to hear explosions from time to time, and the number of explosions began to increase little by little, day by day, until it became like routine. Death was something we came to expect at any moment. When we left the house, we did not know at what moment an explosion might occur.

A few months later, the al-Qazzaz bombing occurred. All those who were in the city when it happened can vividly recollect that deadly day. The thunderous sound of the explosion reverberated throughout Damascus, impacting everyone.

On that day my husband had delayed leaving for work by a few hours, unlike his usual 8:00 a.m. departure time, so we were fast asleep when we were abruptly woken by a massive explosion. The shockwave rattled all the windows and made it seem as if the explosion had occurred in my room. I leaped out of bed, screaming in panic, and hurried to check on my children. I heard the frantic cries of my neighbours, each of them thinking the explosion had occurred nearby because of its intensity. All the parents rushed to the nearby elementary school, to make sure their children were safe. No one knew what had happened or where. I saw smoke billowing over the area. I shouted to the others that the explosion was not at the school, but it was in the vicinity. Parents were reassured that their children were safe. Tragically, however, others weren't as fortunate. The explosion caused hundreds of casualties, injuries, and the destruction of numerous homes.

That view that I adored had become a horror show. I could no longer look at the beautiful houses and smell the scent of jasmine. That fragrance that I delighted in had turned to the smell of gunpowder. Everything had been destroyed by those who do not care about the beauty and the fragrance of roses. Of jasmine. Beauty, for them, is a dirty fragrance; they are addicted to the smell of gunpowder.

The days were so long. I barely opened the curtains, not to see the pigeons fly or even to enjoy sunny days. Fear and terror were always with me – I was terrified at every moment. Gunshots were heard from time to time. Whenever I heard them, I would hide my children in a small corridor in my house where there were no windows. Those damned windows – every room had a big window, and I was terrified of what might come through them. That corridor did not exceed two metres. I used to sit there whenever I heard shots, as I was afraid of stray bullets. We spent our days at home and went months without seeing the bright sun that we were used to. We went out only for necessary things.

I was not able to visit my parents, and they couldn't visit me. The road between my city and Damascus had become very dangerous. They were living in Qamishli, which is a small Kurdish city – a city that has tasted the bitterness of fear for a long time. The Kurds in this city have always been afraid of the current regime. They fear being arrested at any time if they speak about it. Qamishli is an area where the regime was always trying to reduce Kurdish influence because they feared the Kurds had a historical claim and that the land belonged to them. The city never celebrated the day of *Newroz,* the day we note as a day of peace; the regime made it a day of fear, murder, and arrest. I cannot remember celebrating that day without death or the arrest of someone who wanted freedom from the regime.

I could not hear anything except the terrifying sound of the planes that are always flying overhead. Planes that devour the city little by little. They unload their artillery in the vicinity and then fly far away.

Every time a plane flies over my house, I imagine what might happen if her payload falls on my house. The sounds of those planes hurts my mind and soul. Sometimes curiosity makes me watch their movement, to see how they destroy the city.

My house was high up, and from there I was living every moment of the war. From my window, I was able to see the billowing smoke from rockets nearby. I was seeing and hearing everything like a scene from a Hollywood movie.

The scene that used to bring me such pleasure had turned to one of fear and horror. I did not care to watch the movement of the pigeons. I was no longer interested in hearing the chirping of the birds – their beautiful sounds had disappeared and been replaced by the sounds of bombs. I only looked out the window to see if we were safe, that there were no planes in the sky.

Life changed in Damascus. Security barriers were spreading everywhere. Every military site was surrounded by white sand barriers making a wall so that soldiers can hide behind it when they feel at risk. They stood ready for any battle that might happen. You could see the effects of the white dust on their faces, clothes, and their big shoes. They were provided with full military equipment including machine guns and rifles to protect military buildings from attack. I glimpsed them through the car's window when I was passing by. I do not know if they were looking back at me or if I imagined that. Their presence and their looks were frightening.

Checkpoints and security were everywhere, and everyone who moved was inspected. If we went out, we had to expect we would pass by them, and they would ask us for identification and look at the car as if we should feel grateful and thankful for what they are doing. We felt their eyes on us always, even if their gaze was elsewhere.

The scene that used to bring me such pleasure had turned to one of fear and horror.

I felt a similar gaze one day from a man I met when I went for the first time to cast my vote for the elected president. I held my electoral card, which had been issued by my father before I travelled to Damascus. He knew that if I didn't vote, it might be not safe there. I was eighteen at the time and very far from home. Kurdish students have always been the focus of attention from a security standpoint, especially after what happened in Qamishli in 2004, two years before I started university – dozens of people were martyred, and many Kurdish students who stood against injustice in Damascus were arrested.

I held my electoral card and went with my friends to the polling place. The election was in a building that belonged to the campus where I lived. We entered the election hall, which was surrounded by security. It was a large hall, and on one side of it was a table with election officials sitting behind it. Beside them was a poll box. On the other side were some curtains, but those curtains were nothing but a lie – I could not go to that area and cast my vote. This election was just mockery.

Staring at those curtains was also frightening. I had to show them that I was not hesitant to elect the current president, Bashar al-Assad, because this was a duty and not an option. His father was president, and he transferred the presidency to his son, so that the family would rule the country forever. Before the election, there were support campaigns for the current president, where huge celebrations were held, and we were forced to support him. I stood next to the election official, and I did not know what to do as this was the first time I was voting. The employee gave me the ballot paper and told me to put a sign at the word YES. I did not know what was written on the paper because he did not let me read it. I just knew it was the ballot, then he told me to put it in the ballot box. What a farce! Why an election? Why did they ask us to pretend to elect a president who had already been elected? I checked YES without hesitation because I wanted to get rid of this task, and in my heart, I said, "Why is there no respect for a person's opinion here?" Would it not be better for them to forge my paper? At least then I would not see this lack of respect. But it was impossible for me to show any of this on my face. On the contrary, I had to show feelings of gratitude and thanks for what they were doing.

My friends and I went out after we signed that paper. After leaving the room, we felt safe. One of my friends said, in a mocking way, "We were afraid to look at the word NO."

I still hear those words resonating in my ears. Yes, we were so afraid to even look at the word NO. That word could hide me from existence. That word could have me sent to jail if I pronounced it. We must show devotion to the president, and pledge allegiance forever. Security did not protect us before, and they never respected us, and they became more aggressive after some people protested. Their presence was only for suppression.

The general atmosphere affected every detail of our lives. Fear was making us into corpses without souls; it was eating our bodies little by little. I was following the news on TV and watching the same scene in which I was living via live broadcast. Were those watching this scene feeling as I did? Did they know the extent of the fear that I experienced at those moments? Did they hear my heartbeat with every missile that fell? Those living with the horrors of war are not like those who only see it on the news. We dealt with death as a daily meal, and if I thought to ignore the current situation, an artillery strike would come to remind me that I was here, in Damascus. There was no escape wherever I went. All Syrian cities had ignited from the spark of war. I reached the decision to leave Syria, a country in which we never felt comfortable, and that had gone from bad to worse. The Ba'ath regime was a threat to everyone's life, and I could no longer bear to see the destruction anymore. But where could we go and how? It was not easy to decide.

I hate farewells because they are a miniature form of death, but it was time to say goodbye to Syria. Nothing was harder on my heart than that word. But for now, it was time for separation. I applied with my family for an entry visa to Kurdistan Iraq.

After a year and a half of living under terror and fear, we were approved. Those moments were joyful but mixed with tears. How could we leave everything behind us? We studied here, we learned, we grew up. It was not easy to leave, but it was a must – it was the best way to keep my family safe. And there is no safety in a country ruled by a deadly regime.

I wanted to go to sleep the last night before leaving, but the flood of memories did not let up. I tried to cry, but I could not because my tears were frozen. I did not sleep that night. But I no longer had any other choice, and we had nothing left to lose. The sun shone the next morning, and it was time to say goodbye to all our memories. I took one last look at every room in the house. I tried to collect shades of beautiful days I'd lived here, to remember them without any pain. I wanted to relive our beautiful moments as I glanced one last time at the balcony where I used to steal peaceful moments of beauty, but it was too quiet without the voices of my kids. I went back into the room. It was miserable, without a soul. No longer did the sounds of my kids laughing, crying fill the space as before.

It was nine o'clock. Help me, oh heart, to leave. I had prepared everything, but I burst into tears as if I did not know this was happening. I did not hear any explosions that day, as if Damascus was saying goodbye to us, tempting us to stay. But there was no escape. Everything was over and now it was time for us to leave.

We reached the airport to find a crush of movement. It was as if everyone was rushing out of Damascus. A woman was saying goodbye to her grandchildren, her features exhausted by the war, but she preferred to remain alone rather than leave with her family. She whispered hidden words from a burned heart when I asked her what had happened in her city. I had heard so much horrible news about it and wanted to know whether it was true

"Houses were attacked, heads cut in my neighbourhood. I fled with my children in the night without anything, what worse than that can happen?" And then she stopped speaking.

I saw on the other side an elderly man with a white beard who looked as if he wanted to reveal a secret to me. He looked like he was being forced by the war to leave his country after spending all his life in Syria. I saw the features of depression visible on his face. How would he adapt to a new homeland? Did he choose exile for himself, or did destiny choose that for him? The features of fear were visible on every face there. Everyone was like me. None of us had chosen this, but the war was forcing us to leave.

We finished the travel procedures and got on a plane. It was a long and hard day with two kids. The plane rose little by little. I felt a passionate feeling between sadness and joy and the fear of the unknown. Only someone who is forced to leave their home can understand that feeling. I slept suddenly with tears in my eyes. My husband woke me up after two hours, when we arrived in the Kurdistan region of Iraq.

Kurdistan. When we were born, we carried its love with us. Our love for Kurdistan has grown since to become an integral part of us. We feel that we belong to it even though we were not born there. A picture of Mustafa Barzani with the Kurdistan flag behind him hung on the wall in our living room when I was a child. We considered Barzani, a Kurdish military leader, to be a godfather to the Kurds. He strove to create an independent nation for millions of Kurds, and he led the Kurdish revolutions until his death in 1979. I always dreamed of seeing Kurdistan Iraq because it is the only part of greater Kurdistan that is controlled by the Kurds.

Now I was seeing it, and I was seeing the Kurdish flag fluttering high in its sky. How beautiful it is. Thousands of Kurdish people fell for its sake, and now for the first time, I saw it fluttering in the sky. Walking around its streets, I saw men and women in Kurdish clothes, I felt the flavour of freedom that I had lost in Syria. Here there was no Ba'ath regime scaring me just because I am Kurdish.

In war, you only think about death, wondering every day if you are going to survive or die. You never stop waiting and wondering what will happen. You struggle like an exhausted solider who is finally coming home. Do you think everything will be fine when a solider comes home from war? *No.* Because a solider sees everything differently; they struggle to adapt to a normal life, far from war.

When I left Syria, I discovered that fear was still living with me as it lived with the soldier. I was afraid of many things in my new country. I felt insecure when I went outside. Crowded areas made me feel unsafe, afraid that an explosion might happen. It was difficult to open the curtains because I had gotten used to leaving them closed in Syria, and the first sight of planes in the sky increased my heartrate immediately. To this moment, I still prefer to have closed curtains. I do not know if it is because of the impact of those days in Syria or if I am simply used to it now, especially at night when everyone outside can see me and my movements.

We got used to our new life in Kurdistan Iraq, and we did not feel strange there. I spent beautiful days there with my family, and we enjoyed the spring. Now we could celebrate Newroz without fear of death or arrest.

After two years, ISIS started to invade some Kurdish cities in Kurdistan Iraq. Shingal, which is a Kurdish city, was invaded by ISIS. Thousands of its people were displaced, and their property was looted and stolen. They lost all that they possessed. The Kurdish women were arrested by ISIS and sold in the slave market.

> *In war, you only think about death, wondering every day if you are going to survive or die.*

ISIS invaded Kurdish cities in Iraq, and on the other side, Turkey invaded Kurdish cities in Syria. Every day we heard ISIS was close to the cities, and about their crimes toward the people there. They were trying to kill everything that belongs to the Kurdish race, even if it is a small child; to displace the Kurdish people and occupy their homes, such as what happened in Afrin and Serekaniye. Thousands of the finest Kurdish young men and women have been martyred in defense of their land.

My husband went to help people in a refugee camp that the region of Kurdistan provided for those who had escaped from ISIS and needed medical treatment from their long journeys on foot. Fear began to permeate our hearts again, its poison infecting our lives. "Do we not have a right to live in peace? When will the long journey of Kurdish suffering end? How many times will we pack our luggage with our belongings, which grow heavier with the burden of our sorrow and the pain from our past?"

We need a homeland that has not been exhausted by sorrow, destroyed by wars, and taken over by terrorists. There was no choice – we could not return to a homeland that lives between fire and bullets. We needed safety, support, and protection, which are necessary to live naturally. We packed our bags again; the arduous wait began anew.

Our luggage sat in front of the door. We looked around the rooms and took a last look at the fountain in the middle of the courtyard where our kids used to splash water and play in the playground. We carried our heavy bags and left the house.

The airport was quiet. We patiently waited in the queue for our turn with the immigration officer, who scrutinized our passports and visas before returning them to us. As I examined our airline tickets, with our destination and seat numbers, the memory of the day I left Syria came back to me, accompanied by that painful sting that afflicts the heart at the moment of farewell and may last days, or perhaps years. We eventually boarded the plane, and I settled into my seat beside the window. I gazed out as the airplane slowly lifted off the ground and into the sky. The familiar landscape grew smaller and smaller until it had diminished entirely, turned into an unseen point. And then a new sky and a new land unfolded before me.

My journey of searching for safety came to a close when I finally heard the words, "Welcome to Canada."

18

Between Two Worlds

Venera Loshaj-Balaj

IF YOU ARE LUCKY ENOUGH to escape war and settle in a great country like Canada, the struggle doesn't end there. For many refugees, life gets safer, but not easier. For some time, I have been wondering how to answer these questions: Where do I belong? What have I accomplished? Who have I become?

In my garden, beautiful flowers wave on the breeze, greeting the sun in the Canadian sky. I close my eyes and see the house where I grew up, in the village of Carrabreg, in Kosova. The front yard is shaded by grape vines. Birds are chirping on the trellis. Flowers stretch across the thick rock walls. Fragrant climbing yellow roses in bloom greet everyone who passes by. And I, a curious girl, smell them in awe. This is not déjà vu. It was one of the most joyful moments of my life.

I was the first-born child to my parents and the first grandchild to my mother's parents. I got all the love and care that a child could need. Since an early age, I spent a lot of time with my grandparents, my aunt, and my uncles on their large farm. While I was an angel in the eyes of my grandmother, I recall my grandfather, who expressed himself in funny ways, startled in fear when he saw me on top of a mulberry tree while I was filling a bucket and singing. He said, "She is able to choke the devil itself." That always made me laugh; it was his way of saying, "She has a strong will."

I continue nostalgically wandering through the happiest moments of my life: honey harvesting, making lemonade with roses and violets, climbing on the ladder to pick grapes, picking and roasting chestnuts, teasing my sisters while doing chores, and singing and playing with my siblings and cousins in our "castle" home.

Suddenly, other images invade like rancid air. The idyllic home where I grew up doesn't exist anymore. My inner smile drops. I hold my breath as beautiful images shift to horrific ones. Black soot and grey ash cover my childhood home. Half the walls have holes from mortars. With no signs of life, the bones of the family dog lay beside the stairs by the front door. I looked at him while tears fell from my eyes. He did his best to protect our home, his home. In sorrow, I continue wandering around. Cautious of what I might find there, I step inside with fear that part of the walls will collapse on me, or that a land mine will detonate, or that I might discover the corpses of Albanians who were killed by Serbs and hidden in the house where I grew up. It has been bombed and burned. Anything could be possible.

I touched the ash. It was the finest substance I had ever felt, finer than dust.

As I went into the ghost house, I couldn't believe my eyes. It was unreal how such a large house full of things could shrink to only rocks, iron waste, and ashes. Some pieces were unidentifiable, melted and stuck to metal and rock. They looked like sculptures made from volcanic lava. The cellar was filled and almost at level with the ground by the collapse of two floors above. Pieces of concrete, bricks, and rocks were covered in dark soot. A sofa's springs stuck out of the ashes. On the side of the wall, the ash was pale, light grey, and somehow stood like a delicate sculpture or a bubble to be blown away by a child's breath. There used to be our library on that side of the wall, with more than two hundred precious books. I went close, to pay tribute to the stories there, to characters I once knew very closely. They'd shared with me their secrets and advice. I touched the ash. It was the finest substance I had ever felt, finer than dust. It melted in my palm. As if to say goodbye to me forever, the "souls" of the books left and the ash sculpture collapsed.

I feared not only for the safety of my own children but also for my parents and younger siblings. When bombshells suddenly hit my house, my family fled in panic. They managed to drag themselves through a shallow creek with very little water. Crawling on their elbows and knees, they passed a couple of gardens, squeezing under a fence to be farther away from the house. They carried only their heavy clothes, which were soaked in mud. My younger brother was wounded that day; a piece of flesh from his shoulder was removed with his burned clothes when a mortar shell hit the house they were in. Luckily, doctor sister was there helping other people, and she was able to stop his bleeding and later stitched his wound under extreme conditions.

My whole family – parents, brothers, and sisters – was in Carrabreg, and I was living with my husband Esat in Peja, where he was from. Peja was not far from my parents' home, but Esat and I and our two children were locked inside our apartment in the downtown area of the city. Our Serbian neighbours suddenly didn't say hi anymore. They changed from casual clothing to police uniforms, and they carried automatic guns with them and glared at us with angry, hateful expressions. One afternoon while feeding my kids, I heard gunfire, screams, and loud noises like breaking glass on the street below. I jumped, confused. Our balcony had a street view; there was a coffee shop nearby where police and Serbian military troops hung around. I was so scared – bullets were flying chaotically. Slowly, I stretched my arm out and closed the blinds, hiding my body behind the wall as I did. I peeked out at the road below and saw some Serb policemen with guns breaking the windows of the boutiques along the road. One was very mad, cursing at Albanians in his Serbian tongue. From his screaming, I didn't know if he was drunk and crying, too. I was alone and didn't know what to do. There was nowhere to escape to. I expected the Serbian police to break down the door at any minute and kill us or take my children away. It was a nightmare that lasted for a couple of hours.

Later, hearing rumbling and footsteps climbing the stairs, I peeked through the keyhole in the door. I saw police going upstairs, carrying with them loads of new bags and luxury gowns wrapped in cellophane. My children and I kept quiet and turned the lights off, pretending that no one was in the apartment. I had a two-year-old child, a baby who was only a few months old, and a severely inflamed wound from a recent Cesarean delivery. Despite having difficulty carrying my baby, I held him closer on my chest to protect him. In fact, he protected me. He gave me courage. Looking at him breathing in his sleep was a true miracle in that harsh, horrific world.

The situation was escalating. It became increasingly dangerous to leave the apartment, with police curfews being enforced and killings happening on the street every day. Our baby was only seven months old when my husband became convinced that we had to leave before it was too late.

We became refugees in Montenegro. Slipping into this world, our lives didn't get easier; the fear only shifted its source, and my dignity suffered several bad wounds. All I could do was develop thicker skin. We were in the city of Ulqin. Food and rent were expensive, and we depended on support from my sister in New York.

In our quest to settle in a safe country, we had to negotiate options with smugglers. Going to the city of Sarajevo by bus produced futile results. After the first offensive killing and burning of half of Albanian homes, Serbian news outlets were inviting people to return to Kosova. Then, exhausted from changing locations over several months and paying high rent, my husband insisted we return to Kosova, believing the war would end soon. In Kosova, we found our home had been destroyed so we rented an apartment.

Encouraging Albanians to return was a Serb-set trap. Killings and massacres continued, and no journalists were allowed in the country. We were locked inside. I was in deep despair. My only dream was to be able to get out of Kosova with my kids one more time – alive. Finally, when NATO started their bombing campaign on March 24, 1999, it revived our dreadful hope of survival.

In the clear night sky, NATO airplanes flew over our heads. If only the pilots knew how grateful we were, what impact they had on our life. We were out in the dark. Serb forces were located on the hill above our house. Bombshells were dropped on them whenever they made themselves visible. The NATO intervention made the Serbs angrier, and they got their revenge by stealing from and killing civilians, and burning everything Albanian in their way.

A few weeks later, I found myself with my kids on a tractor as part of an ethnic cleansing exodus. We didn't know where the head or the tail of the caravan was; we were somewhere in the middle, among thousands of people. Some were wounded physically, and most were scarred emotionally. On an assembled piece of wood attached to the rear of the tractor, I crunched with my kids among eight people out of ten in our group. My dad stood on his feet, leaning beside the shoulder of the driver, who was his first cousin. Occasionally, to stretch her legs and to give my kids and me more room, my aunt would go and stand on the other side of her husband as he drove the tractor. It was our second evening on the road. We were not sure where the caravan was headed. We only had to follow those in front of us. There were people on foot, old cars, tractors, and horses pulling carriages full of civilians – mostly mothers with children and older people. Beside the road, I could see different kinds of things spread about like a garage sale, but everything was useless. I spotted a video camera thrown on an open suitcase alongside handmade things – doilies, crochet tablecloths, and needlework pieces. My aunt jumped down, looking at them in pity. From the bottom of the pile, she pulled a thick colourfully designed wall tapestry the size of a pillow and made with beautiful hand-knotted yarn.

"What the heck do you need that for?" shouted my uncle, unhappily.

"It's for you," replied my aunt in a calm, convincing tone. "It is dry, and you put it on top of your hard seat."

The camera was seen and ignored by who knows how many people who passed by before us. No excuse would save their life if Serbs caught somebody carrying one. They had to destroy all proof of our existence and their crimes.

The darkness came early, and with it fog and cold. It was the beginning of April 1999. We couldn't see far ahead to know what was going on. Sometimes Serb military vehicles would drive past, inspecting the perfect lineup of people. No one wanted to draw their attention, to give them an excuse to be pulled out of line and be used for their entertainment.

It was a quiet, rainy night. Although we didn't like being wet, the lineup moved very slowly. It was a nuisance, having to listen to the monotonous dripping of raindrops on the abandoned plastic sheet we found on the side of the road, which we'd placed over our heads. Suddenly, a man approached our tractor and spoke to my dad. My dad asked if I could help the man's sick niece, as I hold a degree as a registered nurse. I left my kids like birds in a nest, with my mom, two aunts, my little sister, and my cousin. When I dropped to the ground, I discovered my legs and feet were numb. We passed many families who were behind us. I was in a sweater that I'd been wearing when we escaped. I asked the man, my voice shivering, "How far is your carriage?"

He removed his jacket and threw it across my shoulders. "We are close. About two hundred metres away."

When we reached a large truck covered in a tarp, he asked, "Can you climb up from the back of the cart?"

I put my foot on the wheel and grabbed the metal part of the cart. Hands stretched toward me and I was lifted up and pulled in. I was surprised at how different it looked inside. It was like a tent; more than twenty people were sitting side by side on a mattress, packed together like kernels of corn. It was dark, but the warm temperature felt cozy. It was much better than in our tractor. Someone lit a flashlight to show me the way, and so I could avoid stepping on sets of crunched feet. On the front of the cart was a young girl who lay stretched on one side. She looked tired and in agonizing pain. Her eyes opened shortly and closed again. I recognized her immediately. It was the same wounded girl who I had given an injection to in the village of Isniq. Someone offered me a pair of gloves, a syringe, and an ampule filled with Novalgetol, and then showed me the wound under her ribs. It was a fist-sized open flesh wound with a deeper hole in the middle. I felt nauseated. I suspected there might be shrapnel from a grenade. The bleeding had mostly stopped. I only changed the gauze and injected her with a painkiller. I left her with comforting words; I couldn't wait to get out of that suffocating atmosphere. When I jumped down to leave, the grey-haired man whispered something to a woman. She waved her hand and asked me to wait a minute. Her hands moved surreptitiously in her bag, then she pulled out a piece of bread and stretched her arm toward me.

"For your kids!" she said.

Never in my life had I received a more precious gift than that. It touched my heart. A piece of bread which at that moment I wouldn't have traded for a piece of gold that same size. I rushed back to my kids. The road was quiet except for a few low voices in the distance. The caravan was moving and pausing like a wounded reptile, thousands of people anxious and fearful about what the next day might bring and knowing that some may not make it. If it wasn't for the fear of the Serb military or having people think that I had lost my mind, I would have run. I had seen people starving on TV, but it never crossed my mind that it could happen to me. My tears blended with the rain on my face as I looked to the sky, hiding my precious gift under my sweater.

After a few days on the road, we crossed the border just before dawn and became refugees again, but now in Albania. We were eleven people sharing one small room. We ate and slept on the floor, but we felt safe. After a few months, we hit the road again with the help of the International Organization for Migration (IOM). With the IOM's help, we reached a new world – we had arrived in Canada!

From the moment I set foot on Canadian soil, I was shocked. It was the first week in the welcome house in Downtown Vancouver. To explore our new surroundings, my family followed a walkway that took us to a nice paved area. Benches and flowerbeds were installed along the way. We stopped to sit on one of the benches facing the sea. With the kids on our laps, we stared at people passing by. We must have been the odd ones out in that picture. People seemed happy. Some were talking and laughing with each other as they passed. I noticed a blend of ethnicities. They were good looking, too. I took a moment to appreciate it all: a light breeze, the aroma of the salt water, the beautiful flowers, and even the way the people walked – proudly, relaxed, and with confidence, like this was the land of gods and goddesses. I couldn't comprehend it. For every nice image I saw, my mind revoked it and replaced it with a contrasted one. When people walked by slowly, relaxed and happy, I would see worried people rushing in fear. Sunshine, breeze, the aroma of the ocean – my mind would contrast it all with gloom, smoke, and a burning smell. I wondered how it could be possible in the twenty-first century, on the same planet, in the same period of time, for these two realities to coexist. Perhaps one was an illusion. I knew that pinching myself as a reality check was a joke, but I did it anyways. I felt goosebumps. In excitement and with a big smile, I told my husband, to assure him, "We didn't die back there to wake up in heaven here. We are not dreaming, either."

English was my third language, and I knew very little of it. Trying to communicate by way of chopped words and gestures, sometimes I became frustrated and reluctant. I wanted to learn fast and absorb everything, so during the days that I was busy with my kids, we read children's books together and I put stickers with new English words everywhere on the walls. Sometimes I would get overwhelmed by the amount of new information.

I often cried in my sleep, drenching my pillow with tears. In my dreams, I was always hiding in small spaces or caves, running to escape from Serbian forces while carrying my children in my arms or dragging them behind me. Once in my dream, I screamed. I begged Serb soldiers to release my child, but they took him away from me and killed him. I woke up and I couldn't stop crying. Every time I woke up, I would look up at the ceiling, trying to perceive where I was – Kosova, Montenegro, Sarajevo, or Albania – before remembering that I had recently arrived in Canada. The realization was such a relief. I wasn't used to crying while either awake or asleep, even in the most difficult moments during the war. Despite being exhausted, I didn't like going to sleep to meet with my nightmares. I felt as though they were hiding under a pillow, waiting to torture me. I eventually developed some form of insomnia.

In the living room, I served black Turkish coffee in small cups to my new Albanian refugee friend who lived in the same building. The balcony door was open, and the kids were playing in their bedroom. I was happy to chat with my new friend. We understood each other's struggles, so there was enough to talk about. We shared what we had learned since arriving in Canada. After the first sip, she complimented me for making the coffee perfect to her taste. Sitting on the chair with a small cup in my hand, I don't know if my lips touched the rim of the cup or if I had sipped the coffee already, but I suddenly heard a loud sound. In a split second, I saw myself lying flat on the floor. My brain couldn't process the source or even identify the sound, but I was sure that it meant danger. I had to take action and protect my kids.

On my palms and knees, I rushed toward their bedroom. Both my children were sitting on the carpet with their toy cars around them. They were preoccupied, playing a game. When they lifted their heads to look at me, their calm, focused expressions shifted to surprise. I don't know how I looked, but I must have shocked them, like a terrifying beast with spooky eyes on four legs. I went close to cover them, but one thing didn't make sense. How they looked at me was not what I expected. I was in shock, confused from the huge amount of adrenaline in my bloodstream. My kids explained to me that it was merely a motorbike outside that roared loudly when the engine started. I lifted my arms and stretched my body while remaining on my knees. With a dizzy head and no strength to stand back up, I took a deep breath and my eyes moistened. I saw myself then, coffee spilled all over my clothes and my friend standing there in alarm. I cursed the bike and the biker. I was glad that it was not something worse like I had originally thought, and even more glad that my kids didn't react like me.

Eventually, after several months, I got a job. On the first day of my new job, I met with my employers, a mid-thirties couple who ran a small cleaning business. They told me it was training day. I was surprised and a bit offended. I answered, "Oh, no need for that. I know how to clean."

However, training was required to get a job there. I agreed, and they showed me the tools and handed me two white plastic spray bottles – one was for top surfaces and mirrors while the other was for the sink and toilet. I was told not to mix them. I grabbed both bottles. I didn't recognize either brand. I looked at the other side of one bottle to check the listed chemicals, to find out what it was made of. Suddenly, I heard a burst of laughter from my employer. He was amused, seeing me trying to read the information – chemical terms. In a cynical way, he asked, "Can you understand it?"

Modestly but with a blush, I replied, "I have a degree in chemistry."

He laughed even harder. Perhaps he thought I was joking.

Years later, in 2005, for the sake of our kids and as a reward to ourselves for working so hard at two jobs, we took our first holiday, to Disneyland. While I sat peacefully in a hot tub at our hotel in Anaheim, the water massaging my feet as the sounds of bubbling water blended with the surrounding silence, a big lady jumped in suddenly. She was on vacation with her sister. Two couples, hotel guests, joined her. They were friends. Like my family and I, they too were visiting Disneyland. They engaged in conversation with each other while I innocently listened, politely uninterested in participating.

> *I must have shocked them, like a terrifying beast with spooky eyes on four legs.*

My husband and two kids were in the pool passing a ball to each other. They invited me to join them, but I informed them that I preferred the warmer water. Upon hearing my accent, one of the American ladies asked me where I was from.

"I am from Vancouver," I replied.

She seemed confused, as if my answer was unexpected.

"Oh, we are from Canada, too, but where are you from originally? What is your accent?"

I replied, "I am an Albanian from Kosova."

"You mean Kosovo? Is Kosovo and Kosova the same country where the war happened a few years ago?"

My answers got shorter and took longer as I was forced to translate each question into Albanian and then translate my answer back into English.

With a heavy accent, I replied, "Yes, same country but journalists use Serb maps. In Serbian language it is Kosovo, while in Albanian language it is Kosova."

These questions continued in an interrogative yet compassionate fashion.

"Hm, I see."

"How long have you been in Canada?" the Canadian with a moustache asked.

"Six years."

"Have you ever been back since?"

"My husband went to visit his family, but my kids and I have not been back yet."

"How did you arrive here?"

"We came as refugees. Canada took us."

"Must have been terrible to live through the war," the lady said. She shook her head sympathetically.

"It was," I said. The others agreed, nodding their heads as if they knew what it was like during the Kosova war.

"It was on the news when NATO intervened there, and when refugees first arrived in Canada," the man from Calgary added. "Do you still have relatives there?"

"My parents are here, but my grandmother, who I miss a lot, along with other relatives, are there."

"How is the situation there now?"

"Not so good. The war has ended, but there are no jobs and the country needs to rebuild."

"Must be difficult to live there," said the lady.

"It is," I shamefully admitted as I shrunk, feeling as if the temperature of the water had risen and was boiling me from my French-painted toenails to the hair on my head.

She added, "It's good that you escaped and live in Canada now."

The other man also added, "How do you manage to live in Vancouver? We cannot afford to live there. It is an expensive city."

I replied, "Yes, but we live in a nearby city called Surrey, which is more affordable. I work six, sometimes seven days a week. Plus, my husband works two jobs as well."

"What do you do for work?"

"Esthetician."

"What is that?"

"Beauty therapist," I explained.

"Do you do massages, too?"

"Sometimes. It's part of the job."

"Is that why you wear wrist braces?"

I nodded.

I'd seemingly fed enough of their curiosity, as they engaged in another topic with the American ladies: how the traffic in LA was so heavy. I snuck out of the hot tub, burned from the shame of being there: *Yesterday's refugee, today on a luxury vacation, while people in my home country are still struggling.*

My head was spinning. My right shoulder and arm ached due to a rotary cuff tear. My neck pain worsened; the disk bulge must have been compressed from my cowering. I took an anti-inflammatory pill and went to bed, where I rolled a towel under my neck. As I closed my eyes to sleep, my ego and conscience woke up to fight each other.

Migrants carry past wounds for many years while persevering themselves in survival mode, only to find out years later that those traumas never left them. Twenty years seems like a long time, but some of my memories are fresh, as if they had happened yesterday. As I write this, I have to relive those painful moments, which seem to be glued permanently to me. I attempted to write them a few times earlier in Albanian, and later in English, but reliving the past threw me out of the present function of daily life. To integrate and conform with Canadian society, and with my priorities in mind – raising my children and earning financial stability – I chose to work as I locked the bad memories in the deepest corners of my brain. You may forgive, but you cannot forget, even if you wish to. Keeping busy proved beneficial. It sent me toward liberation and healing. But as I said before, the ghosts of the past sometimes find their way through, at least in my dreams. Last year, when my youngest son left home to live on campus at UBC, I knew that I had done all I could as a mother. Relying on my memories, and after long contemplation, I came to realize that I belong here in Canada, where my family and my future are, where freedom and opportunity can live together. I also belong in Kosova, too, where I was born and raised, surrounded by loving people. Even though things have changed there, I still have relatives, friends, and family graves to visit. Even if I am old when I visit Kosova again, even if no one there knows who I am, the four-hundred-year-old Linden tree in the middle of the village will remember how when I was as a child, I used to sit on its thick roots and play with its leaves and bugs and dust while waiting for my dad to come home from teaching at school.

Seeing my kids on a good path toward finishing university and pursuing their dreams, my capital goal is fulfilled. I hope they will be great citizens, that they will live with dignity and compassion for others. I have become a "master," not in nursing or chemistry but in surviving and thriving. If my grandfather were alive today, I am sure that he would proudly and with a smile on his face say, "I knew that you would beat the devil."

Using my creativity to garden, paint, and write – skills that I inherited from my grandmother, mother, and dad – in my own home is blessing, which Canada offers. I have found my peace and am seizing every opportunity to give back to my family, my friends, my community where I grew up, and my community where I belong here in Canada. Over the last twenty years, I have experienced human kindness from strangers that has touched my heart and moved me in the right direction. I have realized that there is no point in being bitter over my past experiences. Those experiences are a part of the life stories that make us immigrants – resilient and proud to have experiences from two worlds. The ugly past and the promising future, reconciled in a bright and beautiful present.

From Both Sides of the Desk

WHEN I FIRST CAME to Canada in November 2014 as a Syrian refugee, I had to navigate BC settlement support. Around my first anniversary in Canada, I started working full-time on the frontlines of the settlement sector. A lot can change in one night. I went to sleep as a Syrian refugee and woke up the next morning as a resettlement counsellor for Syrian refugees. I now work at the same place that has been helping me start over.

After hours, I became an advocate and a public speaker raising awareness about refugees. I also campaigned relentlessly to reunite my family. Within a short period of time, I became a sought-after international speaker, a two-time TEDx speaker, and have spoken numerous times on TV, in the media spotlight, in front of VIPs and dignitaries. This was my life before the COVID-19 pandemic broke out.

With lockdown and the cancellation of normal life, I spent a lot of time reflecting on my journey and thinking about what I want for the future. Eventually, I decided to become a computer scientist because I am passionate about computers, I'm pretty good at math, and technology is proving to be the future of humanity. Becoming a computer scientist and developing systems that facilitate human interactions across languages will be my contribution to a better Canada and a more peaceful global society.

There are many challenges to sharing your story. The obvious being the language barrier, for it is hard to articulate your thoughts in a language you haven't yet mastered. Language skills aside, there is also the emotional cost of revisiting your past, which can easily trigger past trauma hidden under the surface. Even though the process of life-writing is difficult, it can be immensely rewarding. It is an opportunity to rewrite your story with a new perspective. The more you reflect on your journey, the more you can make sense of the chaotic life events that brought you here to this place and to this moment. Thus, life-writing can be therapeutic and can be practised as a form of self-care.

What I love most about this collection of stories is how they are crafted: we are talking about a selection of autobiographies where every newcomer/ storyteller was put in the "driver's seat" when telling their stories. The task was to write about one's life with the goal of producing a piece that best describes their journey. Writing about personal experiences can be challenging. In fact, I would call it a brave action because it takes courage to revisit past moments that have shaped our present selves, and for that I thank all the daring voices who vulnerably shared their contributions to this

> *Never forget, when all else is gone, you still have hope.*

book. They rose to the occasion and welcomed the challenge. This is the type of addition that is needed in the settlement sector everywhere across Canada. I call on settlement policy makers and leaders across the country to adopt a similar approach: when supporting immigrants and refugees to settle in Canada, let's put them in the driver's seat. Let's do things *with* them and not *for* them.

Finally, when it comes to facing adversity, my advice to others is a message that is evident in every story shared throughout this book: Never lose hope. Never forget, when all else is gone, you still have hope. This may sound cliché, but I promise it works. Hope survives the worst disease. No matter what you face in life, remember: Never let go of hope. Everything can be taken away from you except for hope, so hold tight to your vision and never let go.

HAMOUDI SALEH BARATTA

Chapter 1: "Passport, Please"

Pre-reading questions

What does your passport look like? What words and images are on your passport? What specific meaning do these words and images have for your country?

What rights and privileges does your passport give (or deny) you?

Post-reading questions

What can we learn from Akberet's story about the role of documentation and bureaucracy in newcomers' experiences? What are the consequences of lack of documentation?

How can we read this story through an intersectional lens? How might the difficulties around gaining Canadian status and freedom of movement intersect with the experiences of other marginalized groups and their experiences in Canada?

How would you define resilience? How can we recognize and value resiliency in people?

Chapter 2: Beyond the Mountain

Pre-reading questions

Has someone ever asked you, "Where are you from?" Where and when did this happen? Were you in your home country or in another country?

How did you feel when you were asked this question?

What do you think the person was really asking?

Post-reading questions

"The other passengers gave him angry looks. Some of them were distressed – they were either new to Vancouver or they could not speak English. People felt uncomfortable, threatened, and unsafe."

Why do you think the passengers were "distressed" and gave the man "angry looks"? Why do you think no one spoke up? How are people silenced?

"Today was my first day of English class. The teacher asked everyone to stand up and show their country on the map at the front of the room."

Many ESL classrooms often have a map of the world on the wall so that students can show each other where they are from. How does it make the writer feel when she is asked to point to a country on the map and she cannot?

When Deea begins to explain the history of Kurdistan to the class, her classmates interrupt and disagree with her. The teacher deals with this by saying, "Your time is over." Why do you think the teacher chose this way to deal with the situation? What are other ways the teacher could have responded?

Kurdish people have a saying, "Kurds have no friends but the mountains." What do you think this saying means?

Chapter 3: Saddam, the Fallen God

Pre-reading questions:

When you read the title "Saddam, the Fallen God," what images come to mind? What does it make you think of? What do you think the story will be about?

What do you know about the Kurdish community?

What do you think it means to be internally displaced?

Post-reading questions

Why does Diary not know the date of his birthday even though he has an Iraqi passport? How does Diary's confusion over his date of birth reflect the history of his family and of the Kurdish people?

We hear stories about displacement and refugees in the media, but many stories are not heard. What stories are generally shared? How do they perpetuate stereotypes about refugees?

What role does storytelling play in our work? How do we share stories that do not perpetuate harmful stereotypes about refugees? What stories can we bring forth that are not reflected in media?

Chapter 4: What the Poppies Know

Pre-reading questions

Everyone has painful memories or stories that involve fear and suffering. Who do we choose to share these stories with? Why do we choose to share these stories?

Post-reading questions

This story is one that Shanga has had to repeat many times, from her childhood until now. The Kurds are one of the Indigenous people of the Mesopotamian plains and the highlands in what is now Southeastern Turkey, Northeastern Syria, Northern Iraq, Northwestern Iran and Southwestern Armenia. They were deprived of establishing their nation-state. Imagine how the world knows about them, and what it means to all Kurdish people crossing borders between countries and oceans of life and death. How do you think they feel when a teacher asks everyone in the class to show their country on a map?

How can people working in systems and institutions avoid re-traumatizing asylum seekers?

How can we provide people with the space to share and tell their stories with a trauma-informed approach?

Chapter 5: The Power of Perseverance

Pre-reading questions

What does allyship mean? How would you define it?

How do you define colonization?

Post-reading questions

Muhialdin begins his story with the story of his name. He was "assigned" a Muslim name. According to Muhialdin: "This name imposed on me an Arab/Muslim identity, which would prove, eventually, to be problematic, since I am an African and a Christian."

What other forms of identity are "assigned" to Muhialdin or "imposed" on him? What assumptions do you think people might make about Muhialdin because of his name, his nationality, or other aspects of his identity?

What aspects of Muhialdin's story reflect historical events or the process of colonization?

What does it mean to be in solidarity with someone? How is this different than being an ally?

Chapter 6: Decolonizing Forced Displacement

Pre-reading questions

When has new information caused you discomfort and prompted you to re-evaluate a previously held concept or position?

How has this shaped your values?

Post-reading Questions

What aspects of your experience resonated as you read Sofia's story?

What does losing connection to their ancestral land mean for refugees, and how can this understanding be used to build solidarity with Canadian Indigenous peoples?

What can educators do to teach, build, and nourish communal relationships between Indigenous people and newcomers?

What methods outside of the school setting can be employed to challenge the myth of erasure (i.e., that Indigenous people are only archaeological figures)?

Chapter 7: A New Form of Colonialism

Pre-reading questions

What do you know about international students?

What do you think are some of the struggles they face?

Post-reading questions

What did you learn about the experience of international students in this story?

What exclusionary practices did Nuria describe in her story?

How can we create spaces and systems of inclusion for international students?

Chapter 8: Licensed to Drive

Pre-reading questions

Have you ever faced a much-dreaded assessment?

How did the stress of your dread affect you?

Post-reading questions

What freedom does a driver's licence offer an individual?

How does this story demonstrate some of the hurdles that newcomers face?

Sheela was shocked by the appearance of the RCMP at her door. How can you provide a collaborative non-threatening practice of care/service model?

Chapter 9: Becoming the Person I Admire

Pre-reading question

How would you describe yourself? What contributes to your sense of identity or helps you define who you are?

Post-reading questions

Why does Yuki begin her story by explaining the meaning of her name? Why is this so important to her?

Yuki says, "I was an independent and confident woman before I moved to Canada. That woman did not exist anymore. I started to dislike myself." How does this statement speak to complex identities?

When Yuki decides to become an English teacher, she asks herself, "Should a non-native speaker not teach the language? Were there any advantages for me in teaching the language?" How do personal experiences of being considered different, minoritized, or marginalized work to shape an individual's identity?

Chapter 10: Finding My Place

Pre-reading questions

What do you think it means to be undocumented or to have precarious immigration status?

What do you think are some of the ways this might impact a person?

Post-reading questions:

Ana's family was considered "illegal" and continually moved to escape deportation from the United States. Even though Ana is now an American citizen and says that everything is "easy" for her in Canada, how do you think her family's experience affected Ana?

Immigration involves displacement and shifting identity. What are the implications for children?

Ana's story includes many situations in which she felt she needed to change herself to feel that she "belonged." How can we move away from positioning people as being individually responsible for adaptation and thus build communities of mutual responsibility and equity?

Chapter 11: Amaluna

Pre-reading questions

What have you experienced when you have moved?

How do you define well-being?

Post-reading questions

What motivates people to re-invent themselves? What might be lost or gained in the process?

Angela speaks about her cancer diagnosis and treatment. She struggled to receive timely care, diagnostic services, and to understand diagnoses and treatment plans. What challenges and barriers do newcomers to Canada face as they navigate the health care system in Canada?

If you were a caregiver, a counsellor, or a health professional, how would you address Angela's concerns, provide support, and help her find value?

Chapter 12: Canada Reimagined

Pre-reading questions:

What do you understand about implicit bias? What informs implicit biases?

How might implicit biases affect employment?

What do you think of when you hear the term "systemic discrimination"?

Post-reading questions:

Camille believes that making us aware of our own behaviour, the assumptions behind it, and the effects it may have on others is one of the most effective ways to work toward true equity. What kind of assumptions did people make about Camille? How did she try to raise awareness when she interacted with others? What helped or hindered her?

Most job postings include a statement that the employer "values diversity" and welcomes applications from marginalized groups. Yet employers repeatedly justified not hiring Camille by apologizing and saying, "We're so sorry, but you're not the fit."

What does "not the fit" mean?

What things does Camille feel she has to do to show potential employers that she "fits"?

What is the effect of this ongoing effort to "fit" on Camille?

What is the purpose of a diversity statement? What does Camille's story tell us about the hidden agenda behind such statements?

What practical steps or actions can we take to ensure that all the employment practices in our workplaces reflect the value of diversity and inclusion?

Camille states, "I believe that racism, discrimination, and unfairness take many forms. Our oppressors and bullies hide behind another word that gives them some sort of comfort: 'systemic.'"

What does "systemic" mean? How can we define systemic racism? How can we work to address racism and bullying both individually and collectively?

Chapter 13: Travels to My Here and Now

Pre-reading questions

Where do you experience belonging or exclusion?

What do you know about your ancestors' journey?

Post-reading questions

How does Taslim describe her early attempts to belong? How did her experience of not belonging affect her?

In Warsaw, Taslim says, "Being an outsider removed the problem of not belonging because there was no hope or expectation to belong; no awkwardness or humiliation. And expats were often so much friendlier, so much more open to seeing you as one of them."

> On her return to her home in Yaletown, Vancouver, what gave Taslim a sense of connectedness and belonging?

In spite of her sense of connectedness and belonging, Taslim states that she still feels "conflicted in both heart and spirit."

> What is causing this conflict in her heart and spirit?

How do you describe your identity? Do you think other people perceive your identity in the same way as you do? How is their perception of your identity different? How is it the same? How does that impact your self-concept and self-confidence?

What parts of your identity open doors for you? Which parts do you feel close doors for you? Why?

What do you see as the role of old comers and newcomers in shaping a just and equitable future? What is one way that you could contribute to Truth and Reconciliation?

Chapter 14: Child Soldier

Pre-reading questions

Describe a memorable day of a journey that you've been on.

What did you look forward to at the end of that journey?

What story do you tell yourself about that journey?

Post-reading questions

What strengths do you think would be needed to survive the ordeals Albino experienced? How could an educator or caregiver acknowledge Albino's strengths either implicitly or explicitly and enable him to express them?

As a caregiver, a settlement worker, a counsellor, a nurse, or a teacher, how would knowing something about Albino's background shape your practice?

Despite the hardships of his childhood, Albino ends his story by saying, "My experiences have taught me to look on the bright side and always have hope." How can we build strength-based approaches in our work with newcomers?

Chapter 15: An Uncertain Journey

Pre-reading questions

What comes to mind when you read the title *An Uncertain Journey*?

What does the phrase "comfort zone" mean to you?

Post-reading questions

What comes to mind when you hear the word "refugee"? What do you think are the effects of being labelled a refugee or an immigrant? Are they the same or different? Why?

Much of Jummeiz's story is about the process required to claim refugee status for entry into Canada. First, Jummeiz had to wait for a year to get the application form, and then another year to return it. Then, he had to document his case carefully to ensure that his case fit the established criteria. The process of immigration can be dehumanizing. How do we recognize this and help support people moving forward?

Jummeiz is now a support worker for newcomers and works with multi-barriered people. In a closing message below, he offers some advice to newcomers:

> "If you dwell on your past, it will limit your thinking and slow your ability to pursue your goals and ambitions, and also anchor you to the past. Get *any* job and provide for yourself and your family, and at the same time upgrade your English language skills and evaluate

your credentials. Get enrolled in any program that will enable you to practice your profession. In order to succeed, interact with your informed social network, which will provide you with knowledge and information you will need to motivate you to achieve your goals and dreams."

How can informed social networks be developed? How do we provide encouragement, support, and information?

Chapter 16: Hiraeth

Pre-reading question

Malena came to Canada as a young refugee. What connotations does the word "refugee" have? What image comes into your mind when you hear this word? What do you know about the experiences of refugee youth and children?

Post-reading questions

How does this story explore intergenerational trauma? How can we better understand and respond to this experience in our work?

"Thanks to selfless strangers who we met through the Kinbrace community, which welcomes refugee claimants with housing, education, and support, we found a temporary roof over our head, a food bank card, and a label that would follow us for the next eight years: refugees." What does the use of the word "label" suggest? How does Malena feel about being labelled as a refugee? What kind of interactions with Canadians might have caused her to choose that word to describe her status?

How can we challenge this notion of Canada as welcoming and free from discrimination? Why is it important to do this?

Chapter 17: A Journey to Safety

Pre-reading question

What do you love about your daily routine? What small everyday sights, sounds, or smells bring you pleasure?

Post-reading questions

What sights, sounds, and smells does the writer focus on when she describes the war? How do these details convey the effects of trauma?

When the writer completes her "journey to safety" and arrives in Canada, she continues to experience the effects of trauma. What effects does she experience? Why do you think these effects are related to trauma?

What can you do to respond to people's somatic experiences of trauma? How can you be mindful in your response?

Chapter 18: Between Two Worlds

Pre-reading question

Have you worked in a job you were overqualified for or worked with others who treated you as if you had no knowledge or skills? How did this experience make you feel?

Post-reading questions:

Venera states, "For many refugees, life gets safer, but not easier" in their country of settlement. What is the difference between a "safe" life and an "easy" life?

Venera's priorities after arriving in Canada were "to integrate and conform with Canadian society," "raising [her] children and earning financial stability." What do think about this statement?

Venera describes the employer at her first job as laughing at her for checking the chemical ingredients in the cleaning fluids she was supposed to use. What does this seemingly small incident tell us about the assumptions made about immigrants and refugees?

FURTHER READING

This is not an extensive list but can serve as a launching pad for further self-study.

Books

Abdelmahmoud, Elamin. *Son of Elsewhere: A Memoir in Pieces* (2022).

Aguirre, Carmen. *Something Fierce: Memoirs of a Revolutionary Daughter* (2011).

Al-Rabeeah, Abu Bakr, and Winnie Yeung. *Homes: A Refugee Story* (2018).

Al Solaylee, Kamal. *Intolerable: A Memoir of Extremes* (2012).

Bala, Sharon. *The Boat People* (2018).

Bauder, Harald, ed. *Putting Family First: Migration and Integration in Canada* (2019).

Bezmozgis, David. *Immigrant City* (2019).

Bycel, Lee T., ed. *Refugees in America: Stories of Courage, Resilience, and Hope in Their Own Words* (2019).

Chrona, Jo. *Wayi Wah! Indigenous Pedagogies: An Act for Reconciliation and Anti-Racist Education* (2022).

Fantetti, Eufemia, Leonarda Carranza, and Ayelet Tsabari, eds. *Tongues: On Longing and Belonging through Language* (2021).

Gaucher, Megan. *A Family Matter: Citizenship, Conjugal Relations, and Canadian Immigration Policy* (2018).

Guo, Shibao, ed. *Transnational Migration and Lifelong Learning: Global Issues and Perspectives* (2013).

Habib, Samra. *We Have Always Been Here: A Queer Muslim Memoir* (2019).

Hill, Lawrence. *The Illegal* (2015).

Iqbal, Maleeha, Laila Omar, and Neda Maghbouleh. "The Fragile Obligation: Gratitude, Discontent, and Dissent with Syrian Refugees in Canada." *Mashriq*

& *Mahjar: Journal of Middle East and North African Migration Studies*, 8 (2021): 1–30.

Liu, Simu. *We Were Dreamers: An Immigrant Superhero Origin Story* (2022).

Lowman, Emma Battell, and Adam J. Barker. *Settler: Identity and Colonialism in 21st Century Canada* (2015).

Melnyk, George, and Christina Parker, eds. *Finding Refuge in Canada: Narratives of Dislocation* (2021).

Ramadan, Ahmad Danny. *The Clothesline Swing* (2017).

Suleyman, Chimene, and Nikesh Shukla, eds. *The Good Immigrant: 26 Writers Reflect on America* (2019).

Thammavongsa, Souvankham. *How to Pronounce Knife* (2020).

Thúy, Kim. *Ru* (2012).

Troeung, Y-Dang. *Landbridge: Life in Fragments* (2023).

Walia, Harsha. *Border and Rule: Global Migration, Capitalism, and the Rise of Racist Nationalism* (2021).

Wong, Lindsay. *The Woo-Woo: How I Survived Ice Hockey, Drug Raids, Demons, and My Crazy Chinese Family* (2018).

Websites

New Canadian Media, https://newcanadianmedia.ca/

University of British Columbia Centre for Migration https://migration.ubc.ca/

Toronto Metropolitan Centre for Immigration and Settlement https://www.torontomu.ca/centre-for-immigration-and-settlement/

ABOUT THE AUTHORS

Volume Editors

KERRY JOHNSON has worked with multilingual learners for many years, teaching academic language and communication skills. Kerry's research on the experience of multilingual learners in the Canadian academic environment led to the creation of classroom workshops on cross-cultural communication and exploring diversity. She is grateful for the new perspectives she gained through working with the writers, who challenged themselves to articulate painful and traumatic experiences, in most cases in an unfamiliar language, in the hope that sharing their stories would contribute to critical reflection on Canadian identity and efforts toward positive change.

ZAHIDA RAHEMTULLA is a playwright and short story writer who is currently completing an MA in Adult Education, and who worked for several years in the immigrant and refugee non-profit sector in the areas of housing employment and literacy. Her father came to Canada as a refugee from Uganda after being expelled by Idi Amin, and her mother came as an immigrant from Tanzania. Growing up learning stories about her parents and grandparents' lives and post-settlement experiences in Canada made her interested in projects that assist individuals with authoring their own stories of migration. As an emerging writer herself, her stories have been shortlisted for the Alice Munro Award and longlisted for the CBC Short Story Prize.

RAYMONDE TICKNER is a recently retired English Language Studies instructor from the University of the Fraser Valley (UFV). She has also taught in UFV's TESL teacher training program and is an Instructional Skills Workshop facilitator. Raymonde taught internationally in China at the Harbin University of Science and Technology, in India at UFV's Chandigarh campus, and with Somalian refugees in Dubai, in the United Arab Emirates, during the first Persian Gulf War. She also worked with refugees and immigrants in the Language Instruction for Newcomers to Canada program in Surrey, Canada.

AMEA WILBUR is an assistant professor at the University of the Fraser Valley. She led Vancouver Coastal Health's Access Community through English program, which helped people with chronic mental health issues learn English. She also developed a trauma-informed English as an Additional Language program at Pacific Immigrant Resources Society, which received national recognition. Amea speaks and writes on the topics of literacy and trauma, and is the co-author of *The 6 Principles for Exemplary Teaching of English Learners* (TESOL Press, 2018). Amea is also the coauthor of "Inventive Pedagogies, and Social Solidarity: The Work of Community-Based Adult Educators during COVID-19 in British Columbia, Canada," which was published in the *International Review of Education*.

Contributors

DEEA BADRI was born in Kurdistan-Iraq. She is currently working as a settlement worker with MOSAIC in Metro Vancouver. She joined *Geographies of the Heart* after working for several years in the biggest non-profit publishing organization in Kurdistan as a journal editor and essayist. Making a motivational atmosphere for newcomers was her main goal of being in this book project and sharing her story of genocide, tragedy, hope, and survival.

MUHIALDIN BAKINI is originally from Sudan. He completed a BA in Political Science and TESL from the University of the Fraser Valley in 2018, with distinction, while also working as a Life Insurance Agent for the World Financial Group. After graduating, he joined the Universal Learning Institute in Coquitlam, British Columbia, as an ESL Instructor. In 2021, Muhialdin graduated from the Master of Public Policy and Global Affairs program at UBC and is featured as one of their Changemakers. He is now employed as the Diversity Education and Resources Supervisor with Abbotsford's Archway Community Services, which provides education, resources, and support on diversity, anti-racism, hate, and bigotry.

HAMOUDI SALEH BARATTA, formerly known as Mohammed Alsaleh, had been studying to be a doctor in Syria before he was arrested by the Assad regime for his involvement in the peaceful Syrian uprising. After surviving imprisonment and torture, he escaped to neighbouring Lebanon, where he registered with the UNHCR and came to Canada as a refugee. He is an award-winning human rights advocate and speaker who brings the voices of refugees to the international stage.

AKBERET BEYENE grew up in Eritrea during the thirty-year Eritrean–Ethiopian war. She achieved a Diploma in Mass Communication from the University of Asmara and worked for almost twenty years for the national TV station, becoming well-known for her writing and production of documentaries about social, political, and health issues for women and youth. She fled to Canada in 2011, when the dictatorship relentlessly persecuting journalists threatened her life. In 2019, after years of adjustment and suffering from PTSD, Akberet became a proud Canadian, deeply grateful for life and for the support and opportunities in Canada.

ANA I. VARGAS was born in Tepatitlan, Jalisco, Mexico. She arrived in Canada in 2014 as a visitor. She works for Abbotsford's Archway Community Services Language Services department, which helps adults whose native language is English, as well as immigrants, refugees, refugee claimants, and other newcomers for whom English is an additional language. She joined *Geographies of the Heart* because she had always wanted to say something about her life as an immigrant and how it has helped her to help others.

TASLIM DAMJI's Ismaili family lived in Uganda before they were forced to leave during the Idi Amin dictatorship. They migrated first to England and eventually to Canada. Taslim is an Instructor at Vancouver Community College and at the University of the Fraser Valley. She holds a master's degree from King's College, University of London, and has been working in the field of language, settlement, diversity, and well-being for many years as a consultant, teacher educator, trainer, and facilitator. Taslim has always been interested in identity, perceived identity, and how that shapes our human experience. She designs and delivers courses and training that promote justice, equity, diversity, and inclusion for local and national audiences.

AVA HOMA is a Kurdish writer, editor, and public speaker who was born in Iran. As a renowned transnational author, activist, and lecturer, her impactful fiction and advocacy work have garnered global recognition. Her powerful voice has resonated with audiences worldwide through her contributions to prestigious publications such as the *Globe and Mail,* the *Guardian,* the BBC, the *New Statesman, LiteraryHub,* and the *Literary Review of Canada.*

RASHA HAJ IBRAHIM is a Kurdish woman from Syria. She arrived in Canada in 2017 as a refugee through a sponsorship program run by Living Hope Church. She is a mother of three children. Currently she is studying early childhood education at the University of the Fraser Valley, hoping to become a teacher. She joined *Geographies of the Heart* because she wants people to know about newcomers, their stories, and the difficulties they face in their new country.

JUMMEIZ KAMBIDI was born and raised in Sudan and immigrated to Canada in 2003. He is currently working for a non-profit organization that provides services to newcomers. He joined *Geographies of the Heart* in the hope that his story will be an inspiration to other immigrants.

SHANGA KARIM came to Canada in 2015 as a refugee claimant from Kurdistan, Northern Iraq. She now works as a Vancouver local coordinator for the Shoe Project, where she works for other women, helping to write their stories as newcomers. While a student at UFV, she joined this book project as a continuation of her career. Through her story, she wants to tell what it's like to start again from zero in another country.

VENERA LOSHAJ-BALAJ is an Albanian from Kosova who came to Canada in 1999 as a refugee, after the Kosovo War. As an alumna of the Vancouver Shoe Project, she saw the importance in contributing her story. Surviving as a mother of two small babies during the war, then coming to Canada, shifted her battle for survival into a different mode. She has a degree in chemistry from the University of Prishtina, and in recent years she has found her passion in gardening, painting, and writing.

ANGELA MANETTI moved to Canada from Florence, Italy, in June 2013. She lives in Abbotsford with her husband and daughter, whom she considers her muse and her inspiration for every step she takes in life. Angela currently works at Archway Community Services as a childminding teacher for the Language Instruction for Newcomers to Canada program. She has years of experience in education teaching Italian as a second language and dance to immigrant children.

DIARY MARIF is an Iraqi-Kurdish journalist and political analyst. He has a master's degree in History from Pune University in India. His writing has appeared on a variety of media platforms and he worked with a TV channel in his home country as a documentary researcher. He later moved to Vancouver, Canada, in 2017, and he has been writing non-fiction in English.

CAMILLE MCMILLAN RAMBHARAT was born and raised in Trindad and Tobago and is known for getting into "Good Trouble." She's married to a politician; is a mother of three leaders; and is a training and development consultant, activist, and workplace bullying and harassment survivor. Camille speaks both Trinidad and Tobago and Canadian English.

MALENA MOKHOVIKOVA came to Vancouver as a refugee from St. Petersburg, Russia, in 2012. Her family was fleeing racism and discrimination. She studies Psychology at Douglas College and loves to write, draw, and hike in her free time. She is a mental health advocate and is working toward becoming a clinician and supporting others in overcoming trauma. She hopes her story will connect with those struggling with immigration identity crisis and finding "home."

SOFIA NOORI, an assistant professor at UBC, details her connection to the Indigenous people of Afghanistan and Canada. She recounts details of British and Soviet occupations according to the bedtime stories her grandmother and mother told her. She arrived in Canada at the age of four and explains the impact of settler colonialism on her education and family settlement process in Canada. Sofia provides some insights into the complexities of what it means to be indigenous to one place and to become part of the colonial displacement agenda of another indigenous community elsewhere. She hopes that her chapter will open up dialogue about the role of Indigenous practices of treaties, wampum belts, and other means of decolonizing our citizenship and education processes.

ALBINO NYUOL was a child soldier, one of the 25,000 Lost Boys from Sudan. He migrated to Canada in 2002 from South Sudan. He pursued an education and graduated in 2016 from the School of Social Work at the University of the Fraser Valley. Albino now works for Abbotsford's Archway Community Services as a Settlement Worker. He offers a caring and safe space for newcomers to receive a variety of services, to engage in activities, and to explore educational opportunities.

NURIA SEFCHOVICH is a Spanish-English speaker and a communications and corporate social responsibility strategist originally from Mexico. She is passionate about building bridges that connect people and create bigger legacies that transform the world. In her chapter, "A New Form of Colonialism," Nuria writes about her efforts to preserve her sense of self while learning to navigate a system that determines her identity based on the social construction of immigration.

SUSHILA SHARMA, originally from Nepal, is an acclaimed author of short stories, essays, and poems in both English and Nepali. She completed a master's in Gender and Social Justice from McMaster University, with interests in critiquing mainstream feminism, advocating economic freedom for women, justice movements, and gender parities. Her studies also focus on Indigenous and non-Indigenous women's health and hygiene, and meaningful participation in politics and decision-making. She uses ethnographic and archival research methods to examine her research questions. She is currently working at YWCA Metro Vancouver as a Case Manager and studying for a Ph.D. in Gender Studies at Queens University in Ontario, Canada.

YUKI YAMAZAKI was born in Japan and moved to BC in 2011. She always had a strong interest in education, and she is currently teaching English as a Second Language in the Language Instruction for Newcomers to Canada program at Archway Community Services in Abbotsford, supporting adult immigrant learners in their language learning.

Printed and bound in Canada

Set in Macklin, Apercu, and Adobe Devanagari by
Artegraphica Design Co. Ltd.

Copyeditor: A.G.A. Wilmot

Proofreader: Caitlin Gordon-Walker

Cover design: Martyn Schmoll

Cover photo: Noah Silliman, Unsplash